W9-ANK-670

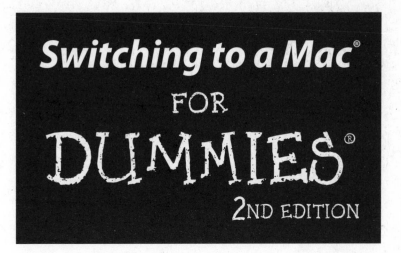

Switching to a Mac® FOR DUMMIES®

2ND EDITION

by Arnold Reinhold

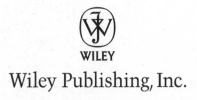

WILEY

Wiley Publishing, Inc.

FEB 22 2010

004.165
R372s2

Switching to a Mac® For Dummies®, 2nd Edition

Published by
Wiley Publishing, Inc.
111 River Street
Hoboken, NJ 07030-5774
www.wiley.com

Copyright © 2009 by Wiley Publishing, Inc., Indianapolis, Indiana

Published by Wiley Publishing, Inc., Indianapolis, Indiana

Published simultaneously in Canada

No part of this publication may be reproduced, stored in a retrieval system or transmitted in any form or by any means, electronic, mechanical, photocopying, recording, scanning or otherwise, except as permitted under Sections 107 or 108 of the 1976 United States Copyright Act, without either the prior written permission of the Publisher, or authorization through payment of the appropriate per-copy fee to the Copyright Clearance Center, 222 Rosewood Drive, Danvers, MA 01923, (978) 750-8400, fax (978) 646-8600. Requests to the Publisher for permission should be addressed to the Permissions Department, John Wiley & Sons, Inc., 111 River Street, Hoboken, NJ 07030, (201) 748-6011, fax (201) 748-6008, or online at http://www.wiley.com/go/permissions.

Trademarks: Wiley, the Wiley Publishing logo, For Dummies, the Dummies Man logo, A Reference for the Rest of Us!, The Dummies Way, Dummies Daily, The Fun and Easy Way, Dummies.com, Making Everything Easier, and related trade dress are trademarks or registered trademarks of John Wiley & Sons, Inc. and/or its affiliates in the United States and other countries, and may not be used without written permission. Mac is a registered trademark of Apple Computer, Inc. All other trademarks are the property of their respective owners. Wiley Publishing, Inc., is not associated with any product or vendor mentioned in this book.

LIMIT OF LIABILITY/DISCLAIMER OF WARRANTY: THE PUBLISHER AND THE AUTHOR MAKE NO REPRESENTATIONS OR WARRANTIES WITH RESPECT TO THE ACCURACY OR COMPLETENESS OF THE CONTENTS OF THIS WORK AND SPECIFICALLY DISCLAIM ALL WARRANTIES, INCLUDING WITHOUT LIMITATION WARRANTIES OF FITNESS FOR A PARTICULAR PURPOSE. NO WARRANTY MAY BE CREATED OR EXTENDED BY SALES OR PROMOTIONAL MATERIALS. THE ADVICE AND STRATEGIES CONTAINED HEREIN MAY NOT BE SUITABLE FOR EVERY SITUATION. THIS WORK IS SOLD WITH THE UNDERSTANDING THAT THE PUBLISHER IS NOT ENGAGED IN RENDERING LEGAL, ACCOUNTING, OR OTHER PROFESSIONAL SERVICES. IF PROFESSIONAL ASSISTANCE IS REQUIRED, THE SERVICES OF A COMPETENT PROFESSIONAL PERSON SHOULD BE SOUGHT. NEITHER THE PUBLISHER NOR THE AUTHOR SHALL BE LIABLE FOR DAMAGES ARISING HEREFROM. THE FACT THAT AN ORGANIZATION OR WEBSITE IS REFERRED TO IN THIS WORK AS A CITATION AND/OR A POTENTIAL SOURCE OF FURTHER INFORMATION DOES NOT MEAN THAT THE AUTHOR OR THE PUBLISHER ENDORSES THE INFORMATION THE ORGANIZATION OR WEBSITE MAY PROVIDE OR RECOMMENDATIONS IT MAY MAKE. FURTHER, READERS SHOULD BE AWARE THAT INTERNET WEBSITES LISTED IN THIS WORK MAY HAVE CHANGED OR DISAPPEARED BETWEEN WHEN THIS WORK WAS WRITTEN AND WHEN IT IS READ.

For general information on our other products and services, please contact our Customer Care Department within the U.S. at 877-762-2974, outside the U.S. at 317-572-3993, or fax 317-572-4002.

For technical support, please visit www.wiley.com/techsupport.

Wiley also publishes its books in a variety of electronic formats. Some content that appears in print may not be available in electronic books.

Library of Congress Control Number: 2009933381

ISBN: 978-0-470-46661-2

Manufactured in the United States of America

10 9 8 7 6 5 4 3 2 1

WILEY

About the Author

Arnold Reinhold has more than three decades of experience in the software industry. His first Apple product was a Mac 512. Arnold helped found Automatix, Inc., a pioneer in robotics and machine vision, and is coauthor of *The Internet For Dummies Quick Reference, E-Mail For Dummies, Green IT For Dummies,* and *Mac mini Hacks & Mods For Dummies.* He developed and maintains `diceware.com`, widely regarded as the "gold standard" in password security, and `mathinthemovies.com`.

Arnold studied mathematics at City College of New York and MIT, and management at Harvard Business School. You can check out his home page at `arnoldreinhold.com`.

Dedication

To Max and Grete, who put me here, and Josh, who keeps me going. B"H.

Author's Acknowledgments

Thanks to Barbara Model, Carol Baroudi, and Barbara Lapinskas for their help and suggestions. And, thanks to the folks at Apple computer and their loyal customers, who keep alive a dream that personal computers, cellphones, and music players are not just utilitarian machines but can be tools that empower and inspire us.

Publisher's Acknowledgments

We're proud of this book; please send us your comments through our online registration form located at http://dummies.custhelp.com. For other comments, please contact our Customer Care Department within the U.S. at 877-762-2974, outside the U.S. at 317-572-3993, or fax 317-572-4002.

Some of the people who helped bring this book to market include the following:

Acquisitions, Editorial, and Media Development

Project Editor: Rebecca Huehls

Executive Editor: Bob Woerner

Copy Editor: Rebecca Whitney

Technical Editor: Dennis Cohen

Editorial Manager: Leah P. Cameron

Media Development Assistant Project Manager: Jenny Swisher

Sr. Editorial Assistant: Cherie Case

Cartoons: Rich Tennant (www.the5thwave.com)

Composition Services

Project Coordinator: Lynsey Stanford

Layout and Graphics: Reuben W. Davis, Andrea Hornberger, Christin Swinford, Christine Williams

Proofreaders: John Greenough, Jessica Kramer, Nancy L. Reinhardt

Indexer: Rebecca Salerno

Special Help: Virginia Sanders

Publishing and Editorial for Technology Dummies

    Richard Swadley, Vice President and Executive Group Publisher

    Andy Cummings, Vice President and Publisher

    Mary Bednarek, Executive Acquisitions Director

    Mary C. Corder, Editorial Director

Publishing for Consumer Dummies

    Diane Graves Steele, Vice President and Publisher

Composition Services

    Debbie Stailey, Director of Composition Services

Contents at a Glance

Table of Contents

Introduction

● ●

*M*aybe you love your iPhone or iPod and are curious about other Apple products. Maybe you've had one virus scare too many and are fed up with Windows. Maybe the daunting prospect of upgrading to Windows 7 has made you open to other possibilities. Maybe you're a Mac fan who wants to show a friend how easy and productive Macs can be. Wherever you're coming from, I hope you find that this book meets your needs.

Apple Incorporated, of Cupertino, California, is over 30 years old, and few brands in the history of business generate such fierce customer loyalty as Apple and its Macintosh line of personal computers. That loyalty runs both ways. Apple knows that the people who decide to buy its products are, for the most part, the ones who have to use them. Offering systems that satisfy and even delight its users is a matter of survival for Apple.

Many virtues of the Macintosh are a matter of taste: its easy-to-use graphical interface, its elegant industrial design, and its integrated suite of software. But one virtue is a simple matter of fact: In recent years, when Windows users endured wave after wave of computer viruses, worms, spyware, and other types of evil software, Mac users were essentially immune. 'Nuff said.

About This Book

Macintosh computers and the OS X operating system have more in common with Windows than all the hoopla would suggest. Still, differences exist, big and little, that can cause problems for the unaware.

In this book, you find helpful guides for every aspect of your switch, from deciding that you do in fact want to switch to a Mac to making buying decisions to setting up everything. You also find help getting started with all the cool software that comes with your Mac, including iTunes for organizing and playing music and media and iMovie and GarageBand for making them. You even find suggestions for what to do with your old PC.

This book looks at switching to a Mac from a Windows user's perspective. You find out the best way to transfer your information from Windows to a Mac, as well as tips on how to do common Windows tasks the Mac way. But most any new Mac user can find help here. Users of older Mac operating systems who want some perspective on switching to OS X can also find assistance in this book, along with a bonus chapter available on this book's Web page, www.dummies.com/go/switchingtoamacfd2e, which was written especially with older Mac users in mind. Similarly, I address the needs of both home and business users who are making or considering a switch.

As with Windows, OS X often provides more than one way to accomplish a task. I try to describe one straightforward method for each task, perhaps with a keyboard shortcut, rather than confuse you with lots of options.

If you have already decided to buy a Mac, you can skip the first chapter. If you already bought a Mac, start with the second part of the book.

Of course, you can read this book from cover to cover, if you're that kind of person, but I try to keep chapters self contained so that you can go straight to the topics that interest you most. Wherever you start, I wish you and your new Mac well.

Foolish Assumptions

Try as I may to be all things to all people, when it comes to writing a book, I had to pick who I thought would be most interested in *Switching to a Mac For Dummies.* Here's who I think you are:

- ✔ **You're smart.** You're no dummy. Yet the prospect of switching to a new computer platform gives you an uneasy feeling (which *proves* you're smart).

- ✔ **You own a personal computer based on an operating system different from Apple OS X.** This book is aimed mostly at Windows XP users, but I think it will be helpful to users of Windows 7, Windows Vista, older Windows editions, Linux, and even owners of older Macs.

- ✔ **You're considering buying or have bought an Apple Macintosh computer.** You want to transition to your new computer expeditiously. I suggest straightforward methods and don't attempt to cover every possible approach.

- ✔ **Alternatively, you're a Mac user who knows OS X well but wants a resource to give (okay, even lend) to friends who are considering abandoning the dark side.** What a good friend you are.

- ✔ **You have used the Internet and know about browsers, such as Internet Explorer, and search engines, such as Google.** I briefly cover getting your own Internet connection in case you're not hooked up at the moment or it's time to update your service.

- ✔ **You're looking to buy a new Macintosh.** While I briefly discuss the used market in Chapter 3, this book addresses only the Intel Macs (ones based on microprocessors from Intel Corporation), which are all Apple has sold since 2006.

Whoever you are, welcome aboard. I think this book can help you.

How This Book Is Organized

I divide this book into the following highly logical (to me) parts. Each is self contained, for the most part. Feel free to skip around.

In Part I, "Informed Switching Starts Here," I explain why the Apple Macintosh is a big deal and why you should consider buying one. I also introduce you to the Apple product line and present a few different approaches to conversion (no dunking in water involved).

Part II, "Making the Switch," helps you decide what to buy and find what you can reuse from your old setup. Then I hold your hand as you make the big leap, moving your computing life to a Mac. OS X is a little different from Windows. I tell you what you most need to know to get started.

Part III, "Connecting Hither and Yon," tells you that Macs are to networking what ducks are to swimming: It comes naturally, but a few tricks are involved. I describe what you need to do to get your Mac online and talking to any other computers you have, including that old PC.

In Part IV, "More Software, More Choices," you find out that your Mac is supplied with a ton (0.907 metric tons) of preloaded software. And, you can buy — or even download for free — a lot more. Windows advocates complain that little software is available for the Mac, but so much is out there that I could write several books. And, yes, lots of cool games are available.

Kids, seniors, and businesses all have a lot to gain from the Mac way of doing things. In Part V, "Specialty Switching Scenarios" I also dive a bit deeper into OS X.

Part VI, "The Part of Tens." If you've read other For Dummies books, you're no doubt familiar with "The Part of Tens," which consists of entertaining lists containing ten (more or less) elucidating elements. They're fun to write; I hope they're fun to read.

There's more! In addition to providing all these elements, I've included a Cheat Sheet in the front of this book and a glossary in the back. The Mac world talks with a vocabulary all its own, and you may encounter other technical terms on your switching journey. (Everything is a journey these days.) I think you'll be happy to have this glossary of words and definitions on your bookshelf.

Typographic Conventions

For the most part, stuff you need to do on a Mac is graphical, but from time to time, I may ask you to type something. If it's short, it appears in boldface, like this: type **elm**. When I want you to type something longer, it appears like this:

```
terribly important text command
```

Be sure to type the line just as it appears. Then press the Enter or Return key. Capitalization usually doesn't matter on a Mac. But OS X is based on Unix (as I discuss in Chapter 19), and Unix considers the uppercase and lowercase versions of the same letter to be totally different beasts.

In the text, Web addresses are shown in this typeface: www.ditchmypc.com. I leave out the geeky http:// part, which Mac browsers don't need you to type anyway.

Apple keyboards have a special key with a fan-shaped squiggle that looks like this: ⌘. It has various nicknames — fan key, propeller key, Apple key — but in the text I use its formal name, the *Command key.*

You also see the Apple logo (⌘) in menu commands. It refers to the Apple menu headed by that symbol in the upper-left corner of your screen.

Icons Used in This Book

A little tidbit that can save you time or money or make life a little easier. "Avoid jackrabbit starts to save gas."

Pay attention. Trouble lurks here. "Never open the radiator cap on a hot engine."

Keep these words of wisdom in mind and save your derriere in the future. "Have your car battery checked before each winter."

Macs keep the gears and pulleys pretty well hidden. This is under-the-hood stuff for the technically inclined; if that's not you, you can skip it.

Where to Go from Here

Hey, it's a Mac. You're set. If you have problems not covered here, lots of resources are available online to help you. You can visit my Web site, www. ditchmypc.com. I'd be happy to hear from you directly at switchtomac@ditch mypc.com. I would love to know what you think of this book and how it can be improved, but I cannot promise individual advice.

Meanwhile, use your new Mac to build a Facebook page, create a business, solve the world hunger problem, write the great novel of the 21st century, produce your first feature film, meet some cool people, or just have fun. After all, the rest of your computing life has just begun.

Part I
Informed Switching Starts Here

The 5th Wave — By Rich Tennant

"He saw your MacBook and wants to know if he can check out the new Mac OSX features."

In this part . . .

Perhaps you're fed up with Windows and are ready to try something different or maybe you're a happy Microsoft user who's curious to read what silly justifications someone might come up with for switching to a Mac. In this part I suggest some reasons for switching that I find compelling and address common objections. Then I introduce you to the Mac family and help you figure out what to buy when you're ready to take the plunge.

Chapter 1

Why Switch? Demystifying the Mac Mantra

Apple Macintosh computers aren't perfect. They can't cure bad breath, save your marriage, or fix a bad hair day. Apple has had its share of product recalls. Talk to enough Mac owners, and you'll find one who thinks he got a lemon and wasn't satisfied with Apple's service. You can probably find a cheaper computer that will do what you really need. The vast majority of computer users get by using Microsoft Windows, and you can, too.

So why even think about switching? Macs offer a far better experience, that's why. Value matters in tight economic times. In big ways, such as security and industrial design, and in countless little details, Apple makes the extra effort to get things right — right for the user, not for some corporate purchasing department. For those of us who spend a good part of our lives in front of a video display, those easier-to-use controls, well-thought-out software choices, and better hardware fit and finish all add up to create a tool that lets us do what we want and doesn't get in our way. For more casual users, the simpler Mac design means less head-scratching while you figure out how you did that task the last time.

Life is too short for Windows aggravation. Computers are now integral parts of our lives: We use them for work, for play, to communicate, to find mates, to shop, to express ourselves, to educate our children, and to manage our money. They help us fix our homes, cure our diseases, and even clean out our attics. No one has time to fuss over them, fix crashes, fight viruses, clean out hard drives, figure out why the printer won't work, reload the software, or press Ctrl+Alt+Delete. We need computers to be there when we want them. And for the most part, Macs are. Macs just work.

Microsoft isn't run by a bunch of idiots. The company is managed by some very smart people, and they hire top-notch engineers. Just getting a product as complex as Windows out the door takes extraordinary talent. But Windows is designed for corporations. A Microsoft engineer revealed on his blog that one of the company's corporate users had 9,000 programs for Windows. The user simply couldn't afford to update them for new releases. Microsoft Windows has to support all the old software that's out there. Apple is better able to let go of the past and is therefore more nimble in developing new ways to make your life easier.

Apple sees its mission as harnessing the rapid advances in computing hardware to create revolutionary new products that improve our lives. The Macintosh, the iPod, and the iPhone are all filled with groundbreaking innovations. They're cool to look at and to own. Why buy boring?

Be Happy You Waited

In many ways, now is an ideal time to switch to a Mac. Windows users who upgrade to the new Windows 7 operating system will have a lot of new stuff to get used to anyway. So one way or another, a switch is in your future. If your PC is more than a year or two old, you'll probably have to buy a new computer or perform a major upgrade of your existing hardware to run Windows 7 — the PC industry is counting on it. Meanwhile, Apple has just gone through a major transition in its product line that makes Macs much more attractive to Windows users. All new Macs now run on Intel microprocessors, the same ones that power most Windows machines. In fact, any Mac sold today is a full-fledged, strictly kosher PC, one that can run the Windows XP, Windows 7, and Windows Vista operating systems as well as any PC on the market. So if you must run software that's available only for Windows, you can use it on a Mac too. Yeah, you have to buy and install Windows separately, but I walk you through that task in Chapter 16.

Take Your Best Shot

The question of which is a better personal computer, a Macintosh or a Windows PC, provokes passion matched by few other controversies. Were the world less civilized, Apple fans would long since have been burned at the stake by more numerous Windows users fed up with hearing how great Macs are. Instead, the debate rages over claims that Macs aren't a suitable choice because they're too this or can't do that. The following sections outline the principal objections.

Steve Jobs' other company

Steve Jobs helped found Apple and is widely credited with creating the company culture of excellence. For ten years, Jobs moonlighted in another job: running Pixar Animation, now part of Disney. There have been many movie studios in the history of film, but few have produced nine smash hits in a row: *Toy Story 1* and *2; A Bug's Life; Monsters, Inc.; Finding Nemo; The Incredibles; Cars; Ratatouille;* and *Wall-E.* All were critically acclaimed box office successes that made extensive use of the very latest in computer animation technology. But the key to their popularity was subordinating the gee-whiz special effects to the telling of a compelling story. Want to know what makes Macs different? Rent one of these movies.

"Macs are too expensive"

These days, every dollar counts. As of this writing, you can buy a new Windows XP computer for as little as $300. Netbooks sell for even less. But a cheap product that causes you years of aggravation — and has to be replaced in a couple of years — is no bargain. When you price configurations from quality manufacturers that match the ones that are standard on a Mac — the difference in price is less and often disappears. In the United States, you can buy a complete and very usable Mac desktop setup for under $600, assuming that you already own a suitable display, keyboard, and mouse; you can buy an excellent MacBook laptop for under $1,000. If those prices are too much for your budget, see the tips in Chapter 3 for getting a Mac for less.

The arguments for buying a Mac are based on quality and total cost of ownership, not on initial purchase price. PCs have hidden costs, such as virus protection software and periodic disk cleaning, and they generally are replaced more often than Macs. Few people boast about how cheap their car is or how little they spent for their home entertainment center. When cash is scarce, quality matters more.

"Switching is too hard"

I'm not saying that switching from Windows to a Mac is painless. If you have been using Windows for a while, you're used to its idiosyncrasies. You made a big investment in learning how to use all that Windows software, not to mention the amount you paid for it. You may find some aspects of the Mac hard to get used to, though I guide you through it all in Chapter 4. But on the whole, it's not that bad. Macs and Windows PCs have more in common than they have differences. All in all, I think you'll find a switch worth the effort.

"I'll be left with no software"

Many Windows advocates claim that less software is available for the Macintosh. The standard smart-aleck Mac user answer is, "Yeah, we really miss all those viruses and spyware programs." But some truth to this objection exists. Certain highly specialized programs in many fields run only in Windows. If equivalents exist for the Mac, you might have fewer choices. On the other hand, thousands of software titles are available for the Mac, and they cover the needs of most users quite well.

Some great software is available only for the Mac. Every new Mac comes with

- ✔ **Apple applications:** Handle your e-mail, instant messaging, address book, calendar, and of course, iTunes.
- ✔ **The Apple iLife suite:** This collection has programs for managing photos, making movies, burning DVDs, creating Web sites, and composing your own music. It even teaches you how to play an instrument.
- ✔ **A built-in camera and powerful videoconferencing software:** All new Macs (laptops and iMac desktops) that have a built-in display have the camera, and the software works with industry standards.

The Mac OS X operating system is built on top of UNIX, and Apple follows the Single UNIX Specification (SUS). A large amount of software developed for UNIX and Linux operating systems can therefore run on your Mac, including many popular, free, open source packages. Much of that software doesn't run in Windows.

Finally, as I mention earlier in this chapter, Macs can also run Windows, so you can still run the odd program for which an equivalent isn't available on the Mac.

"Macs are dying out"

Macs *were* close to dying a decade ago. Their share of the personal computer market was less than 3 percent. However, their share has been climbing steadily, and at last report was 10 percent in the United States. But that isn't the whole story. Consumers buy only about 37 percent of the total number of PCs sold. The rest are purchased by corporations — think of all those PC-based cash registers you see in stores and restaurants. Add in all those office workers who have no say in the computers they use. Apple has little presence in the corporate world. Most companies restrict Macs to the creative departments. So that 10 percent of total sales may represent up to 25 percent of the consumer market — people who buy computers for their own use. And

Apple's share is growing. The success of its iPhone, iPod, and iTunes music store makes more PC users consider Apple. More than half of all new Macs are purchased by people who were using Windows, and 40 percent of college students buy Macs.

"Macs are not expandable"

Since the earliest days of the IBM Personal Computer, PCs have come in big boxes that a user could open to install expansion cards or to add memory and hard drives. Steve Jobs horrified the techie end of the PC world when he built the original Macintosh as a self-contained unit that users weren't supposed to open. Apple later relented and offered the Mac II, which had expansion slots — six of them — but few users filled them. So instead, Apple developed FireWire, a blazingly fast expansion port that lets users attach high-performance devices without opening the box. The PC world responded by developing its own fast expansion port, USB 2.0, which Apple then adopted.

All new Macs offer USB 2.0 ports, and many include a FireWire port, allowing a wide range of accessories to be attached just by plugging them in. Macs also offer networking and wireless capabilities. In case you think you must have expansion cards, the top-of-the-line Mac Pro comes in a big box that you can open to install the same expansion cards (called PCI Express) as modern PCs use. But I doubt that you will ever need to do that.

See Chapter 2 for an introduction to the Mac models now available.

"Macs don't comply with industry standards"

Early in Apple's history, Steve Wozniak, a cofounder of Apple and its engineering genius, came up with a clever way to squeeze more bits onto a floppy disk (an early form of portable data storage). Unfortunately, this design made floppy disks written on early Macs unreadable on IBM PCs. That gave Apple a reputation of being an odd duck, from a standards standpoint, which it has never been able to shake completely, even though it later added PC-compatible floppy drives and is now exemplary in sticking to industry standards. Indeed, Apple was the first to popularize now-ubiquitous computer industry standards such as Wi-Fi wireless networking and the Universal Serial Bus (USB). Other standards gobbledygook that Macs support include Gigabit Ethernet, Bluetooth, IEEE-1394 FireWire, PCI Express, ExpressCard/34 (see Chapter 3 for more details), and now the Intel microprocessor architecture. The Apple Web browser, Safari, now also available for Windows, carefully follows Internet standards — more so than Microsoft Internet Explorer.

"I need Windows for work"

So run Windows 7, XP, or Vista on your Mac. You have to buy a copy, which is an added expense. But both run fine on a Mac, and you can still use Mac OS X when you're not working. Using third-party virtualization software, you can run both operating systems at the same time, with Windows applications appearing on the Macintosh OS X desktop alongside native Mac applications. I tell you more about how all this works in Chapter 16.

"Macs are a poor game platform"

True, more games exist for the PC, but plenty are available for Macs, many of the top titles too, including *World of Warcraft, Call of Duty,* and *Spore.* And many more are coming. The Apple iPhone and iPod touch have proven to be successful portable game platforms, attracting new game developers to the Apple OS X operating system. All low-end Macs include NVIDIA GeForce 9400M integrated graphics processors, MacBook Pro laptops add a second graphics chip, and the higher-end, 24-inch iMac and the Mac Pro can be ordered with top-of-the-line graphics processors, such as the NVIDIA GeForce GT 130 and ATI Radeon HD 4850. And the Snow Leopard OpenCL unlocks the power of these graphics devices for more computing tasks. If you're a serious gamer, you probably know all about the latest graphics processors, but I tell you more about them in Chapter 2.

"Vista, er . . . Windows 7 will kill Apple"

Microsoft spent five years and billions of dollars developing the Vista operating system, in part to end the scourge of computer viruses and spyware that have plagued the PC world for over a decade. After Vista proved to be an embarrassment, Microsoft spent more years and more billions reworking it into Windows 7. In the same period, Apple has been devoting its energy to improving its OS X operating system from the user's perspective. While Windows 7 and Windows Vista were gestating, Apple released five improved versions of OS X, code-named Jaguar, Panther, Tiger, Leopard, and Snow Leopard. (Someone in Apple likes big cats.) Microsoft has indicated that Windows 7 may be its last big operating system release — the race may be too exhausting for Microsoft. Still, it will have to find some way to keep up with Apple.

Will Apple license OS X for other PCs?

A perennial question in the Apple-watching community is whether Apple will license its OS X operating system to run on other PCs. After the Apple switch to Intel processors, there remains no technical reason why this cannot be done. Indeed Apple has to go to some lengths to discourage clever programmers from modifying *(hacking)* OS X to run on personal computers sold by other manufacturers. One scenario has Apple mimicking the Microsoft strategy and selling OS X to anyone to run on any computer that meets minimal standards. One company, Psystar, is selling PCs with OS X installed, claiming that it bought the software from Apple and has the right to install it on any computer. Apple has sued the company, but the courts have yet to rule on the Psystar defense. Every indication says that Apple will continue to try to keep OS X to itself and follow its high-end branding strategy, but Apple is known for creating surprises.

Considering All Aspects —
Advantage Apple

Standard business school theory says that a company that sells the most amount of product can't be stopped because it just gets better and better at what it does, to the point where no one can catch up. But Apple has adopted strategies that give it important advantages over the competition provided by Microsoft.

One neck to wring

Microsoft sells its Windows operating system to dozens of companies that make personal computers. This practice has some benefits in that competition among these PC vendors keeps prices down, but it also means that Microsoft has to support a bewildering number of different hardware designs and components (for example, displays, hard drives, communications adapters, and processor chips). And this includes not just all the variations now being sold but also products no longer on the market but still in use, including PCs made by companies that have left the business. Outside of a brief flirtation with licensing in the mid-1990s, Apple has maintained complete control over the design and manufacture of products that use its software. This *vertical integration* greatly simplifies Apple development efforts, allowing it to bring out new versions of its operating system much more often than Microsoft has been able to.

Vertical integration also has benefits for customers in terms of reliability and service. If you have a problem with hardware or software, Apple has a strong incentive to fix it. With the computer, operating system, and much of the software supplied by a single vendor, Mac users don't have to worry about being shuttled from company to company. ("I'm sorry, but you'll have to contact Fly-by-Night Software to solve your movie-editing bug; it makes that application.") Regardless of the problem with the extensive suite of software that comes with a Mac, it's Apple's problem. There's only one neck to wring.

Apple is the industry thought leader

Anyone who follows the high-tech industry is used to reading articles about amazing new technologies that are going to revolutionize our lives and then never hearing about them again. One of Apple's roles in the computer industry is to pick and choose among those new ideas. For the most part, technologies that Apple picks are adopted by the rest of the industry, particularly Microsoft. Apple may not have invented the graphical user interface, Wi-Fi wireless networking, USB, or the smartphone, but its adoption of these technologies made them industry standards. Apple users get the good, new stuff first.

Appearances matter

Sometimes you *can* judge a book by its cover. Sometimes function follows form. Early in Apple's history, Steve Jobs recognized that aesthetics matter. The design team that created the first Macintosh computer included a fine artist who was involved in everything from graphical interface design to the artwork on the cardboard box that the Mac came in. When Jobs returned to Apple in 1996, he restored artistic quality to prominence at Apple. From the original lollipop-colored iMac to the latest iPod, Apple products have won awards for excellence in industrial design. Figure 1-1 shows the elegant current iMac all-in-one computer.

Quality industrial design means more than arranging all the buttons and jacks in a pleasing way. It means questioning each feature and eliminating unnecessary doodads. The result is something that isn't just easy to look at but is also easy to understand and simple to work with.

A case in point is the optional Apple Remote. Remotes for most consumer products rival an airplane cockpit in complexity; the Apple version has just six buttons.

Figure 1-1:
The iMac —
everything
you need in
one smart
package.

Photo courtesy of Apple, Inc.

Looking forward, not backward

Apple leadership in technology extends beyond picking winners. Apple is also the company that decides when to tell a technology, "You're fired." It was the first to introduce $3^1/_2$-inch floppy disks on personal computers and the first to drop their use as a standard feature. Other technologies that Apple was the first to drop include the RS-232 serial port and the dialup modem. You can still find these features as external add-ons if you really need them, but Apple realized that most of us no longer do. Letting go of old technology wards off the feature bloat that plagues the computer industry. Unneeded features increase complexity and make machines harder to use and more prone to problems.

Getting top-notch products

Apple makes money on the products it sells. Unit for unit, Apple is the most profitable company in the industry. How does the company do that with such a small share of the market? The same way that Mercedes-Benz or BMW or Armani does — by branding. Apple doesn't sell products that are interchangeable with products sold by half a dozen other companies. It sells something unique — products sufficiently superior for which customers willingly pay a bit more. The benefit to you as a Mac buyer is the simple reality that no company can keep such an enviable position in the long run without delivering top-notch goods. You do get what you pay for.

Innovating with the enemy

For most of the personal computer era, Intel Corporation, inventor of the microprocessor and creator of the *x*86 series of microprocessors that power most PCs, was closely allied with Microsoft. The term *Wintel*, a contraction of *Win*dows and In*tel,* was coined to describe a Windows-compatible PC. Over time, however, the interests of Intel and Microsoft have diverged somewhat. Other companies, particularly AMD, have cloned the *x*86. Microsoft keeps its software compatible with all current *x*86 machines. That limits Intel's ability to innovate. Microsoft doesn't readily adopt new features introduced by Intel that aren't supported by other microprocessor makers.

In 2005, Apple announced that it would partner with Intel. Now, all new Macs use Intel chips. Although Apple says it based its decision on the computers Intel already had on the drawing board (Intel's *microprocessor road map*), strong hints have surfaced that Apple expects to take advantage of unique innovations from Intel in the future.

iPod and iPhone

Apple's runaway success with the iPod personal music player, introduced in 2001, has given the company the kind of market dominance that Microsoft has enjoyed in the PC market.

The iPhone has been hailed as a revolution in personal communications. It combines a four-band phone that uses the worldwide GSM standard, allowing its use anywhere, with iPod music and video technology and direct Internet access via Wi-Fi or cellular phone links. Apple includes its OS X operating system in the iPhone, with a well-integrated and easy-to-use interface, all in a spectacularly elegant package.

Apple gives away a version of its iTunes music software that runs in Windows. The company is betting that iPod and iPhone customers who use Windows will be impressed by the iTunes ease of use and will give the Macintosh a closer look when they're ready to upgrade their computers. We tell you more about iTunes in Chapter 11.

Switching Sides Can Sting

The Mac-versus-PC debate ranks as one of the great divides in the modern world. Just because these feelings are whipped up by marketing departments doesn't mean that they lack emotional impact. Your computer choice forms part of your personal identity. Mac users have a reputation for a certain smugness. (You just got a virus? You mean like a cold?) Much of that is defensive, of course. It's no fun being a minority in a PC-dominated world. (You bought a what? Are they still making those?) Few other choices we make in life can be as self-defining — perhaps religion, political party, and sports team to cheer for. People who move from New York City to Boston invariably suffer mental scars inflicted by changing their baseball allegiance from the New York Yankees to the Boston Red Sox. Some never recover and have to live the rest of their lives in sheltered halfway houses, eking out a living writing books for novices about technology.

This kind of psychological trauma doesn't have to happen to you just because you switch computer platforms. Think of it this way: The PC won the great war. Apple was forced to abandon the Motorola processor family and convert to Intel. Macs are now just PCs in a more stylish package with some better software. You're not abandoning your mother's cooking — just sampling a different cuisine.

No matter what I say, you probably won't completely escape the emotional side of switching to a Mac. When you feel the shame of betrayal and the pangs of guilt coming on, repeat this mantra: "It's just a computer. It's just a computer. It's just a computer."

An optional brief history of Apple

You don't need to read this sidebar to make your decisions, but no book on switching to the Mac would be complete without a little history of how the Macintosh got where it is today. None of the science fiction magazines that warped our formative minds dared to predict the level of computing power beneath our fingertips or in our shirt pockets. But no high-tech story is as compelling as the legend of Steve and Bill, two kids from the West Coast of the United States who revolutionized the world.

Apple Computer was founded on April Fools' Day, 1976, by three young men: Steve Jobs, Steve Wozniak, and Ronald Wayne. Their original mission: Sell low-cost circuit boards on which hobbyists would build their own computers, based on the newly invented microprocessor. That mission quickly changed when Jobs found that a local electronics shop wanted more fully assembled systems and gave him an order for several dozen of them. The price of the first Apple product, the Apple I, was $666.66. That sum would now buy a vastly more capable Mac mini. Adjusted for inflation, the Apple I would cost about $1,950 in 2009 dollars, enough for a MacBook Pro or high-end iMac.

The Apple I used a 6502 microprocessor, considered easier to program than the early groundbreaking devices from Intel, and featured a BASIC interpreter. *BASIC* is a particularly simple computer language invented by the Dartmouth professor John Kemeny to help teach programming. A young programmer named Bill Gates dropped out of Harvard — horrifying his parents — to start a business selling software to the fledgling microcomputer industry. He chose the imaginative name *Microsoft* for his venture. A BASIC interpreter for microcomputers was the company's first product, and Apple was among its earliest customers. The choice of corporate names was prophetic: a utilitarian contraction versus a friendly fruit icon.

The Apple II quickly supplanted the primitive Apple I and propelled Apple Computer to early leadership in personal computing. Dan Bricklin wrote VisiCalc, the world's first spreadsheet program, for the Apple II. If you crunch numbers for a living, imagine what the world was like when a spreadsheet was just a wide piece of ruled paper on which calculations were recorded one at a time by hand, and you can appreciate the impact of VisiCalc.

Microsoft got its big break when International Business Machines (IBM) decided to try its hand at making a personal computer and chose Gates' company to supply the all-important operating system. Although IBM is now a well-respected name in computing, back in the 1970s it pretty much owned commercial computing. Almost every major corporation in the world used IBM computers. Young computer professionals were told by older hands that no one was ever fired for buying IBM. Some Apple IIs had made their way into the corporate world because of VisiCalc, but they were soon replaced by beige boxes sporting IBM logos, the Microsoft operating system named DOS, and an even better spreadsheet program — Lotus 1-2-3.

The Apple II was a hard act for Apple to follow. Apple made two disastrous attempts, the Apple III (a souped-up Apple II) and the Lisa. The Lisa was a machine ahead of its time, pioneering the use of a mouse to move a pointer on the screen and letting users initiate actions by manipulating icons representing programs, data files, and hard drives, for example. But this *graphical user interface* couldn't overcome a $10,000 starting price, and few Lisas were sold.

Jobs, fed up with the increasingly corporatized development environment at Apple, led a renegade team to develop a more affordable computer, based on much of the same technology as Lisa. The new Macintosh was announced during the 1984 Super Bowl with what is perhaps the best television commercial ever made. You can view it at `www.uriahcarpenter.info/1984.html`.

Besides its mouse and graphical user interface, the Macintosh was packaged as a single unit with a built-in, high-resolution — for its time — black-on-white screen that crisply displayed the information that would eventually print on paper. IBM PCs offered green letters on a black background in just one font. The higher-quality Mac display enabled a "what you see is what you get" document-creation process and started the desktop publishing revolution. The Mac also introduced 3½-inch floppy disks, and its Motorola 68000 microprocessor could address more memory than the Intel 8088 in the IBM PC, allowing the use of more sophisticated programs.

Microsoft hedged its bets by developing software applications for the new Mac, including the word processing program named Word and the spreadsheet named Multiplan. Jobs and Gates personally negotiated a contract that let Microsoft sell a simplified version of the graphical interface named Microsoft Windows 1.0. When Microsoft later released a full-blown graphical user interface in Windows 3.0, Apple sued, but the courts ruled it was covered by that one-page contract. Word became the flagship word processor for Windows, and Excel, with a graphical interface like Multiplan, drove out Lotus 1-2-3.

Jobs left Apple in 1985 after some disagreements with the board of directors and started a new computer company, NeXT. It built a graphical interface on top of an operating system named UNIX that was originally developed by the American Telephone & Telegraph Company (ATT). UNIX was popular with computer researchers because of its flexible design

and because a version with source code was available.

Apple continued to introduce more powerful versions of the Macintosh, adding hard drives, laser printers, and high-resolution color displays. Its share of the personal computer market continued to decline relative to IBM PCs and their clones. In 1994, Apple switched from the Motorola 68000 series microprocessor to the PowerPC chip, jointly developed by Motorola, IBM, and Apple. The PowerPC was designed to allow programs to run faster than those for the Intel chips, but the theoretical advantage never materialized as Intel chip engineers used innovative techniques to keep up.

In 1997, Apple acquired NeXT and Steve Jobs rejoined the company, soon taking the helm. A year later, he reinvigorated Apple sales with the iMac, an all-in-one computer that echoed the original Macintosh. A flat-panel version appeared in 2002. Apple soon replaced its OS 9 operating system, whose lineage goes back to the first Macintosh, with a new system, OS X, based on the NeXT operating system. The iPod was launched in 2001.

In 2005, Jobs ended the personal computer microprocessor wars when he announced that Apple would switch to Intel microprocessors, a transition completed in 2006. In 2007, Jobs introduced the Apple TV (TV), extending the Apple brand to the living room, and the spiffy iPhone, setting a new standard in mobile communication. The companion iPod Touch shares many iPhone features except the phone and has become a popular game platform. Over 25,000 inexpensive or free applications for the iPhone and iPod Touch are available online at the iTunes App Store. In 2009, Jobs announced he was taking a six-month leave of absence from day-to-day Apple management for health reasons.

Chapter 2

Meet the Mac Family

Switching to a Macintosh means getting a computer manufactured by Apple Inc. No one else currently makes Macs. If you found shopping for Windows PCs a bit bewildering, you're in for a pleasant surprise. Apple has only a few models in each category, and each model generally has a name. Apple gave up using four-digit model numbers to name its products years ago. If you love having many vendors to choose from and lots of catalogs to look through, with the prospect that *something* is always on sale, the Apple experience might require some adjustment. In this chapter, I touch on the various available Mac models and related products. In Chapter 3, I point out your options, including memory size and disk capacity, and help you figure out which model is best for you, overall.

From time to time, Apple upgrades its products, drops old models, and introduces new ones. Check www.apple.com for the latest specifications.

Checking Out Common Features

Apple typically offers three or so versions of each model: a lowest-price basic version, an intermediate version, and a loaded version. Certain features, including the following, are common to all current Mac models:

▶ **Processors:** The processor in a computer carries out the instruction steps and is sometimes called a CPU (for central processing unit) or a microprocessor (because such things once filled large rooms, but now are about the size of a postage stamp). All Mac models use fast Intel microprocessors with two or more processor cores, similar to those used in most PCs, allowing them to perform more than one task at a time. They all support 64-bit operation, allowing main memory greater than 4GB, though not all Mac models let you install such large memory. Unlike in Microsoft Vista, you don't need a special 64-bit version of the operating system to take advantage of this capability. Mac OS X is 64-bit ready and also supports older, more common, 32-bit applications. Apple typically offers a couple of faster processor options for each Mac model.

✔ **Memory:** As with PCs, Macs come with two types of memory:

- *Random Access Memory (RAM):* Stores programs and data while the computer is actively processing them. With one exception, the cheapest Mac mini, all Macs come with at least 2GB (two gigabytes) of RAM. The basic mini has only 1GB. Having more RAM lets you do more things at a time and is especially important if you work with very large files, such as movies.

- *Hard drive mass storage:* For long-term data storage. A bigger hard drive means more space for music, photos, and video files.

✔ **Graphics:** All Macs include a powerful graphics processor unit (GPU) to speed the display of pictures and video. Low-end Macs use an integrated NVIDIA GeForce 9400M graphics chip. Higher-end models add even more powerful GPUs.

✔ **Software:** All Macs come with OS X software, and all Macs except the Apple Xserve servers include the integrated iLife suite of digital lifestyle applications. I introduce you to OS X in Chapter 5. I describe in Part IV the iLife suite and other software goodies you can get for Macs.

✔ **Wireless networking support:** All new Macs have provisions for wireless networking using the latest Wi-Fi and Bluetooth standards, and most models have wireless built in. (Only the most expensive models don't; they're often used in industrial settings where wireless isn't needed.) Apple was the first computer company to embrace Wi-Fi, using Apple's own brand name, AirPort.

This wireless support is especially handy in Mac laptops because lots of places offer Wi-Fi hotspots where you can jump online. Look for hotspots in coffee shops and public libraries, train stations, airline terminals, hotels, shopping centers, and even doctors' waiting rooms. With an Apple laptop under your arm, you're never out of touch.

The Bluetooth networking is a short-range wireless personal networking scheme that connects to nearby electronic devices. Bluetooth connects your Mac to wireless keyboards and mice. If your cellphone has Bluetooth, you can synchronize your OS X address book with your cellphone and even use it to connect to the Internet if your phone and cellular carrier support such use.

✔ **Wired networking support:** All Macs except the minimalist, ultrathin MacBook Air have Gigabit Ethernet jacks for wired networking and connecting to high-speed cable and DSL modems. See Chapter 9 for more on networking the Macintosh way.

✔ **No dialup modems or floppy drives:** Apple dropped the practice of including a built-in dialup modem when it switched to Intel microprocessors. Instead, it sells the Apple Modem, a small, external modem, as an accessory. Macs haven't had internal floppy drives for several product generations. External USB floppy drives are available from third parties.

✔ **Multimedia:** Most Macs can accept infrared signals from Apple's compact FrontRow remote control, allowing you to control them with Apple FrontRow software for comfy media viewing.

✔ **SuperDrive:** All models except the MacBook Air can read, play, and write (burn) CDs and multilayer DVDs, incorporating what Apple calls a SuperDrive. The SuperDrive is slot loading, so you have no slide-out tray to break. Apple offers an optional external SuperDrive for the Air.

✔ **HD support:** Apple is also tying its wagon to the high-definition (HD) video revolution that's under way. Its displays are normally set up with a 16:10 aspect ratio (width versus height), which is ideal for HD video.

Other discriminators between models are screen sizes for laptops and iMacs, memory, and hard drive space. The more expensive models also have bigger hard drives and faster processors, though the speed difference generally isn't dramatic — 20 percent or so.

In the sections that follow, you take a closer look at how the various Mac models are suited for different tasks and uses.

Connecting on the Go with Your Apple Laptop

Laptops are the most popular Mac models. Compact and elegantly designed, they show up more and more at meetings where clunky Windows laptops used to predominate.

One unique feature of Apple laptops is the large *Multi-Touch* glass trackpad on its aluminum models, which understands gestures you make using more than one finger at a time. For example, you can pinch an image to shrink it or swipe with two fingers to scroll or with four fingers to move windows out of the way so that you can see your desktop. The Multi-Touch trackpad registers a click if you push down a little harder on it, avoiding the need for a separate button. If you're wondering about how to work without a second button, a click while you have two fingers on the trackpad of any laptop model is understood as a right-click. (The trackpad on the plastic MacBook supports only two-finger scrolling.)

Another thing that sets apart Apple laptops is their built-in iSight video camera. It's located on the lid, above the display, along with an omnidirectional microphone. Stereo speakers and a headphone jack are also provided. Coupled with easy, high-speed Internet connectivity, and OS X iChat communication software, these cameras let you videoconference from just about anywhere. You can turn off the camera for ordinary audio phone calls if you prefer. No one needs to know what you look like first thing in the morning.

Speaking of the lid, it's kept closed by a magnet — you find no mechanical catch to break. And that's not the only magnetic feature of Mac laptops: The power cord is magnetically attached, too. Apple named it MagSafe because it's designed not to pull your laptop off the table if you trip over the cord. MagSafe is a fine example of Apple's attention to detail.

Apple laptops come with a separate power supply that runs on 100–240 volts AC, 50 to 60 hertz, so they can be used anywhere in the world with an adaptor or power cord for the wall outlets in the country you're visiting. Apple power supplies meet U.S. EPA Energy Star requirements, reducing energy waste. An airplane MagSafe power cord is available as an option.

All Apple laptops come with built-in AirPort Extreme Wi-Fi wireless, supporting the 802.11a, b, g, and draft-n standards. They also support Bluetooth 2.0 with Enhanced Data Rate (EDR). So you can use your Apple laptop with any Wi-Fi hotspot and any Bluetooth device.

Apple divides its laptops into three product lines, the MacBook, the MacBook Air, and the MacBook Pro. I summarize the different Apple laptop models in Table 2-1. Figure 2-1 shows the Apple aluminum laptop lineup, from left to right: MacBook Air, and the 13-inch,15-inch and 17-inch MacBook Pro models.

Figure 2-1:
The Mac
laptop
family.

Photo courtesy of Apple, Inc.

Table 2-1	Mac Laptop Comparison				
	MacBook (White)	*MacBook Pro 13-inch*	*MacBook Air*	*MacBook Pro (15 inch)*	*MacBook Pro (17 inch)*
Screen size (diagonal)	13.3 in	13.3 in	13.3 in	15 in	17 in
Resolution	1280 x 800	1280 x 800	1280 x 800	1440 x 900	1920 x 1200
Backlight	Fluorescent	LED	LED	LED	LED
Finish	Glossy	Glossy	Glossy	Glossy	Matte option
Weight	5 lb	4.5 lb	3 lb	5.5 lb	6.6 lb
	2.27 kg	2 kg	1.36 kg	2.5 kg	3 kg
Thickness	1.08 in	0.95 in	0.76 in	0.95 in	0.98 in
	2.75 cm	2.41 cm	1.94 cm	2.41 cm	2.5 cm
CPU	Core 2 Duo	Core 2 Duo	Core 2 Duo	Core 2 Duo	Core 2 Duo
Speed (GHz)	2	2–2.4	1.6–1.86	2.4–2.93	2.66–2.93
Maximum RAM	4GB	8GB	2GB	8GB	8GB
GeForce graphics	9400M	9400M	9400M	9400M (opt. 9600M)	9400M +9600M
Optical SuperDrive	Yes	Yes	External option	Yes	Yes
Mini DisplayPort	Mini-DVI	Yes	Yes	Yes	Yes
USB 2.0 ports	2	2	1	2	3
Ethernet port	Gigabit	Gigabit	None	Gigabit	Gigabit
FireWire port	400 MHz	800 MHz	None	800 MHz	800 MHz
ExpressCard/34	No	No	No	No	Yes
Wi-Fi	802.11n draft	802.11n draft	802.11n draft	802.11n draft	802.11n draft
Bluetooth	Yes	Yes	Yes	Yes	Yes
iSight Camera	Yes	Yes	Yes	Yes	Yes
Headphone jack	Yes	Yes	Yes	Yes	Yes

Table 2-1 *(continued)*

	MacBook (White)	Macbook (Aluminum)	MacBook Air	MacBook Pro (15 inch)	MacBook Pro (17 inch)
Microphone	Yes	Yes	Yes	Yes	Yes
Audio in jack	Yes	Yes	No	Yes	Yes
Trackpad	Two touch	Multi-Touch	Multi-Touch	Multi-Touch	Multi-Touch
Keyboard back-light	No	Yes	Yes	Yes	Yes
MagSafe power	60 watt	60 watt	45 watt	85 watt	85 watt

Getting just what you need with MacBook

MacBook is the less expensive Apple laptop line. It's built into a sturdy, snow white plastic case. MacBooks come with a powerful graphics processor and lots of ports for connecting peripherals, and have a reputation for great Wi-Fi range, due to the plastic body. They go anywhere, do anything.

If you can't make up your mind about which Mac to buy, get a MacBook. Laptops are versatile, and the low-cost plastic model works just fine for most folks. (However, I'd also recommend a look at the 13-inch MacBook Pro, which only costs a little more and features the cool multi-touch trackpad, backlit keyboard, and SD card slot.)

Figure 2-2 shows a white MacBook. MacBooks are a bit more than an inch thick (2.75 cm) and weigh 5 pounds (2.2 kg).

Details, details

Each MacBook includes the following items:

✔ **Glossy wide-screen display:** The display has 1280-x-800 screen resolution and measures 13.3 inches (338 mm) diagonally. (All computer screens are measured diagonally, a holdover from the earliest days of television, when CRT tubes were round.)

Photo courtesy of Apple, Inc.

Figure 2-2:
The MacBook in white, showing videoconferencing with three other people.

- ✔ **Intel Core 2 Duo processor with 2GB of RAM:** Two SO-DIMM slots support up to 4GB of RAM. More RAM helps you work with bigger files and do more things at a time. I discuss how much RAM you need in Chapter 3.

- ✔ **NVIDIA GeForce 9400M integrated graphics processor with full 3D support:** I explain what you get with low-, middle-, and high-end graphics processors in the section "Getting the Right Graphics Processor," later in this chapter.

- ✔ **Video out port:** You can see full native resolution on the built-in display and even more pixels on an external display, with the second display either extending your desktop or duplicating (mirroring) what's on the built-in screen, for use with a projection screen, for example. The MacBook has a Mini-DVI port that can display up to 1920 x 1200 pixels on an external monitor. I say more about video output options in Chapter 3.

- ✔ **Standard-size keyboard:** The keyboard includes 12 function keys and 4 arrow keys.

- ✔ **Scrolling trackpad for cursor control:** The trackpad on the plastic MacBook supports two-finger scrolling — the glass trackpad on the aluminum models understands Multi-Touch gestures.

✔ **Plenty of hard drive space:** The plastic model comes with 120GB of hard drive space, but you can order one with up to 500GB of storage. This is the memory you need to store your pictures, music files, and more. I discuss how much to get and the solid state option in Chapter 3.

✔ **Lithium-polymer battery:** The battery provides as much as five hours of battery life with wireless in operation.

Ports

All MacBook cable connections line up along the left side. See Figure 2-3 for the white version.

Figure 2-3:
Connections
to the
MacBook.

MagSafe power connector | Mini DVI external video | USB | Audio in | Kensington cable lock

Ethernet | FireWire | Headphone (Audio out)

Connections include

✔ MagSafe power connector.

✔ Gigabit Ethernet.

✔ External video port.

✔ FireWire 400 port, which enables you to transfer pictures and video quickly, if your camera supports FireWire. You can also use it with higher-performance FireWire external hard drives.

✔ Two USB 2.0 ports, which you can use to plug in any number of devices, including a mouse, external drives, flash memory cards, a printer, and more.

✔ Combined optical digital audio input/audio line in — 3.5 mm minijack.

✔ Combined optical digital audio output/headphone out — 3.5 mm minijack.

✔ Kensington cable lock slot for physical security.

Traveling light with MacBook Air

The MacBook Air is the ultraportable laptop for road warriors. Apple has stripped out components that aren't generally needed on the road in an effort to keep size and weight to a minimum. MacBook Air features include

✔ An Intel Core 2 Duo processor with 2GB of RAM. A slower processor with only 2 GB of memory maximizes battery life.

✔ A glossy widescreen display with 1280-x-800 screen resolution, measuring 13.3 inches (338 mm) diagonally.

✔ A very thin but strong aluminum case that can slip inside a manila mailing envelope.

✔ An NVIDIA GeForce 9400M integrated graphics processor with full 3D support.

✔ A single USB 2.0 port.

✔ A backlit keyboard for easy texting at night.

✔ A smaller, 45-watt AC power module.

✔ An NVIDIA GeForce 9400M graphics processor; see the section "Getting the Right Graphics Processor," later in this chapter, for details.

✔ A 120GB hard drive or 128GB solid state disk drive, if you prefer.

✔ A full-size backlit keyboard, including 12 function keys and 4 arrow keys (inverted *T* arrangement).

✔ A Multi-Touch trackpad for cursor control.

✔ An optional external dual-layer-burning slot-loading SuperDrive.

✔ An optional wired Ethernet to USB adapter.

✔ A lithium-polymer battery that provides up to 4.5 hours of battery life.

The MacBook Air cable connections include

- ✔ Analog audio output/headphone out — 3.5 mm minijack
- ✔ MagSafe power connector
- ✔ USB 2.0 port
- ✔ Mini DisplayPort external video

Taking the high ground with MacBook Pro

The MacBook Pro is the more expensive laptop line, with a number of features that set it apart from the MacBook:

- ✔ A choice of display screen sizes (13, 15 or 17 inches)
- ✔ An aluminum case
- ✔ Faster processors with more memory
- ✔ Two graphics processors on some models for even faster gaming and 3D support
- ✔ Faster FireWire 800 port
- ✔ Two USB 2.0 ports; three on the 17-inch model
- ✔ SD card slot (13-inch and 15-inch models) or ExpressCard/34 slot (17-inch model)
- ✔ Backlit keyboard for easy use at night
- ✔ Heftier, 85-watt AC power module on some models (can also power a MacBook, but the 60-watt power module that comes with the MacBook isn't powerful enough to supply the bigger MacBook Pros)

Details, details, details

Each MacBook Pro includes these items:

- ✔ **A glossy wide-screen display:** The 17-inch model can be ordered with a higher resolution of 1920 x 1200. (Table 2-1 lists standard resolutions.)You can order the 17-inch model with a reduced glare screen rather than the standard glossy model. Many graphics designers find that glare interferes with precision color editing. All MacBook Pro displays feature a screen that lights up using light-emitting diodes (LEDs) rather than fluorescent lamps, which contain trace amounts of mercury, a hazardous material.
- ✔ **Intel Core 2 Duo processor:** Two SO-DIMM slots support up to 8GB of RAM.
- ✔ **A GeForce 9400M graphics processor:** The more expensive models add a 9600M and graphics memory; see the section "Getting the Right Graphics Processor," later in this chapter, for details.

✔ **A 160GB hard drive on the 13-inch model; 250GB on the 15-inch; 500GB on the 17-inch:** You can order your MacBook Pro with larger disk drives or solid state disk drives if you prefer.

✔ **Mini DisplayPort video out**

✔ **Full-size backlit keyboard:** Includes 12 function keys and 4 arrow keys (inverted *T* arrangement).

✔ **Scrolling Multi-Touch trackpad for cursor control**

✔ **Lithium-polymer battery:** Provides up to 7 hours of battery life on the 13-inch or 15-inch model and 8 hours on the 17-inch model.

Ports

The MacBook Pro cable connections include

✔ MagSafe power connector

✔ Gigabit Ethernet

✔ FireWire 800 port

✔ Two USB 2.0 ports (three on the 17-inch model)

✔ Mini DisplayPort external video

✔ Combined optical digital audio input/audio line in — 3.5 mm minijack

✔ Combined optical digital audio output/headphone out — 3.5 mm minijack

✔ SD card slot (13-inch and 15-inch) or ExpressCard/34 slot (17-inch)

✔ Kensington cable lock slot for physical security

Furnishing Your Lair with Mac Desktops

Laptops are great, but sometimes you want more permanence in your setup, whether it's your workplace, home office, or entertainment center. Apple offers a range of desktop models — from the petite but well-equipped mini to the graceful all-in-one iMac to the industrial-strength MacPro and Xserve — that you can use to build just the computing environment you want. In the sections that follow, I describe the different models. Their features are summarized in Table 2-2.

Table 2-2		Comparing Mac Desktops			
	Mac mini	*iMac 20*	*iMac 24*	*Mac Pro*	*Xserve*
Screen size (diagonal)	None	20 in	24 in	None	None
Resolution built-in	N/A	1680–1050	1920–1200	N/A	N/A
Resolution external	2560 x 1600	2560 x 1600	2560 x 1600	2560 x 1600	N/A
Screen finish	N/A	Glossy	Glossy	N/A	N/A
Weight	2.9 lb	20 lb	25.4 lb	41 lb	31.7 lb
	1.31 kg	9.1 kg	11.5 kg	18.7 kg	14.4 kg
CPU	Core 2 Duo	Core 2 Duo	Core 2 Duo	Quad-Core Xeon	Quad-Core Xeon
Speed (GHz)	N/A	2.66–3.06	2.66–3.06	2.26–2.93	2.8–3.0
Maximum RAM	4GB	8GB	8GB	32GB	32GB
GeForce graphics	9400M	9400M	9400M	GT 120	GT 120
Optional graphics	N/A	N/A	GT 120/130 or Radeon HD4850	Radeon HD4780 up to 4 GPUs	N/A
PCI Express slots	None	None	None	3	2 + 1 for GPU
Optical SuperDrive	1	1	1	1 or 2	1
Mini DisplayPort	Yes	Yes	Yes	Yes	No
DVI port	Mini DVI	No	No	Dual link	Mini DVI
USB 2.0 ports	5	4	4	5	3
Gigabit Ethernet	1	1	1	2	2
FireWire ports 800 MHz	1	1	1	4	2
RS-232 serial port	No	No	No	No	1

	Mac mini	*iMac 20*	*iMac 24*	*Mac Pro*	*Xserve*
Wi-Fi	N draft	N draft	N draft	Optional	Optional
Bluetooth	Yes	Yes	Yes	Yes	No
iSight Camera	No	Yes	Yes	No	No
Headphone jack	Yes	Yes	Yes	Yes	Yes
Microphone	No	Yes	Yes	No	No
Audio in jack	Yes	Yes	No	Yes	Yes

Starting small — the Mac mini

The mini is Apple's least expensive Macintosh model. As its name implies, it's quite small, about the size of an external CD or DVD drive. Aimed, in part, at PC users who are considering switching to Mac, it doesn't come with a keyboard, mouse, or video display. It can work with most video monitors. You can also use your USB keyboard and mouse, if you like, or order new ones from Apple.

The mini's small size ($6^{1}/_{2}$ inches square by 2 inches high) and unobtrusive package fit almost anywhere and make it ideal for living room home entertainment centers. It makes almost no noise and uses very little power when it's idle. Apple has adopted the mini's quiet styling for other products, including the Airport Extreme base station and the Apple TV. In Figure 2-4, you can see the mini as well as the optional FrontRow IR remote control (on the left).

Figure 2-4: The Mac mini with optional FrontRow remote control.

Photo courtesy of Apple, Inc.

The mini has an Intel Core 2 Duo processor with up to 4GB of memory and an NVIDIA GeForce 9400M graphics processor with the ability to drive two high-resolution displays. The low-price version has a 120GB hard drive and a SuperDrive that can read, play, and burn CDs and DVDs. You can special-order one with a 320GB hard drive. Both models include AirPort Wi-Fi networking, Bluetooth, and IR port for optional FrontRow remote control.

The mini's power button and all cable connections are on the back, as shown in Figure 2-5. These connections include

 ✔ Power connector for cable from separate power adapter
 ✔ Gigabit Ethernet
 ✔ FireWire 800 port
 ✔ Mini-DVI external video
 ✔ Mini DisplayPort external video
 ✔ Five USB 2.0 ports
 ✔ Combined optical digital audio input/audio line in — 3.5 mm minijack
 ✔ Combined optical digital audio output/headphone out — 3.5 mm minijack
 ✔ Kensington cable lock slot for physical security

Figure 2-5:
The Mac mini's back, showing cable connections.

Photo courtesy of Apple, Inc.

The lowest-priced mini comes with only 1GB of RAM. You'll probably want more. You can order it with more memory, have a computer store add memory for you, or install more memory yourself. The mini isn't designed for user servicing — you need a putty knife to open its case and a screwdriver to remove the hard drive and SuperDrive assembly — but videos on the Web describe the process. If you're not into hardware hacking, spend a few bucks and get a pro to add the memory for you.

Speaking of hardware hacking, many people have developed interesting mod-
ifications that customize the mini for fun or specialized uses. See *Mac mini
Hacks & Mods For Dummies,* by John Rizzo, with contributions from yours
truly (published by Wiley). Some interesting ideas described there include

   ✔ Upgrading the hard drive and RAM

   ✔ Building a home theater around a mini

   ✔ Modding the mini's case

   ✔ Automating your home with the mini

   ✔ Using the mini in the kitchen

   ✔ Installing a mini in your car (maybe even a Mini Cooper)

Getting it all in one box: The iMac

The Apple iMac continues a tradition that goes back to the first, revolutionary Macintosh — packaging the computer and display as a single unit. Having
it all in one box means a single power cord, fewer connecting cables, nothing
to tuck under the desk, and less clutter all around. And who couldn't do with
less clutter in their lives?

The current iMacs take this idea one step further. All you have on your desk
is what looks like an ordinary flat-panel display. Well, not quite ordinary:
With an aluminum case and sculpted stand, it's well turned out. But that's all
there is. The computer is tucked inside the display. All connections are in the
back. Figure 2-6 shows the two iMac model sizes: 20 inches and 24 inches.

Figure 2-6:
The iMac
family.

Photo courtesy of Apple, Inc.

Although the computer is out of sight, it has plenty of mind. The iMac can keep up with most desktop machines on the market.

Like Apple laptops, iMacs sport a built-in iSight camera for videoconferencing and chat. Both have Intel Core 2 Duo microprocessors, AirPort Wi-Fi, Gigabit Ethernet, built-in microphone, and audio in and out. The built-in stereo speakers are powered by a 24-watt digital amplifier, with ample volume for watching videos or listening to music. Both come with a keyboard and Apple's Mighty Mouse, which are wired, but you can order wireless models.

Both have four USB 2.0 ports and one 800 MHz FireWire port. All ports are neatly lined up along the bottom-left of the iMac as you face the rear — no groping under the desk to get at cable connections. The wired Apple keyboard has two more USB 2.0 ports built-in, though it uses up one of the USB ports on the back of the iMac.

Note that the lower-cost model is good enough for most ordinary uses. The next model up offers a lush, 24-inch display, more RAM, and a larger hard drive for not that much more money. If you have more to spend, you can order up to 8GB of RAM, a terabyte of hard drive space, faster CPU chips, and more capable graphics processors. See the section "Getting the Right Graphics Processor," later in this chapter, for the advantages of more powerful graphics. The larger screen on the 24-inch model lets you have more open windows onscreen when you're doing complex tasks like editing a video or researching a paper.

Computer displays aren't as bright as flat-screen televisions, but if you don't mind dimming the lights in your living room, you can build a complete home entertainment center with a 24-inch iMac and an HDTV tuner, such as the eyeTV from `www.elgato.com`. It's a helpful solution for a small apartment.

Maxing out with a Mac

If you have a big budget and need lots of computing power, Apple has the answers. In the following sections, you find out about the stand-alone Mac Pro and the rack-mounted Xserve.

Mac Pro

As its name suggests, the Mac Pro is Apple's most capable Macintosh. Maxed out, it can hold dual Intel Xeon quad-core processors, 4 terabytes (4TB) of hard drive space, and 32GB of RAM in eight DIMM slots that incorporate error-correcting codes (ECC) for greater reliability.

Although most Macs are designed with the expectation that their cases will never be opened, the Mac Pro is a major exception. It's built into a full tower–size case that opens easily to gain access to most Mac Pro components. Figure 2-7 shows the Mac Pro the cabinet splayed open to reveal its insides.

Figure 2-7:
The Mac Pro, opened up.

Photo courtesy of Apple, Inc.

Also unlike with other Macs, you have room for expansion. The units contain four hard drive bays, and you can install dual SuperDrive optical drives. You have your choice of either of these graphics cards:

✔ NVIDIA GeForce GT 120 with 512MB of GDDR3 memory, one Mini DisplayPort, and one dual-link DVI port. As many as four GT 120 cards can be installed.

✔ ATI Radeon HD 4870 with 512MB of GDDR5 memory, also with one Mini DisplayPort, and one dual-link DVI port.

Three additional full-length PCI Express (PCIe) slots are available for plug-in cards, which allow expansion of your Mac's capabilities. These are the same types of expansion cards used in newer PCs. They aren't, however, compatible with the older PCI, PCI-X, or ISA cards. The PCIe slots can hold high-speed communications cards, such as fiber channel, or as many as three more graphics cards, for a maximum of four, total. Three hundred watts of power are available just to power these cards. The whole Mac Pro can draw 12 amps at 120 volts — half that at 240 volts. If your office is a bit chilly, convince your boss that you need one of these puppies under your desk, fully loaded, and it will keep you toasty warm.

The Mac Pro has two connector panels: a main one in back and a smaller one in front. The rear panel includes

- ✔ Three USB 2.0 ports
- ✔ Two FireWire 800 ports
- ✔ Optical digital audio input and output Toslink ports
- ✔ Analog stereo line-level input and output minijacks
- ✔ Two independent Gigabit Ethernet ports

The front panel conveniently supplies

- ✔ Two more FireWire 800 ports
- ✔ Two more USB 2.0 ports
- ✔ Stereo headphone minijack

Bluetooth is standard on the Mac Pro; Wi-Fi is optional.

Now serving OS X — the Xserve

People who buy servers — the computers that provide the information we consume for the Internet — consider different factors than consumers do in making their purchasing decisions. Issues such as reliability, packaging density, hot-swappable components, and remote management become paramount. Server owners want their machines to be up all the time. When something like a hard drive or power supply fails, they want to replace it without shutting down the machine. The server is often located in expensive server-farm real estate, and the space it takes up becomes an issue.

The Apple server offering is Xserve, and you'll find that it offers appealing answers to each of these criteria, especially that of space. Apple's Xserve is a *1U* device, which means that it's quite thin and maximizes the number of Xserves that can fit in a single rack. That makes server farmers happy — more cows in the barn. Figure 2-8 shows three Xserves and an Apple RAID storage unit in a minimalist rack.

Back in the 19th century, as the railroad and telephone industries got going, folks realized that a lot of electrical equipment had to be installed in their offices. Mounting equipment in vertical "relay racks" with side bars spaced 19

inches apart became a standard that's still used today. Even the location of the screw holes is standardized, and the devices that fit in these racks have heights measured in units (U). The shortest height unit that can still span a pair of standard mounting holes is designated 1U.

Photo courtesy of Apple, Inc.

Figure 2-8:
Three Xserves and a RAID mounted in a 19-inch rack.

Each Xserve features the following:

- ✔ One or two Intel Quad-Core Xeon Nehalem CPUs
- ✔ Up to 32GB of ECC RAM, banked in four channels for high memory throughput
- ✔ NVIDIA GeForce GT 120 processor card with Mini DisplayPort output
- ✔ Two available PCI Express 2.0 slots
- ✔ Hot-pluggable SATA and SAS mass storage (three independent bays)
- ✔ SuperDrive
- ✔ One USB 2.0 port on the front panel
- ✔ Two FireWire 800, two USB 2.0, and two independent Gigabit Ethernet ports in back
- ✔ Optional second power supply for redundancy
- ✔ Integrated processor for lights-out management and supporting software

✔ A license for Mac OS X Server software, with no limit on the number of clients

✔ Optional 24/7 AppleCare service

Also lurking in back is an old-fashioned DB-9 serial port. Most commercial server-hosting facilities use DB-9 serial ports for console monitoring from a remote station using KVM technology. They're also needed for some uninterruptible power supplies.

Xsan and RAID

Xsan is Apple's storage-area network (SAN) software. A *storage-area network* aggregates all disk drives in the local-area network into a single entity, allowing all servers to access that data at the same time. It can support up to 2 petabytes of data. That's 2 million gigabytes. It can be used with commercial RAID (Redundant Array of Inexpensive Disks) systems such as the VTrak from `www.promise.com/apple`.

Getting the Right Graphics Processor

In modern personal computers, a graphics processor (GPU) takes over from the central processing unit much of the work of generating visual displays. All current Apple models come with GPUs designed to perform the intricate mathematical calculations needed to render three-dimensional objects realistically at speeds fast enough to keep up with real-time game play, and can drive two HD displays simultaneously at full resolution. Virtual reality becomes more real than life. Apple supports a variety of models in its Macintosh line:

✔ **The low end:** Low-end Apple models use a graphics processor from NVIDIA that's integrated with its support chip set for the Core 2 Duo processor line — the GeForce 9400M. These graphics processors are fast and quite respectable for editing videos, engaging in moderate 3D game play, or visiting 3D virtual reality worlds such as *Second Life.*

✔ **The middle range:** The MacBook Pro adds a second graphics processor to some models, the NVIDIA 9600M, and you can order your 24-inch iMac with a choice of optional graphics engines, including

- NVIDIA GeForce GT 120 graphics processor with 256MB of GDDR3 memory

- NVIDIA GeForce GT 130 graphics processor with 512MB of GDDR3 memory

- ATI Radeon HD 4850 graphics processor with 512MB of GDDR3 memory

You'll appreciate the better quality of these processors if you're into serious game play or professional video work.

✔ **The high end:** If you need the highest performance, the Mac Pro blasts out graphics with top-end PCI Express graphics cards. You get your choice of the following:

- NVIDIA GeForce GT 120 with 512MB of GDDR3 memory, one Mini DisplayPort, and one dual-link DVI port. Up to four GT 120 cards can be installed.

- ATI Radeon HD 4870 with 512MB of GDDR5 memory, also with one Mini DisplayPort, and one dual-link DVI port.

ATI, now owned by AMD, and NVIDIA vigorously compete for king of the graphics hill. Each has loyal fans. You likely have used one or both of these companies' products in your PC experience, and you may have your own opinions.

✔ **The previous generation:** Early low-end Apple models with Intel computers used a graphics processor from Intel that's integrated with its support chip set for the Core Duo processor line — the GMA 950 graphics processor, which wasn't good for 3D game play. To a large extent, Apple's dual CPU design made up for this lack because the second CPU can perform the 3D calculations fairly rapidly. Apple no longer ships the wimpy 950, but you may find older models at remainder prices, or consider a used machine. If you're mostly doing light 2-D graphics or light game play (I know someone who did quite well in *World of Warcraft* with an older MacBook), the 950 should meet your needs.

Adding On and Filling In

Apple is judicious in its choice of peripherals and other accessories it provides. For example, although it was among the first to sell laser printers, it no longer brands its own printers, but supports most models made by others. Apple does offer displays and other hardware, software, and support packages, which may come with your Mac or which you can purchase as an add-on. The following sections explain the more popular options to help you decide what you might want — or want to ignore.

Apple displays

Apple sells two attractively styled, but pricy, flat-panel displays:

✔ 24-inch LED Cinema Display, 1920 x 1200 resolution

✔ 30-inch Apple Cinema HD Display, 2560 x 1600 resolution

The 24-inch display is designed to serve as a docking station for Apple aluminum laptops. It includes an iSight camera, a microphone, speakers, a built-in power supply that can charge any Apple MagSafe laptop, and a three-port powered USB 2.0 hub for your keyboard, mouse, and other accessories that stay put, such as a backup hard drive. The display's cable has three plugs that go to the laptop: MagSafe power, USB, and Mini DisplayPort. The last connection doesn't work with the white plastic MacBook or older models, but if you can afford this display, you can afford one of the aluminum MacBooks. You can use the 24-inch display with the Mac mini or Pro or as a second display for your iMac (it looks just like an iMac) and still use the MagSafe as a charger for your laptop.

The 30-inch display is packaged in anodized aluminum with a narrow bezel, so you can put two displays right next to each other. It includes a FireWire 400 hub and a USB 2.0 hub, each with two ports. The video signal connects via a DVI cable, and requires an adapter for Macs with Mini DisplayPort video out.

An optional VESA mounting kit, available from the Apple Store, meets the Video Electronics Standards Association (VESA) Flat Display Mounting Interface (FDMI) standard, allowing you to attach your Apple display to a third-party VESA mounting device.

Time Capsule Wi-Fi base station and backup disk

The Apple Time Capsule combines a Wi-Fi base station and a 500GB or 1TB backup hard drive. Wi-Fi connects computers and other devices in your home or office without running wires. Those computers, PCs and Macs, can access the Time Capsule hard drive over your wireless network. Macs can also use Time Capsule for automatically making backups with the Apple Time Machine backup software, described in Chapter 5.

In a normal installation, you run an Ethernet cable from the back of the Time Capsule, shown in Figure 2-9, to your high-speed Internet modem — cable, DSL, or satellite. If you're in a school or an office with a direct Internet connection, plug your Ethernet cable into that connection.

Figure 2-9:
Time
Capsule,
from the
back.

Photo courtesy of Apple, Inc.

Time Capsule comes with these features:

- ✔ **Support for all Wi-Fi standards:** Time Capsule supports all current Wi-Fi standards, including 802.11a, b, g, and n-draft. It should work, therefore, with just about any Wi-Fi-equipped computer and other Wi-Fi devices, such as the iPhone and Apple TV.

- ✔ **Two frequency bands:** Time Capsule operates on both Wi-Fi frequency bands, 2.4 and 5 GHz, simultaneously for maximum range and performance.

- ✔ **Broad support for security standards:** The security standards basically keep anyone parked on the street or your next-door neighbor from hopping onto your network to use your Internet access. Time Capsule supports all the Wi-Fi security standards — WEP, WPA, WPA2, 802.11X, Radius, and so on — and includes a firewall. I tell you how to turn on Wi-Fi security in Chapter 10.

- ✔ **Parental controls:** You can set permissible times for access for each authorized computer, which is great for limiting kid access.

- ✔ **Even more ports:** Time Capsule does more than just supply high-speed Internet to any Wi-Fi device within range, which by the way is about 150 feet (50 meters), though your footage may vary. In the rear (refer to Figure 2-8), it has three local Ethernet ports so that you can hook up computers that require a wired connection. It also has a USB 2.0 port that lets you attach a printer that can be shared by your network. Or, you can attach a second USB hard drive that is then shared over the network.

What's that? You want *both* a printer *and* a hard drive? Don't be so greedy. Okay, okay. But you need to get a USB 2.0 hub. It's inexpensive, and you can then have multiple printers and multiple hard drives. Go wild.

Time Capsule is styled like the Mac mini and the Apple TV. It's 7.7 inches (197 mm) square (same as the Apple TV), weighs 3.5 pounds (0.753 kg), and runs on 100–240V AC.

AirPort Extreme Wi-Fi base station

AirPort Extreme is basically a Time Capsule without the built-in hard drive. As supplied, AirPort Extreme provides the same Wi-Fi base station services as Time Capsule and has the same set of connectors on its back, including the USB port for a printer or hard drive. Add a big hard drive and you get the Time Capsule backup functions, but with more boxes and wires.

The AirPort Extreme is also styled like the Mac mini and the Apple TV. It fits in the same footprint as the mini, 6.5 inches (165 mm) square, and weighs 1.7 pounds (0.753 kg). It comes with an AC power adapter, but runs on 12 VDC, so you can put one in your car to run a Wi-Fi network at your next geek picnic.

AirPort Express, a Wi-Fi relay

The AirPort Express is smaller and simpler than the Airport Extreme. Kind of like the latté grande at Starbucks — it's the small model. The AirPort Express looks like the Apple laptop power supply (see Figure 2-10). It even has the same "duck's head" snap-off power connector.

Although AirPort Express can function as a Wi-Fi base station to share an Internet connection, it's intended more as a relay and an interface to your stereo so that you can pipe music from iTunes to your home entertainment system. It supports the 802.11b and g signaling speeds.

AirPort Express has just four connections:

✔ An AC wall plug — just stick it in any outlet

✔ An Ethernet port

✔ A USB port

✔ A combined optical digital audio output/headphone out — 3.5mm minijack

The USB port supports a shared printer. The audio port can connect to your stereo. You just need a 3.5mm stereo phone plug–to–RCA phone plug adapter cable. You can get one from the Apple Store or your local Radio Shack. If you have more than one sound system, you can install multiple AirPort Express units.

You can take the AirPort Express in your suitcase and use it to create a Wi-Fi network in your hotel if the hotel has only wired Internet.

Figure 2-10:
The AirPort
Express,
plugged in.

Photo courtesy of Apple, Inc.

iPod and iPhone

If you haven't yet heard of the Apple iPod portable music player or the revolutionary iPhone, please return this book for a full refund. They're everywhere and have changed the way we listen to music and use our cellphones.

Although iPhones and iPods work fine with PCs, they are particularly well integrated with Macs and their digital lifestyle applications, including mail, address book, iChat and iPhoto. I talk more about the iPod, iPhone, and its mother ship, the iTunes Store, in Chapter 11.

Apple TV

Apple TV is a box that bridges your Macintosh and the Internet with your big-screen home entertainment center. It has a 40GB or 160GB hard drive inside to automatically store movies and TV shows that you downloaded to your iTunes library. You can also display your photos at high definition in your living room. Apple TV connects your home computer network (Mac or PC) to your living room electronics suite in several ways:

- ✔ High-Definition Multimedia Interface (HDMI) for high-definition video and audio.
- ✔ Component video for HDTVs that accepts separated red, green, and blue (RGB) signals, but no single-cable composite video — it's not designed for conventional TVs.
- ✔ Optical audio for the latest sound systems.
- ✔ Analog RCA stereo audio for just about any home audio system ever made.
- ✔ 10/100 Base-T Ethernet if you prefer a wired connection to your computer.
- ✔ USB 2.0.
- ✔ AirPort/Wi-Fi 802.11n for fast access to your wireless network.
- ✔ Infrared receiver for use with the Apple Remote — one comes with the Apple TV.

The Apple TV is styled like the Mac mini, as you can see in Figure 2-11, but is a bit larger: 7.7 inches (197 mm) square, like Time Capsule. It weighs 2.4 pounds, a bit more than a kilogram. Its power cord connects directly to a wall outlet or a power strip, with no space-hogging power adapter. We don't need *their kind* in our living rooms.

Figure 2-11:
Apple TV,
hooked up
to a high-
definition
television.

Photo courtesy of Apple, Inc.

Support

Apple doesn't just sell hardware — it *supports* that hardware (and software). Most Apple products come with 90-day free telephone support and a one-year warranty on the hardware, subject to the usual fine print that says it's limited and doesn't cover products hurled into active volcanoes or used to stop stampeding elephants, and other forms of abuse. In my experience, Apple gives customers the benefit of the doubt.

Each Apple retail store includes a Genius bar — a section at the back of the shop where Apple-trained experts are available to answer your questions and provide technical support for Apple products. The service is free, but it's best to make an appointment, which you can do online at www.apple.com/retail/geniusbar.

The following sections introduce you to the three big support programs Apple offers as add-ons.

AppleCare

AppleCare extends the phone service and warranty that come with your Mac, usually to three years, but always check the terms before you buy.

Service policies are a form of insurance. If they're priced properly, you pay a bit more for the policy than your losses are likely to be on average. But the term *on average* is the kicker. If something goes wrong with your computer after the warranty expires, repairs can be very expensive — often a good fraction of the cost of a new machine. Portables, like laptops and iPods, take a lot of abuse. For a new Mac user, I think the free phone support and the peace of mind justify the added cost.

OS X upgrades

OS X is included with new Macs. The version you get has a number, such as 10.6.2. Here's what that number means:

- ✔ The *10* refers to OS X. *X* is the Roman numeral ten.
- ✔ The *.6* is a major release; 10.6 is also known by its Apple not-so-secret code name Snow Leopard.
- ✔ The *.2* is a minor upgrade, known as a point release, that typically includes bug fixes, minor enhancements, and support for new hardware.

Apple traditionally provides point releases and other minor changes, such as security patches, for free via its Software Update service. You're notified about the availability of such changes once a week unless you change the settings.

Expect major releases every 18 months to two years. Apple charges for these; in the past, each one cost about $129. You could also buy a family pack with five licenses for about $200. When an upgrade comes out, it's usually a good idea to wait a bit to see whether it receives negative reviews or whether the upgrade breaks programs you use. But Apple upgrades have been relatively painless, and the added features are usually worth the expense. So expect to buy an upgrade at least once in the lifetime of your Mac.

MobileMe

MobileMe is an online Apple service that's integrated with Mac OS X. It isn't an Internet service provider, but it does offer e-mail, chat, groups, Web page hosting, a photo and video gallery, and 10GB of storage space. It costs $100 per year, and a family pack is available. Keep in mind, though, that you can often find a lower price for MobileMe by shopping around, such as at Amazon.com.

The Internet-based storage service iDisk shows up on your computer's desktop along with your local disk storage. You can use it to back up files or to share files with others.

Green Apples

Many people insist that corporations they buy from must address the impact of the corporation on global warming and other environmental problems. Apple takes these concerns seriously and has moved aggressively to make its products more green. Some of the steps Apple has taken include

- ✔ **Improve the energy efficiency of its products, especially when they are in Idle or Standby mode.** Idle computers consume substantial amounts of electricity, and much carbon dioxide — a major cause of global warming — is released, generating electricity. All Macs meet stringent EnergyStar 4.0 requirements. See www. energystar.gov.

- ✔ **Design its products to be easy to recycle.** Apple fabricates the chassis of most new Macs from the metal aluminum, which is particularly easy to recycle and commands a high scrap value.

- ✔ **Switch its displays to use LED backlighting.** it's more energy efficient than the fluorescent lamps that it and others previously used. LEDs are also mercury-free.

- ✔ **Eliminate hazardous chemical use when making circuit boards, cables, and other**

components for its computers. These are now free of BFR and PVC and comply with European Union hazardous material reduction regulations (RoHS).

- ✔ **Reduce the size and waste in its packaging.**

- ✔ **Provide a carbon lifecycle analysis of its products.** This is something that few companies do. You can find these reports at www.apple.com/environment/ resources/environmental performance.html.

- ✔ **Take back old computers and displays (even PCs) when you buy a new Mac.** Apple recycles computers collected in North America at carefully vetted facilities in North America; it doesn't ship equipment overseas for disposal. To find out about its recycling programs, see www.apple. com/environment/recycling.

For more information on green Apples, visit www.apple.com/environment. I suggest other beneficial ways to use your computer in Chapter 21.

The MobileMe service enhances several applications in the Apple iLife suite, which is the subject of Part IV. It can also be used to synchronize two or more computers' address books and appointment lists. And, photocasting lets you send pictures to other Macs — perfect for grandparents. See Chapter 18.

Application software offerings

Although Macs come with an impressive array of easy-to-use applications that are ready to go, Apple sells a number of additional software tools. They break down into three groups, roughly by price and power.

Small, extra-cost upgrades

Apple has a few of these, including QuickTime Pro and JamPacks, that add music and tools to GarageBand.

Advanced applications

These applications typically sell in the $80-to-$300 price range and are suitable for quality, commercial work. They include the following:

- ✔ **Aperture:** The top-of-the-line Apple solution for professional photographers.

- ✔ **BentoBox:** This simple-to-use, inexpensive but powerful personal database that syncs with a version for the iPhone and iPod touch.

- ✔ **FileMaker:** This full-featured database application is also available in a fully compatible version for Windows.

- ✔ **Final Cut Express HD:** A big step up from iMovie (the video-editing component of iLife) because it captures, edits, and outputs HDV (high-definition video).

- ✔ **iWork:** This Apple office suite includes the Pages word processor and page-layout program, Numbers spreadsheet, and Keynote, Apple's answer to Microsoft PowerPoint presentation software.

- ✔ **Logic Express:** A powerful music-creation package.

Pro applications

These applications are world-class solutions that hold their own against any solution on the market and are generally less expensive than their top competitors:

- ✔ **Final Cut Studio:** Everything you need to edit and post-produce a full-length feature motion picture or a TV series. Movies edited in Studio have won an Emmy and received one Oscar nomination. The package includes

  - *Color:* Adjust the tone and color values of your film.

  - *Compressor:* Convert between formats.

  - *DVD Studio Pro:* Make professional DVD masters.

  - *Final Cut Pro:* Use native HDV and real-time editing.

- ✔ **Logic Pro:** A powerful music composition tool that I don't begin to understand.

Server software solutions

Mac makes a mean server version of OS X, and the full version is licensed without the per-seat head tax that brand-M imposes. Server products include

- Apple Remote Desktop
- FileMaker Server, which doesn't require OS X Server
- Mac OS X Server
- WebObjects for Java server applications
- Xsan Storage Area Network (SAN) for Mac OS X

Chapter 3

Deciding What to Buy

*B*uying a computer can be a bewildering experience. Stores are stuffed with oodles of models in different shapes and sizes, and they're offered in a wide range of prices. Many of the options you're asked to select involve options that only a geek could love, like the number of bytes of RAM to buy (what if I don't like lamb?) or the hard drive capacity (what if I prefer a soft drive?).

Computer store sales staff can be helpful, but all too often they give questionable advice. Many aren't knowledgeable about the latest features and software. Sometimes they receive financial incentives to sell in-stock models that aren't moving.

Buying a Macintosh simplifies things quite a bit. Apple has only half a dozen or so models and relatively few options for each one. It doesn't sell cheap, lowball models that require expensive upgrades to do anything useful. The lowest-price Apple models can more than meet the needs of most users.

Still, you need to make choices, and you generally should make your decision (or at least narrow it to a couple of possibilities) before you go off to the store or log on to Apple.com. In this chapter, you find tips that can help you decide which type of Mac suits your needs. (If you skipped the two preceding chapters, be sure to check out the detailed introduction to the different models in Chapter 2.) Switching to a Mac may also affect how you connect your computer accessories and access the features you need, because your new Mac is likely an upgrade to better technology and some ports and options on new Macs are different from those on older Windows computers. In this chapter, you find the most important concepts you need to know, and I provide a section at the end that helps you decide where to buy.

Selecting a Conversion Strategy

Time to take a deep breath. Before I dig into which model and which options to buy, I want you to think about what you're trying to accomplish and then consider the best way to get exactly what you want. (I'm just talking about computers here — don't get excited). There's more than one way to peel an Apple.

To begin, answer the following questions honestly (the mind-reading chip in the spine of this book is automatically disabled when you're on this page, so no one will know your answers):

- **How often do you use your computer?** Is it less than once a week, several times a week, every day, or hours each day?

- **What do you use your computer for?** Do you crunch numbers in a spreadsheet, write *For Dummies* books, check social networking sites such as Facebook.com, surf the Internet, text friends, look for soulmates, download music, or play games?

- **Which new tasks do you want to use it for?** Do you want to organize photos, develop a Web site, podcast, or edit movies?

- **Where do you use your computer?** Do you use it in a den or office, anywhere in the house you feel like, at work, at work and at home, or on the road?

- **What's your budget?** Do you want to spend less than $1,000, $1,000 to $2,000, or whatever it takes?

Depending on your answers, you have several different switching approaches to consider. I try to group them sensibly and give the categories cute, easy-to-remember names.

I'm not a big fan of computers for small children. They spend, and will spend, too much of their lives in front of video screens as it is. But if you're buying a computer for your kid or kids, make sure that you understand how to set limits (by using parental controls). OS X has some useful features to help you enforce them. Before buying anything, be sure to look carefully at the section that discusses Macs for kids in Chapter 17.

Taking it slow

No need to rush things. The Mac mini is perfect if you're the cautious type who wants to convert gradually and not spend a lot of money. Start out with worry-free Internet surfing and switch over additional applications as you become more comfortable with OS X. Of course, you can use the spiffy iLife applications that come with the Mac mini as soon as you set it up. Taking it slowly, which can be the lowest-cost conversion strategy, assumes that you already have a fairly up-to-date PC set up with a good-quality CRT or flat-panel display. All you really need to buy is a Mac mini. The tiny mini doesn't take up much room — it's not much bigger than an external CD burner. Just find a spare outlet for it on your power strip.

If you don't have a compatible USB keyboard and mouse, you can add those items to your shopping list — literally. Many supermarkets now carry these accessories.

For extra convenience, purchase a USB *KVM switch,* which lets you share a keyboard, mouse, and display between two computers. (More expensive KVM models can support more than two computers.) In a KVM setup, you can work on the PC and, after pressing a special key combination on your keyboard, quickly switch to the Mac and check a Web site and then return to the PC with another key press. Be sure to buy a USB KVM switch, not the more common PS/2 type. (I'm assuming that your PC is new enough to have a USB port. If it isn't, you need a separate keyboard and mouse for your Mac.) I tell you more about which items to buy later in this chapter, and I describe how to hook up a KVM switch in Chapter 4.

If your PC is already part of a Wi-Fi wireless network, you can easily incorporate the mini into the network. If you don't have one, you may need an Ethernet router and a cable — inexpensive items. See Chapter 9 for details.

Macs tend to keep their resale value longer than PCs, so you aren't taking much of a financial risk with this approach. If you aren't happy with the Mac mini, you probably won't have any trouble unloading it on eBay or craigslist.

Living on the go

If you travel a lot or simply like to work or be online in different parts of your house, a MacBook or MacBook Pro laptop may be just right for you. If you need to bring your computer to work and also have it at home, you probably already have a laptop, but maybe you want something more up-to-date.

Mac laptops are complete, powerful computer systems. They're elegant-looking and priced competitively with all but the cheapest PC laptops. You can buy one and still keep your PC setup intact. They can network with your PC, just like the mini, and you can even hook one up to a KVM switch when you have it at home, so that you can use your keyboard, mouse, and display with the Mac laptop.

Why not Linux?

You have another way to escape the clutches of Microsoft that's cheaper than buying a new Mac. You have no doubt heard of Linux, an operating system developed by volunteer computer programmers. Linux is closely related to the Unix operating system that underlies Mac OS X, but differences exist. Linux was once a toy for übergeeks, but it has come a long way. Some people now use it as their only personal computer operating system. You can probably use it with your existing PC hardware. But Linux still lacks the polish and ease of use of a Mac or even a Windows PC. If you're technically inclined and want to find out how operating systems work, by all means give Linux a try. Readers of this book are probably better off with a commercially supported operating system. The good news is that much of the software that runs on Linux also runs on Macs. See Chapter 19.

Giving your PC the heave-ho

Maybe you're the type who just dives into the pool without dipping your toe in first. You may as well plan on just replacing your PC with a new Mac. I tell you how to transfer all your files in Chapter 6. Either the iMac or MacBook model can take your old PC's place in the home:

- ✔ **A desktop iMac can fit on your desk where the PC display now sits.**

  If you have a good-quality video display and enough room, you can keep your display on your desk and plug it into the iMac for two-screen computing. You need a video adapter cable, and all you have to do is tell the iMac where the other display sits relative to the iMac so that OS X knows how to match them up to allow you to drag windows from one screen to the other, across the adjacent screen edges.

- ✔ **If your only computer is a laptop, switching to a MacBook or MacBook Pro is simple.** If the PC laptop has Wi-Fi networking, the two laptops should talk to each other without much ado, allowing you to transfer files. (See Chapter 9.) Otherwise, a simple Ethernet cable should do the trick. If the laptop is so old that it has no network port, you have to get a bit more creative, and I cover those details in Chapter 6.

Spending lots of dough

If you have the money, I recommend a Mac Pro with the large Apple Cinema Display — or, even better, two Cinema displays. (Al Gore has three.) It'll knock your socks off. And while you're at it, grab a thin, light MacBook Air laptop to take with you on trips and some MacBooks that other family members can use. (You weren't going to stick your kids or spouse with that old PC, were you?)

Gaming glow

Does playing computer games, particularly those with detailed three-dimensional visuals, dominate your computer use? Your life? If so, you can get by with the lower end of the Mac line (the mini, the MacBook, and the low-end iMac), all three use a built-in NVIDIA GeForce 9400M graphics processor that's quite powerful. But for higher performance, most MacBook Pros, the high-end iMac, and the Mac Pro blast out 3D imagery with more powerful graphics engines. The Mac Pro accepts graphics cards from either ATI or NVIDIA.

Relaxing as a couch potat-oh

Computers are invading our living rooms. The home entertainment center is going online. Channel surfing is merging with Internet surfing. If nothing on the tube is worth watching, try YouTube. If you want to integrate your Mac with your TV watching, you have these options:

- **Set up a few cables and then relax:** All Macs have video outputs designed to display stunning images on large-format, high-definition TVs and displays — though you probably need adapter cables. See the section "Ports that require an adapter for Macs," later in this chapter.

- **Integrate your computer and TV:** The simple-to-use Apple Remote coupled with a Mac mini can let you effortlessly switch among broadcast content, Internet feed, home movies and slide shows, and other video material.

- **Never get off the sofa:** Alternatively, you can buy the $229 Apple TV (TV), which connects with Macs and Windows PCs around your house by way of wireless (or wired) Ethernet. You can play downloaded digital content — movies, TV shows, music videos, songs — as well as home videos and photos right on your large-screen HDTV or projection system. It's all controlled by the same tiny Apple remote.

Following the KISS principle

KISS stands for keep it simple, stupid. Whichever way you go, I recommend that you start with your Mac configured pretty much the way it is when it comes out of the box. You can customize lots of settings, and you can download software add-ons. But the less of this you do, the less likely you are to get into trouble and the easier it is to obtain support. I mention a few customizations that I think are worthwhile later in this book.

Getting a Mac for less

Bargain hunting is harder in the Mac world than it is in the PC world. Generally, price reductions happen most often when the inventory of a product is too high or when a new product is about to be introduced. Because so many PC manufacturers exist, these supply problems happen often for PCs. Apple, however, has better control of its distribution chain and tries very hard to keep Macintosh clearance sales from happening. They still do appear, but nowhere nearly as often as with PCs, and even when they do, the price cuts are rarely as dramatic. If you're ready to buy a Mac, it's not worth waiting months for one of these sales. Peripheral devices such as printers, scanners, and hard drives are another matter — they're often discounted. Apple also sometimes offers refurbished Macs at its online store. They typically come with the standard Apple warranty. You can search the Apple Store with the keyword *refurbished* to find what's on sale.

Apple often offers an education discount, so if you have an affiliation with an educational institution (student, teacher, staff member), bring ID with you when you visit the Apple Store. In my experience, the store staff is liberal in which types it accepts.

I also don't recommend buying a used Mac in most cases. There's something about unpacking a brand-new machine and setting it up that builds confidence. You know the stuff was recently tested at the factory and should work. You have Apple tech support and, possibly, the people at the retail store to call on if you

have trouble. In the worst case, you can return the Mac for a refund. Switching from one computer system to another is a complex enough task without having to worry about possible hardware problems. And you may not find much of a bargain — Macs tend to command higher prices on the used market than PCs of comparable vintage. But if you want to try your luck on the used market, here are some tips.

✔ Buy locally, such as from `www.craigs list.com` or someone you know, and pick up your Mac in person. That way, you can check it out before you hand over money. You also avoid the risk of product damage during shipping.

✔ Buy only a used Mac that has an Intel processor. Select the About This Mac option from the Apple () menu to see the processor type. Macs sold before 2006 use a different microprocessor, the PowerPC, or, if it's really old, a Motorola 68k series. These models are significantly slower, and Apple support for PowerPC machines is winding down. (The 68k models are for antique computer collectors only — a fun hobby, but not what this book is about.)

✔ If possible, find a machine that has time remaining on an AppleCare contract.

✔ Don't pay more than the price of a new, low-end Mac. A new Macbook will likely approach or better the performance of a used MacBook Pro, for example, and you receive all the benefits of a new unit.

Figuring Out What's on Your Windows Computer

Before deciding what to buy, figure out what's on your existing computer. You want your new Mac to have at least the capabilities of your present computer, plus lots of room to grow. You may know some of this information, and much of it may be on the sales receipt or the original box your computer came in. Of course, if you have added options and peripherals, that info may be out-of-date.

If you're having trouble with your PC, skip this section for now and see the section on recovering data from a damaged PC in Chapter 6.

The easiest way to find the information on your current configuration is to ask Windows to give it to you. Follow these steps:

1. **Choose Start⇨My Computer.**

   The My Computer window should appear, and you should see a section labeled Hard Disk Drives. If more than one drive is shown, start with the drive labeled C:.

2. **Select your C drive and then choose File⇨Properties. (Or, you can right-click the drive and choose Properties.)**

   Figure 3-1 shows the Drive C: Properties window, which tells you how much disk space is used and how much is available.

3. **Make a note of the drive's total capacity and how much of it is used space.**

   The numbers to the right, shown in gigabytes (GB), are all you need. You can organize your notes in the following form:

Drive letter	C:_____	_____	_____
Total capacity	_____	_____	_____
Used space	_____	_____	_____

Figure 3-1:
The
Windows
XP Drive C:
Properties
pane.

 4. **When you're done, click the Cancel button to close the drive's Properties window.**

 5. **Repeat this procedure for any other hard drives shown in the My Computer window.**

 6. **You should see, at the bottom of the My Computer window, the Control Panel icon. Click it.**

    Alternatively, you can select the Control Panel directly from the Start menu. When the Control Panel window appears, double-click the System icon.

 7. **On the General tab of the System Properties dialog box that appears (see Figure 3-2), make a note of the following information:**

    • Operating system (for example, Microsoft Windows XP)

    • Edition (for example, Home)

    • Last installed service pack (for example, SP2)

    • Manufacturer and model number

    • Speed (for example, 1.8 GHz)

    • Amount of main memory (for example, 224MB RAM)

Figure 3-2:
Windows
XP system
information.

Navigating from PC to Mac Ports

When you're deciding which Mac model to buy (and what you can afford), you need to figure out which of the devices you already own will work with your selected model. Unfortunately, few things about computers are as confusing and annoying as the bowl of spaghetti wiring underneath the desk. That's why you find in this section a quick guide to what goes where in the Mac world. Much of it is the same as on a modern PC, but some old favorites are no longer with us. In many cases, you can buy adapters to make the necessary connections; in other cases, well, it's time to move on.

Finding your way in the back of a Mac

When you're trying to figure out where to plug things in, the good news is that Apple keeps things simple by limiting the number of ports it uses, and it has a good track record of picking the most useful ones. In the sections that follow, I summarize the ports available in new Macs now on the market. Except as noted, the ports in this section are common to all current Macs. They're also common on late-model PCs.

If a plug doesn't fit into a jack with a firm but modest push, don't try to force it in. Triple-check to make sure that the shapes and icons match up exactly, and then look for dirt or other obstacles in both the plug and jack.

Audio input and output

All Macs come with two little round jacks that look like the earphone jacks on a portable radio or an iPod. One of them is marked with a tiny pair of earphones. The other is a *line-in* jack, which accepts audio from other devices. Both accept $1/8$-inch (3.5 mm) stereo plugs, and you can buy a wide variety of cables, adapters, and other accessories that work with them at your local Radio Shack. But these diminutive jacks are much cleverer than that. They also can work with newer optical digital audio devices that use the *TOSLINK* standard, which is becoming more popular in the world of consumer electronics. If you shine a light down the little hole, you can see the tiny optical port in the center shining back at you.

Ethernet

Ethernet is the most popular technology for enabling computers to talk to each other over a wire. Ethernet came from the same Xerox lab that developed the graphical interface that the Mac first popularized. Ethernet is available in 10, 100, and 1,000 Mbps versions. Macs support all three, except for the Macbook Air, which requires an optional, separate adapter for wired Ethernet.

Ethernet connectors look like fatter versions of the connectors used on most telephones in North America. Just like with the telephone connectors, you find a little, easy-to-break plastic tab that you have to squeeze to pull the connector out. Be gentle.

Don't plug your telephone line into this port — it could damage your computer. Current Macs don't have built-in telephone modems. Apple sells an external modem that plugs into a USB port.

ExpressCard/34 (17-inch MacBook Pro only)

The ExpressCard/34 is a standard for expansion modules, which are basically cards that you can slide into personal computers, though they're mostly used with laptops.

Only the 17-inch MacBook Pro has an ExpressCard/34 slot. Figure 3-3 shows a MacBook Pro with an ExpressCard/34 card installed to access Verizon wireless Internet service. Accessing such a wide-area network is probably the most common use for the ExpressCard/34 slot.

As its name implies, the ExpressCard/34 card is 34 millimeters (mm) wide, about two-thirds the size of a credit card. It replaces an older standard known as CardBus PC card, or PCMCIA card. You can also find bigger ExpressCard/54 cards (54 mm wide), but no current Apple models support them. See www.expresscard.org for more info on which devices are available in this format. But before buying one, make sure the manufacturer offers Mac drivers.

FireWire

Apple created a different serial bus, *FireWire,* to support connecting high-speed devices. Also known as IEEE-1394, it comes in two speeds: 400 megabits per second (Mbps) and 800 Mbps. A number of camcorder manufacturers adopted FireWire 400 (Sony calls it *i.Link*), but USB 2.0 is almost as fast and most non-tape video recorders now use USB 2.0. Only the white plastic MacBook has a FireWire 400 port. High-end Macs sport FireWire 800 ports, which use a different connector, although 800-to-400 adapters are available and inexpensive.

Figure 3-3: ExpressCard/34 for wide-area networking installed in a MacBook Pro.

Infrared

Infrared (IR) is a form of invisible light that's used in most remote controls supplied with televisions, stereos, and other devices. When you press a button on the remote, it projects a beam of invisible light out the front that's coded with a signal that tells the TV or other device which button you pushed. A magic spot on your TV or device receives these IR signals, and if you point the remote in its general direction, the device should do what you wanted. A Mac can work with its own, optional Apple Remote, so it has a magic spot too.

Mini DisplayPort

Older (analog) methods of sending signals to displays limit the quality of pictures that can be shown. A Mini DisplayPort sends images to the display in digital form, preserving the images' full fidelity for viewing on flat-panel computer displays and high-definition televisions (HDTVs). The white MacBook uses a variant, the mini-DVI connector. The mini has both. Apple and other vendors sell converter cables that let you hook up Mini DisplayPort and mini-DVI ports to most digital and analog video displays, including most large-screen television sets.

PCI Express (Mac Pro and Xserve only)

Peripheral Component Interconnect Express (PCI Express or PCIe) is the newest, blazingly fast incarnation of the classic open-the-cover-and-plug-a-card-in-the-motherboard expansion model. Only the Mac Pro and the Xserve now have these slots. The Pro has four of them, one of which is typically occupied by the graphics card. You can use the slots to add more graphics cards or for ultra-high-speed communications cards, and they're handy for other specialized applications. These capabilities excite video producers and serious gamers, but if you don't know why you need expansion cards, you probably don't need one.

PCI Express isn't compatible with the older PCI or PCI-X cards. Xserve has three slots that can accept a PCI-X card, one of which is occupied by a graphics card.

Universal Serial Bus (USB)

Intel invented USB technology to let a wide variety of low- and medium-speed devices connect to a computer using only one type of port. Apple was the first to popularize it for use with keyboards and mice. USB is a *bus* because more than one device can share the same port. *Serial* means that all the data marches down a single pair of wires. The current version, USB 2.0, can support high-speed devices such as disk drives. All new Macs have two or more USB 2.0 ports. Older USB 1.0 and 1.1 devices should plug in and work fine in a USB 2.0 port, though they can slow it down.

Wi-Fi and Bluetooth

Strictly speaking, Wi-Fi and Bluetooth aren't ports in that there's no place to connect a wire. That's because they support *wireless* communications. Wi-Fi is mostly used for networking computers within a home or office, and is essentially Ethernet without wires. Bluetooth has a shorter range and is mainly for connecting small devices, such as printers, wireless keyboards and mice, and for wireless headsets of the type used with cellphones. Macs generally support both, though Wi-Fi is optional on the Mac Pro.

Ports that require an adapter for Macs

If you have a device with a connection type that a Mac doesn't support directly, you might still be able to connect your device by using an adapter. This section covers the types of connections that Macs no longer support, but that you can still use with an adapter. By adding the adapters you need to your list of items to buy, you can get your new Mac setup running quickly, with less hassle.

Before you buy any adapter, make sure that the manufacturer supports the latest version of Mac OS X. Many don't support Mac, and some support only Mac OS 9 or old versions of OS X. Also realize that when an adapter maker says that it supports OS X, it doesn't guarantee that your printer, scanner, or digital bread maker will work perfectly. If you're buying new stuff, avoid peripherals that require an adapter.

Camera memory cards: The 13- and 15-inch MacBook Pros come with an SD card slot, where you can plug in the SD memory cards used in many digital cameras and camcorders. Many other card types are out there, but Apple apparently chose not to clutter its spiffy boxes with half a dozen camera card slots. USB adapters that accept most card types are inexpensive and readily available, and you can always hook up your camera by using a USB cable.

Fiber Distributed Data Interface (FDDI): This high-performance data network sends information over optical fibers rather than wires. You need a Mac Pro or Xserve and a PCI Express FDDI card, which Apple sells and supports.

High-Definition Multimedia Interface (HDMI): HDMI input is standard on most flat-panel and high-definition televisions. Although many also allow analog input, HDMI is the input to use if you want the video quality you're paying those big bucks for. Apple and other vendors, such as Monoprice. com, sell adapters that let you connect a Mac to that HDMI port. You may also need a separate connection for audio. You'll be amazed when your Mac's display fills your living room wall. You'll also need a separate cable for audio. See RCA audio later in this list.

Musical Instrument Digital Interface (MIDI): This music industry standard was introduced in 1983 for connecting musical keyboards (the ones with black-and-white ivories, not the kind you write e-mail on). The Apple Core Audio offers strong MIDI support in software. Many new MIDI devices use USB or FireWire interfaces and work directly with Macs that have the appropriate interface. Older instruments may have a 5-pin DIN connector and, yup, you need an adapter.

Modem: Macs no longer come with dialup modem ports (the type you can plug a phone line into). Apple sells a modem built into a short cable that plugs into a USB port for about $50. Other USB modems are on the market, some cheaper, but make sure that they support Mac OS X.

Parallel printer (IEEE-1284): This printer interface is also known as a *Centronics* port, named after a long-defunct company that made printers for minicomputers back when Richard Nixon was president. If you have a printer you love that talks only parallel port, Keyspan.com makes a USB–to–parallel port adapter that supports OS X.

RCA audio: This simple connector (which dates back to the early 1940s) is common on home audio systems. Belkin Monoprice.com and Radio Shack sell a cheap cable that plugs into your Mac's 3.5 mm stereo audio output and has a pair of RCA plugs at the other end that can be inserted in your stereo. For RCA video, see the S-Video bullet, near the end of this list.

Small computer system interface (SCSI): Apple popularized this interface for hard drives with the Mac Plus, and SCSI (pronounced "scuzzy") is still used in high-end applications. However, Apple has long since adopted the Serial ATA standard used by most PC manufacturers. USB-SCSI adapters are available, but they generally don't work with OS X. Ratoc Systems, Inc. (`www.ratoc systems.com`), sells a FireWire-to-SCSI adapter that it claims does work with OS X. It's a tad pricey, and it uses the latest UltraSCSI connector, so you will need special cables for first-generation SCSI devices. That old SCSI scanner had better be worth it.

Serial port (RS-232, RS-422): Apple largely dropped serial ports in favor of USB ports when it introduced the first iMac. (A serial port is provided on the Xserve back panel because the server world expects one.) Several companies sell USB–to–serial port adapters. Try Keyspan.com and Serialio.com. You can also buy Bluetooth-to-serial adapters that let you control serial devices without running wires.

S-Video: Apple sells an inexpensive adapter that converts your Mac's video output to S-Video and composite video (an RCA jack), the two most common analog television standards. With one of these adapters, you can show your photo collection on any TV with a video input jack.

Video Graphics Array (VGA) and Super VGA: VGA and SVGA are by far the most popular ports for connecting older analog computer monitors. Apple offers adapters that connect VGA/SVGA displays and other devices to the Mac's video output port. This adapter is free with some Mac models and an extra-cost (about $20) option with others.

Stuff that won't work

You may have some plug-in cards that do specialized tasks in your PC. Sorry, but unless they're PCI Express (PCIe), they don't work on a current Mac. Much of the functionality that these cards were used for, such as Ethernet networking, is built into Macs, and USB and FireWire devices replace other uses.

Using Your Old Equipment with a Mac

If you've been a PC user for a while, you probably have purchased a number of accessories. Some of them may be usable with your new Mac, saving you the expense of buying new stuff. Whether a particular device is Mac compatible depends on its port interface — the type of cable you use to hook it to the computer — and whether Mac software is available that works with the device.

You might also consider the device's age and whether your new Mac will offer a different and improved way of accomplishing what your old, familiar accessories do. Older devices may not have that much life left in them, and worse, they may simply be obsolete. Maybe you have a SCSI Zip drive. The storage capacity of a Zip drive was impressive in its day, but it's now dwarfed by the capacity of a cheap CD-RW disc that's usable in any Mac, so it may not be worth finding an adapter that lets you hook it up to your new Mac unless you have a large collection of Zip disks — and even then, you're probably better off copying them to your PC and then transferring them to the Mac. Or, you could look for a Zip drive with a USB connection. It should work on a Mac with no fuss.

I can't possibly discuss every combination of Mac model, non-Apple device, and software version, so check with the device manufacturer where possible.

Displays and projectors

If you're buying a mini or Mac Pro, using the display you have can save you money. A high-end display often costs more than a computer. Even if you're buying a Mac with a built-in display, an extra display is handy. A Mac can use it as an extension to the desktop area, letting you drag an icon or window from one screen to the other. Or, you can set up the second display to mirror what you're seeing on your main display — handy for letting others see what you're doing. (Select System Preferences from the Apple menu and click the Displays icon to set it all up.)

The following sections help you assess what you need in order to connect your Mac to commonly used displays.

CRT displays

CRT (cathode ray tube) displays are rapidly going the way of the dinosaur, perhaps for the same reason: They are too big and consume too much energy. Still, if you have a good-quality display and a tight budget or if you need the richer color fidelity that CRTs offer for high-end graphics work, using that old CRT might make sense. The good news is that almost all computer-grade CRTs produced since the 1990s use a VGA cable that should work fine with the Apple VGA adapter.

Otherwise, you should replace that CRT with an iMac, saving you acres of space on and under your desk — and you have no display cables to worry about. See how to recycle your old CRT safely in Chapter 22.

Flat-screen displays and HDTVs

Flat screens work fine with Macs, including those with built-in displays. The same goes for flat-panel or high-definition television sets. The only question is whether to connect your Mac to your flat-screen display or HDTV using a digital or an analog interface (that is, the available port where you connect the cable from your Mac to your display). In either case, make sure that you have the right adapter cables. Digital and analog interfaces are described in this list:

- ✔ **Digital:** Digital connections generally produce better results. For a digital interface, see which video output connector your Mac has (see Chapter 2) and which connector or cable your display has. You may need more than one cable. For example, if your Mac comes with a Mini DisplayPort (most do) and your HDTV has an HDMI connector on the back, you need to get a Mini DisplayPort to dual-link DVI cable and a DVI-to-HDMI cable. Check the booklet that came with your display and the booklet that came with your Mac for details about your specific equipment. Also see the list of connector types in the section "Navigating from PC to Mac Ports," earlier in this chapter.

- ✔ **Analog:** You need a VGA adapter that you plug into the DVI port on your Mac. Some Macs come with these adapters; otherwise, order one from Apple.

Projectors

Big-screen projectors and PowerPoint presentations dominate business communication these days and are rapidly taking over our schools. We hate to contribute to this cultural disaster, but the truth is that these projectors generally work with a Mac. Most take VGA, so you need that VGA adapter.

Keyboard and mouse

When deciding whether you can use a keyboard or mouse that you already have, here's the short version of the story:

- ✔ **If you have a two-button scroll wheel mouse with a wire coming out of it that has a USB connector:** If you have this flat, rectangular, metal plug (which is about the size of a fingernail) at the other end, it's something worth keeping.

- ✔ **If you have a Windows keyboard with a USB connector:** It works fine, but a couple of keys are labeled differently from Mac keyboards, and that may make it more trouble than it's worth.

- ✔ **If you have a cool keyboard or mouse or another pointing device that you like:** You might have wireless, for example — read on for the longer story.

- ✔ **If you have some old piece of junk:** Skip this section and buy something new.

Connections, connections

Check how your keyboard and mouse connect to your PC. The three most common methods are a USB cable, a PS/2 cable, and wireless:

- ✔ **A USB cable** should work just fine with your Mac.

- ✔ **A PS/2 connector** is round and has a pastel-colored shell. PS/2 doesn't work with your Mac.

These days, many manufacturers make only USB keyboards and mice and include an adapter that converts it to PS/2. So take a closer look at what you think is a PS/2 plug to see whether it's just one of these adapters, in which case you're in luck — just pull the USB plug from the adapter and plug it into your Mac.

- ✔ **Wireless devices** have a built-in radio transmitter rather than a wire. The receiver is often in a finger-size pod that plugs into the computer, or it can be built in. Some devices transmit using technology that's proprietary to the maker; others use Bluetooth. All Macs come with Bluetooth inside, and Bluetooth devices generally work with Bluetooth-equipped Macs. But you may need special software to take full advantage of this feature on a Mac. A wireless device that uses a USB receiver module and a proprietary transmission scheme may need special software as well. Check with the manufacturer in either case.

Keyboard layout

Mac keyboards have two special keys in the lowest row, to the left of the spacebar. One is labeled *Option,* and to its right is a key with an Apple logo (🍎) and a fan symbol (⌘), known as the *Command key* in Apple-ese. On PC keyboards, these two keys are the Windows key and the Alt key, respectively. If you just plug a PC keyboard into a Mac, the Windows key works as the Command key, and the Alt key works as the Option key. Unfortunately, their positions are reversed from where they are on Mac keyboards. Because you're new to the Mac way of doing things, you don't need this tactile confusion. You can buy the DoubleCommand software (http://doublecommand.sourceforge.net), which lets you reverse these keys.

If all this seems more trouble than it's worth (I think so), buy a Mac keyboard. Apple offers both wired (USB) and wireless keyboards. You can choose a wired keyboard with or without a numeric keypad. Figure 3-4 shows an Apple wireless keyboard, with its special keys.

Figure 3-4:
Apple
wireless
keyboard.

Courtesy of Apple Inc.

KVM switch

A *KVM switch* lets you share your keyboard, video display, and mouse between two computers — more than two with fancier KVM models. Some KVMs also let you share a set of audio speakers or headphones. Two types of KVM switches are available, based on the type of connection they use for the keyboard and mouse: USB and PS/2. *Buy only a USB KVM switch.* Most recent PCs accept a USB input connection for the mouse and keyboard.

Many USB keyboards and mice come with USB-to-PS/2 adapters. The adapters aren't general-purpose converters, however. The USB keyboards and mice are smart enough to also talk PS/2, and the adapters just take the wires from the USB connector and jigger them into a PS/2 plug. Don't expect one of these adapters to convert the USB output of your KVM switch to PS/2.

Relics of days gone by

The mice and keyboards supplied with computers in the 1980s used RS-232 serial port connections. They're useless. Old Apple USB keyboards work fine on current Macs. If you have an older Apple keyboard or mouse with a round plug (Apple Desktop Bus), you can get an ADB-to-USB converter, but it's probably not worth the bother.

Printers, scanners, and fax machines

If you want to use your current printer, scanner, or fax machine with your new Mac, you may not have to buy anything extra or you may need an adapter. The following tips can help you figure out what you need to do:

✔ If your PC printer is of reasonably recent vintage and connects with USB, Ethernet, or Wi-Fi, it probably works with your Mac with little fuss. Macs come with oodles of drivers installed for current devices, though it never hurts to check for updated Mac drivers at the printer manufacturer's Web site.

✔ Older printers with parallel ports require USB–to–parallel port adapters, and chances of them working are a bit more iffy.

✔ All-in-one units generally work, but some features, such as receiving faxes to your hard drive, may not work with the Mac. (Get an Apple USB modem if your all-in-one's fax feature doesn't play Mac.)

The mantra again is to check with the manufacturer.

The scanner story is much the same. Recent USB and FireWire scanners should be fine, the latter assuming that your Mac has a FireWire port. Older SCSI devices need a pricey SCSI-to-FireWire adapter and still may not work. I wouldn't bother.

I talk about how to set up printers in OS X in Chapter 5.

External hard drives and flash drives

External hard drives and *flash drives* are those storage devices you can plug into your computer by using USB or FireWire connections. If you have one of these drives, you know how handy it is for storing backups or transferring files. USB and FireWire external hard drives should work fine, even if they were been formatted for your PC. Just plug them into the appropriate Mac port, and a drive icon appears on the desktop, which you can then click to access your files. The same goes for USB flash drives.

All Macs except the MacBook Air come with a CD and DVD burner — the *SuperDrive.* Apple sells an external SuperDrive for the Air.

An external USB or FireWire DVD reader or burner can come in handy if you want to watch DVDs from countries outside your zone. (The movie industry has obnoxiously chopped up the world into six zones, and Macs can play DVDs from only one zone.)

Internal drives

Because new drives have so much more capacity than those from even a couple of years ago, reusing internal hard drives may not be worth the bother. If you have an internal drive that you want to use in your new Mac, you can also buy hard drive enclosures that let you install your PC's internal hard drive and then plug it into your Mac via USB 2.0 or, if you have it, FireWire. You need to know which type of connection your hard drive uses.

Networking devices

Most of the hardware you use to create a home network (technically, a *local-area network,* or *LAN*) for sharing broadband Internet access should work with a Mac, including the items described in this list:

- ✔ **Ethernet switches and routers and Ethernet cabling:** Create a network with wires.

   If you decide to buy a new Ethernet router or hub, be sure to get a model that supports at least 100Base-T speeds (1000Base-T is blazingly fast but expensive and probably more than you need). If you own older 10Base-T equipment, you can use it, if you like.

- ✔ **Cable modems and DSL modems:** These modems come with high-speed Internet connections from your cable or digital subscriber line (DSL) provider, respectively. In all likelihood, you don't need any different hardware to use your existing Internet connection with your Mac.

- ✔ **Wireless routers and access points:** Set up the popular Wi-Fi wireless networking. The 802.11a, b, g, and n standards also work with a Mac. The *n* version is the fastest, and *b* is the slowest.

Wi-Fi networks work at the speed of the slowest device on the network, so an older laptop that supports only 802.11b is best left off the network when it isn't needed.

The Wi-Fi standard 802.11a operates in a different frequency band (5 GHz) from *b* and *g* modes (2.4 GHz). The radios in Wi-Fi-equipped Macs can operate on the 802.11a band as well, and newer models can work both bands simultaneously.

Digital cameras and camcorders

Macs and OS X provide extensive support for digital photography. Macs work with most digital cameras and support the *RAW mode* that high-end cameras produce when you want the best-quality images from them. The most common way to connect a camera to your Mac is by using a USB cable. The 13- and 15-inch MacBook Pros come with an SD card slot, the most popular high-end camera memory card. Macally.com sells an ExpressCard Media Reader that works with a 17-inch MacBook Pro. (For details about ExpressCard technology, see the section "ExpressCard/34," earlier in this chapter.)

Digital video recorders are also well supported. Some use USB 2.0, and others use FireWire, though manufacturers may call it IEEE-1394 or i.Link (the Sony brand name). USB works fine on all Macs; for FireWire, you need a FireWire-equipped Mac and, likely, a FireWire 400 to FireWire 800 adapter. The movie-editing software that comes with new Macs also supports the new high-definition (HD) camcorders, so you're ready for the latest in videography.

PC cards

PC cards, also known as PCMCIA cards, are about the size of credit cards, though a bit thicker, and they're designed to plug into special slots on PCs — primarily, laptops. The good news is that many of the capabilities that PC cards were typically used for, such as adding Ethernet, are built into Macs or can be added in other ways, such as with the Apple USB modem.

If you need to add functionality to your Mac by using a card, you have a couple of options:

- ✔ **Get a MacBook pro with ExpressCard/34.** ExpressCard/34 slots are basically the latest version of the PC card technology. With the introduction of Intel-based laptops, Apple switched to this newer standard. The ExpressCard, which is a little smaller than a PCMCIA card but has a much faster connection to a computer's innards, is available for many other uses because newer PC laptops come with ExpressCard slots, too.

ExpressCard/34 is available only on the 17-inch MacBook Pro.

✔ **Get a USB PC card reader that works with your card.** If you depend on a PC card for what you do, this may be your only choice. You insert your PC card into the reader and then plug the reader into your Mac by using the USB port.

Portable music players and cellphones

Needless to say, iPods and iPhones work hand in glove with Macs — after all, Apple makes both items.

Most other music players can connect to your Mac by way of USB so that you can at least transfer music files in an open format (such as MP3) to the player. Non-Apple players don't play songs purchased from the iTunes Store directly under OS X; however, you can burn a playlist to CD and then read it back in and transfer the files to your player.

The Microsoft Zune music player doesn't even have this USB option. Some third party may create a way to transfer files between Macs and Zunes, and of course, you can run Windows on the Mac and transfer files that way. But if you're seriously considering purchasing a Mac and a Zune, you may be reading the wrong self-help book.

Miscellany

You probably have accumulated a pile of computer-related items. Some of them are still useful, and others can be given away or recycled. This list gives you the rundown:

Blank discs: Keep full-size blank CD-Rs and DVD-Rs. Miniature discs and discs the size of credit cards don't work in the Mac's slot-loading drive (don't even try it), though they work in external tray-loading optical drives. Blank floppy and Zip disks can go away unless you work with folks who still use them and can get hold of an external drive that supports them. (Save one floppy disk to show your grandchildren.)

Cables: Ethernet, USB, and FireWire cables are worth hanging on to. Serial, SCSI, and proprietary cables can go. The ubiquitous 3-pin power cords used with most desktop PCs (IEC–C13) don't fit most Macs. One or two are always handy to keep around, however, for peripherals.

Computer furniture: A desk is a desk, and switching to a Mac can free some space on one, but if yours doesn't have good ergonomic design (see www. apple.com/about/ergonomics) or just looks terrible, it may be time for an upgrade.

Floppy disk holders: Holders for the ancient 5^{1}/$_{4}$-inch floppy disks are handy for CDs and DVDs. Holders for 3^{1}/$_{2}$-inch disks are good for organizing tchotchkes such as flash drives, the Apple Remote, camera memory cards, and small cable adapters.

Power strips and surge protectors: You always need more of these.

Printing supplies: You can use your printer paper, address labels, and ink or toner cartridges for your printer, if you're keeping it.

Uninterruptible power supply (UPS): Some of these connect to your computer to tell it to shut down when the power goes out. Check with the UPS manufacturer to see whether it has Mac software to support this feature. If not, you can still use it to supply backup power.

USB and FireWire hubs: Connect more than one device to a single port. Don't forget to save the matching power supply, if you have one.

Getting Ready to Buy

After you review the different approaches to switching and consider which items you can use from your PC, you're most likely ready to decide what to buy. I tell you about the different Apple models in Chapter 2. It's time to take out a sheet of paper and work up a couple of configurations that meet your needs, compare them to your budget, and pick one. The rest of your computing life begins today.

Choosing options for your new Mac

All the Macs that Apple sells are complete, usable systems, but some options and accessories are worth considering. Apple typically stocks three or four configurations for each model, and you can custom-order additional options. The following sections walk you through the key decisions you need to make when you order.

Hard drive size

The hard drive is where your computer retains information that you want to keep. If you plan to manage your photos, movies, and music on your Mac or if you plan to run Windows, you want lots of hard drive space. You can buy an external drive (and you want one for the Apple Time Machine backup feature), but it's handy to have your main files in one place. On some models — the Xserve, the Mac Pro, and, surprisingly, the low-end MacBook — adding a bigger drive is easy, but most models require a technician to install one.

Bottom line: Spend a little more for a bigger hard drive, but save some money in your budget for an external unit, too.

Processor speed

Apple charges a little extra for the fastest versions of the Intel processors it uses. Computer reviews tend to dote on 10 percent differences in speed, when most users hardly notice the difference. All Macs have more than one central processing unit (CPU) — the part of the chip that carries out program instructions. Most have two, but the highest-performance models have four or more. If you don't know why you would need that much processing power, you probably don't.

Random access memory

Random access memory (RAM) is where your computer temporarily stores information so that the CPU can quickly (in billionths of a second) access the data while it's working on that data. Other terms used include DRAM and SDRAM. When your computer runs out of RAM, it writes to the much slower hard drive the data it hasn't used in a while.

Adding memory reduces the need for these memory swaps and can typically improve performance more than getting a faster chip. The 1GB of RAM (one billion or so characters of information) that low-end Mac minis are supplied with is barely adequate. Other models come with 2 or 4GB. Getting at least 4GB is usually worth the money.

Selecting other accessories

Configure your computer the way you want it when you buy it. You can buy other accessories with your purchase or later, when you need them.

AppleCare

A Mac typically comes with a one-year warranty and 90-day free phone support. You can extend the warranty and phone support by signing up for AppleCare. Although you can do this at any time before the warranty expires, extending the warranty when you buy is best; otherwise, you may forget. Alternatively, mark your iCal calendar about a month before the warranty expires. Also see ProCare at the end of this list.

Apple could change its terms, so verify the warranty info in this section before you buy — don't take my word for it.

External floppy drive

If you have a collection of 3¹/₂-inch floppies, your best bet is to read them all onto your PC's hard drive and then back them up, either directly to a CD or DVD or to your Mac when you transfer the rest of your files (see

Chapter 6). But if you accumulate too many of them and don't want to spend the time, get an external USB floppy drive. Your Mac should be able to read PC floppies using an external drive.

External hard drive

If you don't already own a high-capacity external hard drive, get one — at least 500GB worth. It's pretty much a must-have item if you want to get decent use from the Apple Time Machine backup software. The external drive is also handy for transferring files from your PC. External hard drives offer capacities in the half-terabyte (500GB) range for less than $100. You can buy a terabyte (1,000GB) for less than $150. If your Mac supports FireWire, you should get a hard drive with both FireWire and USB 2.0 interfaces, giving you maximum flexibility. They typically cost a bit more, but that way, you can use USB 2.0 with your PC and use the faster FireWire with your Mac.

Flash drive

If you don't already have at least one of these tiny, inexpensive USB mass storage units, it's time you got one. It's also known as a thumb drive or keychain drive. A typical unit is shown in Figure 3-5, with a peanut for comparison. There's nothing like knowing you have the files you need in your pocket. Get at least a 4GB unit.

Figure 3-5:
A flash drive (USB plug at the top) and a peanut.

Microsoft Office

Microsoft Office is still the most widely accepted tool for creating text documents and spreadsheets. You can safely send documents back and forth between the Macintosh version of Office and the Windows version. If you feel you need Microsoft Office, for work or school, check on whether special deals are available with the purchase of a new Mac. Unfortunately, you cannot transfer your Windows license to OS X.

MobileMe

MobileMe is the Apple data storage and sharing service, offered in an annual subscription for $99 per year. You get an e-mail address ending in .mac.me. com and 20GB of online storage space that shows up as another hard drive on your desktop and that you can use to store your Web site, photo and video gallery, calendar, and backup files, all subject to a terms-of-service agreement (no naughty stuff). Many iLife programs have features that take advantage of MobileMe, such as a gallery for your photos and video, if you have it. Apple typically offers new Mac customers a 30-day free trial, so you can check it out before buying.

Modem

Current Mac models don't include a modem. If you need dialup Internet access at home or on the road, or if you need to send fax documents from your computer, get the tiny Apple USB modem, which sells for about $50.

Networking equipment

If you already have high-speed Internet access and maybe even a home network, your Mac plugs right in. If not, see Chapter 9, where I tell you about the various options:

- **Wireless:** If you're buying a laptop or just don't want wires strung all over your den, consider getting a Wi-Fi router. The Apple offering is the AirPort Extreme Base Station (AirPort Extreme is Apple's name for the 802.11n draft Wi-Fi standard). However, just about any 802.11g or n router will do.

- **Ethernet (wired):** If you plan to use wired networking, check to see whether you have an extra Ethernet port available on your router or cable modem. If not, you might need an Ethernet router. Getting one that also includes Wi-Fi doesn't cost much more, however.

Another handy accessory is a USB *hub,* a small box that multiplies the number of USB devices you can plug in at the same time. You may already have one, but make sure that it supports the faster USB 2.0 standard. If not get a new one, preferably the type with a separate power supply, so it can power additional devices.

Printer deals

When you buy a new Mac, you're typically offered a reduced price or rebate on a new inkjet printer. Sometimes the rebate covers the purchase price of the printer, so even if you already own a printer, it may be worth getting a new one as a spare or to give to someone else.

How big is a gigabyte?

The international metric system prefix *giga* means 1,000,000,000 — a billion in North American English — so a gigabyte is a billion bytes, right? Well, in the computer world, it's not so simple. A gigabyte (or GB) sometimes refers to that amount, and sometimes it's 1,073,741,824 bytes. (You can make any geek's day by asking him why.) The latter version is always used for RAM. Hard drive manufac-turers use gigabyte to mean 1,000,000,000 (1 billion) bytes. It's kind of the opposite of a baker's dozen — they put one less donut in the bag. Pretty much every manufacturer does this the same way, so you aren't being cheated. And, you should buy at least twice as much hard drive space as you think you need, so none of this really matters.

There's no such thing as a free lunch, however. Printer manufacturers sell their printers cheap and force you to buy ink or toner from them at prices that work out to a few cents per page for a text document to a half-dollar or more for a color photograph — in effect, a tax on every page. New printers often come with "starter" cartridges that print fewer pages than a purchased cartridge, so you might as well buy a cartridge with that new printer and save yourself a trip to the store.

Most inkjet printers use ink that runs when wet, but some are more smear-proof than others. Ask to have a sample page printed and apply a drop of water or saliva to the printing. If you need a relatively waterproof print, go with a laser printer.

If you have a printer you like and it's supported by OS X, you might forgo the printer deal and shop for a new one when you need it.

ProCare

For about $100 per year, Apple sells the premium service plan *ProCare,* which offers a number of services that are not included in the standard warranty, nor in AppleCare. You buy ProCare only at an Apple retail store (not online). It entitles you to personal training, priority repairs, advance registration at the in-store Genius Bar, and a yearly preventive maintenance tune-up. (You find out more about the Genius Bar in the section "Visiting the Apple Store," later in this chapter.)

If you also purchase your Mac at an Apple retail store and buy ProCare as part of the package, the folks at the Apple store can set up your Mac for you, including transferring files from your PC to the Mac. The PC has to be working and must have an Ethernet port and at least Windows 98 — and of course, you have to schlep it in.

Look for the Mac logo

Macs work with most USB, FireWire, and networking devices — such as printers, scanners, and wireless base stations — so don't be afraid to try what you already own. But if you're buying new equipment, make sure that the package says it's designed for Mac and OS X. If you do, you're more likely to own a product that works with little or no fuss. And, if you run into problems and don't find the solution in this book, you're more likely to find useful help from that vendor's customer service department if the box specifies that it supports Macs.

Be sure to request complete setup service when you purchase your Mac; Apple gives you only a ten-day period in which to ask for it.

Travel accessories

If you're planning to travel with a Mac laptop, here are some other accessories worth considering:

- **Airplane power adapter:** If you take long plane trips, you might want to get the Apple airplane power adapter. Many airlines provide laptop power outlets, though less often in economy seating. You can find out which seats on your flight have power adapters at www.seatguru.com. Note that the Apple adapter powers your laptop but doesn't charge its batteries.

  If you're traveling to other countries, the good news is that the power adapter that comes with Mac laptops runs on any AC power source in the world — 100–240 volts, 50 or 60 hertz. However, you may need to buy a travel adapter to plug it in. You can buy one at Radio Shack and many travel stores. You don't need the transformer type.

- **Three-way extension cord:** Those of us who travel spend untold hours in airports, and most of them have only a few power outlets, usually located for the benefit of the cleaning crew. When you do find a pair of outlets, another road warrior has probably already claimed them for his laptop and cellphone. But most people are willing to share the outlet if you ask nicely and produce your three-way cord.

- **Security cable:** If you plan to use your Mac laptop at work or school, consider buying a security cable that lets you lock it up when you have to leave it unattended. You can find a variety of such locks at www.kensington.com.

Shopping for Your New Mac

You might be fed up with choices by now, if you've read the entire chapter, but you have one more decision to make: where to buy your Mac. Here's the gist of it: You can buy online or in a traditional brick-and-mortar store, and you can do either one directly from Apple or from an independent retailer. Both have pros and cons, and the sections that follow can help you decide.

Wherever you go to buy your Mac and its accessories, make sure that you take a list of all the specs and accessories you know you need, based on the information you gathered earlier in this chapter. Your list should include not only which Mac model you want, but also how much RAM you need, what size hard drive you want, and which options to choose (such as whether you want a higher-end graphics card). By having all these notes at the ready, you're much more likely to stay within your budget (if you have one) and get no more or no less than what you need.

Shopping at your local computer store

The nice thing about going to a computer store is that you can see the various models before you make your final decision. You can also ask the friendly salesperson questions and maybe even get useful answers. Assuming what you want is in stock, you get to take your new toy home with you. And, if you have a problem, most stores have a place where you can talk to someone face-to-face. (Ask your salesperson to show you the service department before you buy.)

Not all computer stores carry Macs. Apple is choosy about which establishments it does business with. It doesn't want Macs stacked along the wall with all the Windows models in a department staffed with salespersons pushing the PC that happens to be on sale that week. You can find a list of authorized Apple resellers near you at www.apple.com/buy. Call ahead to see whether what you want is in stock.

Visiting the Apple Store

Frustrated with the way its computers were being sold, Apple defied conventional business wisdom and built its own chain of computer stores. Designed with the usual Apple panache, and propelled by the success of the iPod, this venture has made its customers and stockholders very happy. If you choose to buy your Mac at the Apple Store, you find that the stores are well stocked with most Apple models and attractively displayed — although you probably won't see an Xserve, and the inexpensive minis are usually tucked away in a corner. The stores carry lots of accessories, both from Apple and third parties — printers, external hard drives, carrying cases, software, games, and, of course, iPods, iPhones, Apple TVs, and the growing list of Apple consumer electronics.

The coolest thing about the Apple Store is its *Genius Bar,* a section staffed with people who know their Macs and can answer your questions. After you buy your Mac, the Genius Bar can take your hardware for repair, if necessary. If the store is busy, and it usually is, you have to sign in and wait a bit. Most stores give you a pager so that you can shop elsewhere or visit the food court if the Apple Store is in a mall, as many are. You can visit the Genius Bar and bring in your Mac to the Apple Store for service regardless of where you purchased it originally. You have to pay for service, of course, if your Mac is no longer under warranty or isn't covered by AppleCare.

Apple claims that a large chunk of the population of North America is within a 45-minute drive of an Apple Store. And, you find Apple Stores in many other parts of the world. You can find the ones near you by looking at `www.apple.com/buy`.

Buying your Mac online

Assuming that you already have an Internet connection, buying online can be very convenient. Pick out the model you want and enter your shipping address and credit card number, and in a day or so, depending on how cheap you were about shipping, your computer arrives. If you don't have an Internet connection or your PC is so riddled with viruses that you don't trust it with your credit card, most online stores also have toll-free phone numbers and even printed catalogs you can request.

Surfing to the Apple online store

You can buy all the products Apple makes from its electronic Apple Store at `www.apple.com` (or by calling 1-800-MY-APPLE). You can even watch the latest Apple TV ads.

The online Apple Store is your best bet if you want to buy a build-to-order configuration. Select the Buy Now option on the model you want, and you're presented with all possible options for that model. Of course, you aren't committed to buy anything until you enter your credit card information and confirm your order.

Other online retailers

A number of other online stores sell Macs, including Amazon.com, MacConnection.com, and MacZone.com. Again, you can find a full list at `www.apple.com/buy`. These stores sometimes offer discounts or deals on extra memory. They may stock only the more popular configurations, however.

Apple and netbooks

Netbooks are small, inexpensive laptops that have become quite popular. But they make a number of trade-offs to keep prices low, including having a small screen, slow processor, shrunken keyboard, limited battery life, and no ability to read, much less write, CDs and DVDs. Some models even use the Linux operating system, avoiding the added expense of a Windows license. At the time this book was written, Apple didn't offer a netbook. Apple CEO Tim Cook has said that Apple doesn't want to compete in this market unless it has something other than a low-quality, cheap product to offer and that the iPhone and iPod Touch offer many of the capabilities of netbooks in an even smaller package. Many in the industry believe that Apple is developing an innovative product to compete with netbooks, perhaps a media tablet that can connect to the Internet by way of the cellular telephone network and Wi-Fi — something like an large iPhone. Check my Web site, `ditchmypc.com`, for the latest information on these developments and how they affect your Mac-buying decision.

If you live in the United States, you may be able to avoid paying sales tax by purchasing from one of the independent online stores. The independent store has to collect sales tax only if it has a business presence in the state where you live. (Apple has such presence in most states, so it has to collect sales tax.)

Part II
Making the Switch

The 5th Wave   By Rich Tennant

"It's been two days, Larry. It's time to stop enjoying the new computer smell and take the iMac out of the box."

In this part . . .

You did it. You got a Mac. Now what? This section guides you through setting up your new Mac and introduces you to the Apple OS X operating system. I suggest ways to move over your files and help you deal with the most important application programs you need in order to get started.

Chapter 4

The Big Day: Setting Up Your Mac

....

In This Chapter

▶ Unpacking and hooking up the hardware

▶ Gathering information for setup

▶ Configuring your Mac by using the Startup Assistant

....

Congratulations! You've done it. You bought a Mac. A new world is about to unfold. Apple does an excellent job of making the task of setting up a new Mac simple and painless, and it usually is. But computers are by far the most complex consumer product ever sold, and things can go wrong. Also, some simple preparations can make the setup process smoother and much less stressful. So resist the temptation to start hooking things up, and read on.

Unpacking and Setting Up

You are now ready to unpack your new Mac. (If you did this as soon as you got it home, please just gather all the pieces in one place and pretend that you didn't.) I hope you notice the attractive presentation. Apple has elevated packaging to an art form, with everything snugly in its place. I also hope you notice the tiny manuals that come with the Mac. They explain the basics but leave plenty of demand for aftermarket books such as this one. Thanks, Apple.

Getting organized

The first thing to do is to make room for the new machine and clear away the clutter on your desk or work table so that you can keep track of everything. Next, find a shoebox or plastic storage container so that you have a place to store the discs, manuals, and other bits of stuff that come with the Mac. A friend of mine services computers in his apartment complex and is forever telling people to put the discs and papers in a safe place when he sets up a new computer. When he has to go back some time later, his clients can never find the stuff. So think of a place you'll remember and write down the location here, in the margin of this book.

Hooking up your computer

It's time to put your computer together. Looking through the manual that comes with your Mac for the latest info is always a good idea, but the following sections provide a quick guide on what to do, depending on your computer model.

iMac

The iMac is an easy setup. Apple once ran an ad showing a 7-year-old putting together an earlier model. If anything, the task has become easier. I don't recommend letting a 7-year-old lift an iMac out of its box, however, particularly if you buy one of the bigger screens. The largest weighs almost 25 pounds (11 kg), and you really don't want anyone to drop it. Don't be ashamed to ask another adult for help. Here's what you need to do:

1. **Plug the keyboard into one the USB ports located on the back.**

   Your iMac comes standard with a wired keyboard and mouse.

2. **Plug the mouse into one of the wired USB ports on either side of the keyboard.**

3. **Plug the power cord into the power socket on the back of the iMac and plug its other end into an AC wall outlet or power strip.**

4. **If your power strip has a switch, make sure that it's set to On.**

   You're done.

Wireless mice and keyboards

If you purchased a Bluetooth wireless mouse or keyboard, you have to install the batteries and introduce the keyboard and mouse to the computer. No, I'm not making a joke here; the process is called *pairing*.

The details are in the little booklets that come with the wireless devices, so hang on to them or visit www.apple.com/support/bluetooth. To get started, you need a wired USB mouse to run the Bluetooth Setup Assistant utility — your PC's USB mouse will work fine.

Always check and double-check which way the batteries are inserted in any electronic device. Look for the + and − marks inside the case, and don't assume that you know. Inserting batteries improperly is the most common cause of small electronics not working.

MacBook, Macbook Air, and MacBook Pro

Apple laptops require little setup:

1. **Plug the power adapter into an AC outlet or power strip.**

   At the other end of the power adapter, you find the MagSafe power connector.

2. **Remove the power connector's little plastic protective cover and then just hold it horizontally and bring it near the power receptacle, located on the left side of your laptop, near the display hinge.**

   When it's close, the connector snaps into the laptop as though it were magnetic — because it is. It doesn't matter which side of the MagSafe connector is up; it works properly either way. The MagSafe connector has a tiny light, and when you first apply power to your new laptop, the light should be green and then promptly switch to orange, indicating that it's charging the batteries. When the battery is fully charged, the light turns green again.

   A good friend of mine trashed a nice Apple PowerBook, the predecessor of the MacBook Pro, by tripping over the power cord and sending her laptop crashing to the floor. It never booted up again. The MagSafe connector is designed to prevent such tragedies by popping out if you tug on it, without imparting a big enough jerk to pull the laptop off a work surface. Still, pulling on the cord isn't the best way to unplug the MagSafe connector from your machine. Apple recommends that you grasp the connector itself and pull, but that sucker sticks on tight. The easy way to remove it is to gently lift it from the bottom — it tilts up pretty easily — and then pull it out.

3. **While you're waiting for me to tell you to press the On button, take a moment to examine the power adapter.**

   After you take off all the clear plastic wrapping, you see two little tabs on either side of the power cord that swing out to form a cradle on which you can wind up the power cord. Also, at least in North America, two power blades swing out and plug directly into a power outlet. They're mounted in a small module that Apple calls a *duck's head,* which you can pull free and replace with the longer power cord that comes with the Mac (see Figure 4-1). The U.S. power cord has a grounding plug, so if you're working in a place with older wiring, the duck's head may be more convenient because it fits into just about any outlet.

4. **Okay, press On now.**

Figure 4-1:
The
MacBook
power sup-
ply with
duck's head
detached.

Mac mini, Mac Pro, and Xserve

The top and bottom of the Mac line are both a little more complicated to set up because neither has a built-in display; you have to supply your own and hook it up to the computer. That brings up the ugly question of adapters:

✔ The ultra-light Mac mini has both a Mini DisplayPort and a mini-DVI port video output connector and comes with a mini-DVI-to-DVI adapter. Apple sells a DVI-to-VGA adapter, along with Mini DisplayPort adapters.

✔ The Mac Pro is heavy — 42 pounds (19 kg) — but it has conveniently placed carrying handles on top that make it easier to lug. The standard Mac Pro has a Mini DisplayPort and a dual-link DVI port. It comes with no adapters.

✔ The Xserve is designed to fit into a standard 19-inch electronics rack. It weighs as much as 38 pounds (17 kg), depending on options, and comes with the necessary mounting hardware. Consider getting a technician to help you install it, though. Xserve comes with a VGA adapter.

Selecting the right adapters can be confusing — you may even need more than one.

✔ **If you're hooking up to your PC's monitor:** You probably want a VGA adapter, but first check your display's service manual to see whether your monitor has DVI input. It's better to use the latter, if it's available.

✔ **If you're hooking up to a high-definition TV (HDTV):** You probably need a DVI-to-HDMI cable. The online Apple Store sells one, but you might use Google to search for a less pricey model. A better option might be the Mini DisplayPort to HDMI adapter sold by monoprice.com. In either case you will also need an 35 mm stereo to RCA stereo audio cable if you want sound through your TV. Monoprice sells these as well.

DVI, HDMI, and VGA cover most displays on the market, but you may have something different. And older TVs with analog input only are not supported by the latest Apple computers.

✔ **If you plan to use two displays:** You need two adapters — of different types. For the Mac mini, you need one adapter that plugs into the Mini DisplayPort and one that plugs into the MiniDVI port.

Network

If your PC is connected to the Internet using a Wi-Fi wireless network, you're all set. If you have a wired Ethernet network at home, plug your Mac into it. You likely have such a network but don't know it. If you have high-speed Internet (via cable TV, DSL, or satellite) and your PC is connected by a wire with a plug that looks like a telephone plug but is fatter, that's what you have. You need an Ethernet router or switch to share this connection. If you don't have one, don't worry. You can unplug the connection from your PC and plug it into your Mac for now and pick up a router the next time you're near a computer store, or you can order one online. See Chapter 9 for more on networking your Mac.

KVM

A KVM box lets you share a keyboard, video monitor, mouse, and speakers between your Mac and your PC, as shown in Figure 4-2. You don't need one, but they're handy if you plan to continue using your PC. Hooking up the box involves a lot of wires, but the idea is simple enough. With luck, you got a USB KVM. It should say so on the package. If it doesn't, or if it says *PS/2,* return it and get a USB unit.

The following steps walk you through the setup process:

1. **Plug your monitor, keyboard, mouse, and speakers into the KVM box.**

   Normally, the monitor and speakers have only one possible connection apiece. You should find two USB jacks, one for the keyboard and one for the mouse, but it shouldn't matter which goes where.

   You also have two sets of cables — more if you bought a multiport KVM.

Figure 4-2:
KVM wiring.

2. **Plug one end of each cable into the KVM box.**

   The other end of each cable has a set of plugs.

3. **Plug the other end of one cable into your PC and the other end of the second cable into your Mac.**

Turning your Mac on and off

The power switch on most Macs is a round, white, or silver button marked with the *discus interruptus,* a circle broken at the top with a short, vertical line. This is actually the international symbol for a *soft power switch,* one that tells the equipment to go on or off but doesn't control the power directly.

As with a Windows computer, you should always tell your Mac to turn itself off whenever possible, lest you lose data or damage the operating system. The Shut Down command is on the Apple menu (the one headed by the Apple logo:). After you choose Shut Down, you're asked whether you really want to shut down your computer. If you choose Restart, you see a similar message.

OS X is quite a stable operating system, but if it doesn't seem to do anything after you tell it to shut down, you can try a couple of things. First, be patient; some programs, particularly the Apple Safari Web browser, can take a while to close. Also, look at your screen to see whether an application is asking whether you want to save a file, for example.

If all else fails, you have two last-resort options: You can hold down the power button for about six seconds, and if that doesn't work after a couple of tries, remove the power cord or, on a laptop, remove the battery as well. Restore power and press the power button, and you should be back in business.

4. **Plug the speaker cables into the speaker outputs of each computer, and plug the USB plug (you should see only one per cable) into an available USB socket on the computer.**

   Finally, you have a VGA video plug to contend with.

5. **The VGA plug on the PC cable should find a matching jack on the PC. For the Mac cable, you need a MiniDisplayPort-to-VGA adapter or a mini-DVI–to–VGA adapter (Apple sell both).**

After you have everything set up, switching between the Mac and PC should be easy. Check the manual that came with your KVM box for the details on which method it uses to control the switching.

Configuring Your New Mac

You're almost ready to turn on your Mac. Before you do, I recommend that you gather some information so that you have it ready during the initial setup.

Collecting information you need

After you get your Mac plugged in and turned on, your Mac starts asking you a bunch of questions. Things go more smoothly if you collect the answers ahead of time, so the following sections discuss the information you need. With a few exceptions, you can change the information later, but you might as well get it right the first time, if you can. Make notes of your choices in the margin of this book (assuming that you're not still browsing in the bookstore).

Name

This information seems straightforward enough. But give some thought to how you want your name presented: Mary Smith, Mary Ann Smith, M. Smith, or M. A. Smith. If you're setting up the computer for a youngster, you might not want to include his last name, but don't use a too-cute nickname that the child will outgrow in a couple of years.

If the family is sharing the computer, remember that you can easily set up individual accounts for each member. The first account should be the person who will be in charge (the *administrator*) of the computer, though this can be changed later and you can have more than one administrator.

Short name

This entry is the name of your *home directory,* and it can't be easily changed. Your Mac proposes the full name you gave, in all lowercase letters and with no spaces. I suggest you pick something shorter, such as `msmith` or `mas`.

Password

This is the password you use to log on to your Mac. You're asked for it at other times, too, such as when you install new software or change security settings. You can use the password you've used for everything else in your life, but I suggest you pick something stronger. The security of your computer begins with a well-chosen password. When you see the screen that asks for the password, look for a little key icon next to the password entry box. Click it, and OS X suggests a password. Pick one of its suggestions, write down the password, and keep it in a safe place. I explain why and give some tips on other easy ways to make up a password and not forget it in Chapter 10.

Wi-Fi network name and password

If you already have a Wi-Fi network, your Mac will probably pick up yours, along with a couple of others if you live in a built-up area. It helps to know your network's name. If you have WEP or WPA security enabled, you need your Wi-Fi password, passphrase, or key. If you have long forgotten them, see Chapter 9 for information on how to reset your access point and set up new security.

If you're setting up a new Wi-Fi network, look over Chapter 9 to decide whether you need to enable security. If so, see Chapter 10 for how to generate a strong passphrase to protect your network. Might as well have the passphrase ready before you begin.

Apple ID

If you purchased music or other items from iTunes, you already have an Apple ID and password that lets you sign in to the iTunes Store to make your purchases. Take a moment to look them up.

Internet account information

Have the following information handy:

✔ The name of your Internet service provider

✔ Service type: cable, DSL, satellite, dialup, or other

✔ Account name

✔ Password

✔ The ISP's customer service number

✔ The phone number your computer dials (if you have dialup)

E-mail service information

If you check your mail online using your browser — say, if you have an account with Yahoo! or Gmail — you needn't do anything. Otherwise, check the Web site of your e-mail service to see whether it has any special instructions for Mac users. Keep handy the following info for every e-mail service you plan to use:

✔ Provider name

✔ Customer service number

✔ E-mail address

✔ E-mail password

✔ Type of account: POP (the most common), IMAP, or .Mac

✔ Mail server address

✔ SMTP server address

Getting through the Startup Wizard

Finally, it's time to press that power button. As your Mac powers on, you hear a soft "boing" that has long been part of the new Mac experience. Next, follow these steps:

1. **When the Select Main Language screen appears, choose the language you prefer.**

   You see the message `Starting Mac OS` and then a "welcome" video. You're then asked to select the country or region you're in. If you chose English as your main language, the Mac presents English-speaking countries. (If you're somewhere else, select the Show All check box to view the complete list, including Heard & McDonald Island and the Holy See.)

   Either way, make your choice and click the Continue button.

2. **Select the country or region you're in.**

   You see the choices: US, Canada, UK, AZ, NZ, IRE. You can ask for more choices.

3. **Answer the question: "Do you already own a Mac?"**

   You're asked this question because you can transfer information from another Mac if you already have one. If not, click the Do Not Transfer My Information button and then click the Continue button.

4. **Select your keyboard layout.**

   Select U.S. or Canada (you can add other keyboard versions later), and then click the Continue button.

5. **Select a wireless service.**

   Things start to get exciting now. If you have Wi-Fi at your location and you aren't using exotic security tricks to make your network invisible, your Wi-Fi base station should show up on the screen, along with any others your Mac has found.

   If you have security enabled, you need to know the WEP or WPA password or key to connect. If all goes well, at this point you're now online. If you're not, don't worry; just move on for now. I go over networking your Mac in more detail in Chapter 9.

6. **Enter your Apple ID and its password if you have an iTunes (or a MobileMe) account. Click the Continue button.**

   You can skip this step and enter this info later using iTunes or the MobileMe pane in System Preferences.

7. **Supply the requested registration information, and then click the Continue button.**

8. **Continue with some optional questions from the assistant. (You can decide whether Apple is being too nosy.)**

   The questions include where you will use the computer and what "best describes what you do."

Deselect the Stay in Touch check box if you don't want e-mail announcements. Then click the Continue button.

9. **In the Set Up This Account screen of the assistant, verify the account name and enter your password.**

   Make sure that the account name is the one you want. This is one thing you can't easily change later; you have to rebuild the whole computer. Enter the password you prepared (twice). If you didn't have a password ready, click the key icon next to the password entry field, and Password Assistant suggests some passwords. Pick one and write it down on a slip of paper that you will keep in a safe place. (See Chapter 10 for more on how Password Assistant works.) Finally, click the Continue button.

10. **Select a picture, if you want, for this account.**

    If you have a Mac with a built-in camera (the iMac, MacBook, MacBook Air, and MacBook Pro all have one), the Startup Wizard now offers to take your picture to use as an icon for this account. You can retake the photo if you don't like the results, and you can change it later by choosing System Preferences➪Accounts. Alternatively, you can choose from a picture library.

11. **Select a time zone, click the Continue button, and then set your date and time, if necessary.**

    Macs are supplied already set to Pacific standard time (PST) and Cupertino-USA, Apple's hometown. Click the map or select the closest city from the list. After your time zone is set, the date and time displayed are likely to be close to correct. If you're connected to the Internet, your Mac sets itself by using a time server traceable to the U.S. government's atomic clock.

Are we there yet?

If all went according to plan, you should see an OS X desktop waiting for you to work or play with. And, if you have a modern Internet hookup, you should be online as well. I give you an introduction to OS X in the next chapter. Later chapters tell you more about getting online, setting up e-mail, moving files over, increasing your computer's security level, and solving any problems you may encounter. You also find out more about the various neat things you can do with your Mac. Chapter 22 suggests some creative (and some mundane) things you can do with your old PC.

Dive on in!

Maintaining parental control

As I said in Chapter 3, I'm not a big fan of computers for small children. But even teenagers need limits on computer use — games and networking sites are highly addictive. Be sure to read Chapter 17, which tells you how to use OS X parental controls, before you hand over a computer account to your child. It's very hard to introduce those controls later, when you realize that she's spending way too much time in front of the screen.

Chapter 5

Mac OS X for Windows Users

· ·

· ·

As a PC user, you're already familiar with the operating system known as Windows. It is a complex piece of software developed by Microsoft, and some version of it comes with most personal computers now sold, with one big exception: Apple doesn't sell its Macs with Windows software. Instead, Apple equips its Macintosh computers with Apple's own operating system, Mac OS X. Apple pronounces it "oh ess ten," as in the Roman numeral ten. (The previous Apple operating system was OS 9.) Apple computers are stylish and well made, but OS X is the main reason to buy a Mac. (You can have Windows on your Mac in addition to OS X, but you have to buy it and install it yourself, as I explain in Chapter 16.)

Apple and Microsoft are locked in a battle over which company can produce an operating system that offers a better experience for the user. Both companies are forced to keep improving their offerings. Most Mac users believe that Apple keeps coming out ahead.

PC and Mac: We Have a Lot in Common

Microsoft adopted many Mac OS features when it created Windows, so you find much that's familiar when you try OS X. The fundamental idea is much the same: The operating system

   ✔ Stores data as files that have names

   ✔ Organizes files in a hierarchy of folders

   ✔ Runs applications

✔ Talks to external devices such as printers, scanners, music players, and cameras

✔ Connects to other computers by way of local-area networks and the Internet

You interact with the computer by using a *graphical user interface (GUI),* which presents a simulated desktop on the screen, with icons you can move around and click. Information appears in rectangular windows, and you can select from pull-down menus. You use a pointing device, such as a mouse or trackpad, to move a cursor around the screen. The cursor is normally an arrow, but it sometimes changes its shape to reflect what's going on.

Over the years, the computer industry has adopted numerous standards to ensure that different products can work well together. Nowadays, Apple is at the forefront of this process, adopting most standards and frequently contributing some new ones that other companies adopt. Here's a quick rundown of the alphabet soup of standards that Mac OS X shares with Windows and other operating systems:

✔ **Data formats:** ASCII, H.294, JPEG, MP3, MPEG, PDF, TIFF, Unicode, and UTF-8

✔ **File systems:** Apple HFS+, ISO 9660 CDs, Microsoft FAT, Microsoft NTFS (read-only), NFS, UDF 1.5 DVDs, ZFS, and $3^1/_2$-inch HD floppy (with external drive)

✔ **Input/output:** Bluetooth, FireWire/IEEE-1394, PCIe (Pro and Xserve), TOSlink audio, USB

✔ **Networking:** Bonjour, Ethernet, HTTP, LDAP, POP mail, RSS, S/MIME, TCP/IP, and Wi-Fi

✔ **Security:** AES, HTTPS, RADIUS, SSH, SSL/TLS, WEP, WPA, and WPA2

✔ **Software standards:** BootP, BSD, CalDAV calendering, DHCP, EFI, Java, JavaScript, LP64 64-bit, Microsoft Exchange, OpenGL graphics, POSIX, PPPoE, Ruby on Rails, SOAP, UNIX 03, X11, and x86

This list isn't complete, and I don't expect you to know what all these geeky acronyms mean. I explain the more important ones in Chapter 3 and other ones as I go, and you can check the glossary for the rest. But I'm about to dive into all the differences, and I want to emphasize how much overlap exists between the two operating systems. After you get used to a few new concepts and some different terminology, you'll feel right at home using OS X.

Adjusting to the Differences

You do, of course, encounter differences between Windows and Mac OS X. Some are merely a matter of terminology. Others just take getting used to, and a few you might find annoying. For most of those annoying issues, I point out, in a reasonably familiar way, ways to accomplish what you want to do.

Comparing Windows- and Mac-speak

Computers seem to run on jargon. Many of the buzzwords used on Macs are exactly the same as those used in Windows: *files, users, log on, log out, open, close, shut down, help,* and most networking and Internet terms. Terms used to describe the graphical interface are mostly the same, too: *menu, check box, dialog* or *dialog box, radio button, drag, click,* and *double-click.* Table 5-1 provides the equivalent terms or types of programs for each platform.

Table 5-1	Windows Terms versus Mac Terms
Windows	*Mac OS X*
Control Panel	System Preferences
Ctrl+Alt+Delete	Option+⌘+Esc
Exit or Close (Alt+FX)	Quit (⌘+Q)
Hourglass cursor (busy signal)	Spinning beach ball or gear (busy signal)
Internet Explorer	Safari
My Computer	Finder
My Documents	Documents folder
My Music	Music folder
My Pictures	Pictures folder
Notepad	TextEdit
Outlook Express	Mail
Recycle Bin	Trash Can
Right+click	Secondary click
Settings	Preferences
Shortcut icon	Alias
Taskbar and tray	Dock
Windows Explorer	Finder window
Windows Update	Software Update
Wizard	Assistant

Some things, thankfully, have no equivalent in the Mac world. No activation is required in order to use OS X; you can skip registration, if you like. You find no Windows Genuine Advantage checking and deciding (sometimes inaccurately) whether your copy of Mac OS X is authentic, and no animated paper clip offering inane help (unless you're using Microsoft Office). And you don't run into DLL files or any equivalent of the Windows Registry, both notorious sources of problems.

Seeing the big picture: The desktop and menus

After you answer all the startup assistant's questions, you see the Mac desktop, shown in Figure 5-1.

The basic idea is the same as on the Windows desktop: Most of the screen is filled with a pattern or an image that resembles a tablecloth on which you see various icons that represent files, storage media, and applications. You also find an arrow cursor that you can move around by using the mouse or trackpad. You can move icons around by placing the arrow cursor over them, clicking the mouse or trackpad button, and holding down the button as you move the cursor.

Figure 5-1:
The Macintosh OS X desktop screen.

The big differences between the Mac and PC desktops are at the top and bottom. On the top, you find all OS X menus. Each application has a different menu set. The menu set shown is for the application whose window is in front — that application is said to *have focus* or to be the *current application*:

- The first menu on the left is always headed by an Apple logo (🍎) and is called the Apple menu, naturally. It has system-related stuff, such as System Preferences and Shut down.

- The next menu over is headed by the name of the current application (Finder; refer to Figure 5-1). That menu is where you find entries that change preferences and quit (exit) the application.

- Continuing from the left, you typically see File and Edit menus that work much like the corresponding Windows menus. The Help menu is always on the right.

At the bottom of the screen, you see a bunch of largish icons (you can make them smaller or hide them, as explained later in this chapter). This area, the *Dock,* roughly corresponds to the Windows taskbar and tray. Here's what you see:

- Each icon on the Dock represents an application or a folder; you click an icon once to start or open it. Click a folder or *stack* on the Dock and its contents spring out in a graceful arc (refer to Figure 5-1), or as a grid, if there are too many items.

- If you don't know what an icon represents, move your cursor over it and a label appears.

- Open applications have a little black triangle underneath their corresponding icons on the Dock.

- You add applications and folders to the Dock by dragging them there.

I say more about menus and the Dock in the following sections.

Pointing the way: The mouse and trackpad

One of the great divides between Apple and Microsoft was over whether computer mice should have one or two buttons. You may think it bizarre that adults would fret about such a thing, but the debate invoked great passions. Apple touted the simplicity of having a single button, avoiding the need to explain what each button does. Microsoft eventually found a good use for the second button — the one on the right. It displays menus of possible actions appropriate to the window in which the right-click occurred. Later, scroll wheels appeared, allowing users to move up and down in a window using intuitive finger action. Apple added similar functions to its operating system and eventually introduced its own multibutton mouse, which it named Mighty Mouse.

Mighty Mouse comes with the iMac and Mac Pro. You can order a wireless Bluetooth version as an option. At first glance, this mouse looks like a single-button mouse with a tiny ball toward the front. Here are a few pointers on using the Mighty Mouse:

- ✔ The ball acts like a scroll wheel, but it can command horizontal as well as vertical scrolling.

- ✔ The top of the Mighty Mouse is a single shell. To perform a right-click, you press only on the right half of the shell. Regular (left-) clicks, the most common action, can be on the left or both sides simultaneously.

- ✔ The scroll ball can also be pressed down to signal a third type of click.

  Each side of the Mighty Mouse has a button you squeeze to represent a fourth click.

- ✔ To activate these extra buttons, select ⌘⇨System Preferences⇨Mouse. You see many choices for each button. I set the top button to Application Switcher and the side buttons to Exposé – Desktop.

So Apple has gone from one button to four, but in a way that still looks like one.

If your Mac came with a Mighty Mouse, by all means give it a try — I think it's slick. But if yours didn't or if you find the Mighty Mouse too confusing, I suggest that you stick with a standard, two-button, USB, scroll-wheel mouse. If you already have one you like, great. If not, go buy one. Wired (as opposed to wireless) optical mice are inexpensive, and almost any will do fine. Just plug it in to a free USB port or your USB hub. You don't even have to turn off the computer. Apple keyboards have extra built-in USB ports (one on the left and one on the right) for the mouse. No setup is necessary. Apple software uses the left button for primary clicks, the scroll wheel to scroll up and down, and the right button to bring up context-sensitive menus, just as Windows does. If you're a left-handed user, you may want to switch the buttons by using the Keyboard & Mouse pane in System Preferences.

Apple laptops also feature a single button. PC laptops generally have two buttons. You can signal a right-click on a Mac laptop by holding down the Control key and clicking the trackpad button. Another way is available, however. The Apple trackpad is clever enough to notice when you have two fingers resting on it rather than just one. Check out these trackpad tricks:

- ✔ **To scroll,** move two fingers up and down on the trackpad.
- ✔ **To right-click,** rest two fingers on the trackpad when you click.

For the trackpad tricks to work, you need to adjust your settings. To do so, choose System Preferences from the Apple menu (in the upper-left corner of your screen) and then choose Keyboard & Mouse. Select the Place Two

Fingers on Trackpad and Click Button for Secondary Click check box and then close the window. Note that Apple can't even say the words *right-click*, but that's what I call it whenever I want you to make it happen. Of course, you can use your two-button USB mouse with your laptop, too. Just plug it in.

Gesturing with Multi-Touch

Apple has taken the two-finger trackpad gesture idea a step further. Apple laptops, except for the white plastic MacBook, which recognizes only two fingers, feature a large, glass trackpad that can tell whether one, two, three, or four fingers are touching it. The entire trackpad surface also functions as the click button. Here are some gestures you can express with your fingers:

✔ *Two fingers:*

Swipe to scroll up, down, left, or right.

Rotate pictures by twisting your thumb and forefinger.

Pinch or spread two fingers to zoom out or in.

✔ *Three fingers:*

Swipe left or right to change pages, if you have more than one page open in the Safari Web browser.

✔ *Four fingers:*

Swipe up to move all windows off the desktop; swipe down to bring them back.

Swipe down to show all windows; swipe up to restore their previous positions.

Swipe left or right to see all active applications.

You can use keyboard shortcuts for many of these features.

The key to keyboards

Apple keyboard layouts look much like standard Windows keyboard layouts. The biggest difference is in the two keys on either side of the spacebar. On a PC, the keys closest to the spacebar are labeled Alt; the next ones over sport a Windows logo. On a Mac, the keys closest to the spacebar have an icon (⌘) that looks like a four-bladed propeller or electric fan. The Mac world calls them the Command keys; they have the same function.

The Command key (⌘) is used in almost all keyboard shortcuts. It's one of the most important things to know about the Mac.

The next one over is the Option key (⌥). It's often used as a modifier along with the command key.

Another key that may not be familiar to PC users is in the upper-right area on Apple keyboards. It's the eject button (⏏) for the optical drive (the drive that reads and writes CDs and DVDs). You see the same symbol on the eject button on home audio devices. To the left of the ⏏ key, you find two keys that raise and lower the volume and a key with only a speaker symbol; this key turns the system sound on and off. It's a mute button, in effect. Next to the Escape key (esc) on the far left, you find brightness controls and two keys with funny symbols, one a box of boxes that shows all windows that are open and the other looking like a fuel gauge brings up the Dashboard, which I describe later in this chapter. The sound-control, screen-brightness, and other controls are also the function keys. To make these keys to work as function keys, you hold down the Fn key while pressing the function key you want. Older Apple keyboards may have different arrangements.

Backspace versus Del versus Delete

Fasten your seat belts for this one. The large key on the right end of the numeral row on PC keyboards is labeled Backspace. Of course, it doesn't really back space; the left-arrow key does that. Instead, the Backspace key deletes the character to the left of the insertion point, which is the blinking vertical line that tells you where in a block of text you're editing. Long ago, Apple decided to label this key Delete because that's truly what it does. The problem is that PC keyboards have another, regular-size delete key in the group above, or sometimes next to, the arrow keys. This delete key deletes the character to the *right* of the insertion point. Apple laptops and standard keyboards omit this key. The optional Apple keyboard with numeric pad includes the second delete key, also labeled Delete. It has on it a standard delete symbol that looks like a boxy arrow pointing to the right with an *x* in it. The big delete key doesn't have a symbol on it, though one exists, and it has the same boxy arrow pointing to the *left*. On keyboards that don't have a second delete key, you request the right delete function by holding down the function key (Fn) when you press the lone Delete key.

Keyboard shortcuts using the Command key versus the Ctrl key

Keyboard shortcuts are little incantations combining a couple of key presses that carry out a task without your having to plow through the menus. PCs have two kinds of keyboard shortcuts. For some, you hold down the Ctrl key and a letter key; for others, you press the Alt key and type one letter from each menu item name — often, but not always, the first letter. Mac keyboard shortcuts are similar to the first type, but you use the Command key (⌘) rather than the Ctrl key. The following examples show some Mac keyboard shortcuts:

Keyboard Shortcut	Action
⌘+C	Copy
⌘+X	Cut
⌘+V	Paste
⌘+F	Find
⌘+G	Find Again
⌘+A	Select All
⌘+S	Save
⌘+Z	Undo

Replacing the Ctrl key press with the Command key (⌘) also applies to most Ctrl-key shortcuts in programs such as Microsoft Office.

The letters in keyboard shortcut combinations are always shown capitalized in this book and onscreen, but don't hold down the shift key unless it's explicitly called for. Thus, ⌘+Q means to quit the current application and ⌘+shift+Q is the Log Out shortcut.

Although the Mac OS X menu layout appears to be intuitive and easy to follow, it's fair to say that Apple gets a little carried away with shortcuts. It has dozens of them. Don't try to remember them all. The most important shortcuts are the ones already mentioned, many of which you probably already know from Windows. Pick up others as you need them, and take advantage of the Cheat Sheet in the front of this book.

OS X displays the available shortcut for each menu item directly on the pull-down menu itself. Some combinations use different and even multiple modifier keys. Apple uses other symbols in addition to the ⌘ symbol and symbol to indicate these keys. Here's a quick guide (also see the Cheat Sheet):

- **Option (⌥):** This key often modifies a shortcut or menu item by telling it to do more. For example, pressing ⌘+W closes the front window. ⌥+⌘+W closes *all* windows for the front application. Shortcuts can be complex: The shortcut in TextEdit for Edit⇨Paste and Match Style is ⌥+Shift+⌘+V.

- **Control (⌃):** This key's symbol looks like a hat. You press the key in combination with a mouse click to create a right-click.

- **Shift (⇧):** Either the right or left Shift key can be used. Pressing the Caps Lock key has no effect on shortcuts that include a Shift key.

- **Escape (⎋):** This key's symbol looks a lot like the power button icon, but it's different. The line is at an angle and has a little arrow pointing out. Escape is a shortcut for Cancel in dialogs.

Many other Mac keyboard shortcuts exist. Open the Apple menu and choose System Preferences⇨Keyboard & Mouse and then choose Keyboard Shortcuts to see a list. The Keyboard & Mouse pane has many other options for customizing your input experience. Explore, but don't get carried away.

If you have difficulty holding down combinations of keys, you can activate the Sticky Keys feature in the System Preferences⇨Universal Access pane. See Chapter 17 for other accessibility tips if you have difficulty using computers.

Special characters and other languages

Macs let you enter text in a wide variety of languages. Select ⇨System Preferences⇨International⇨Input and select the check box labeled Show Input Menu in Menu Bar. While you're there, check the boxes for Character Palette, Keyboard viewer and any other input methods shown that interest you. On the menu bar, in the upper-right corner, you should see a little national flag, corresponding to the language of the keyboard you selected during the startup process. For example, the Stars and Stripes appears for the U.S. keyboard. If you click this flag, a menu of options appears. Select Show Character Palette. You can browse through all available characters in OS X — thousands of them exist. Click the small triangles next to the Character Info and Font Variation options to discover the name of each character and which fonts contain it.

You can add keyboard layouts for other languages from the Apple menu by choosing System Preferences⇨International and then choosing Input Menu. Each language you select shows up as a menu option under the flag icon on the menu bar.

Select Flag–>Select Show Keyboard Viewer, and a small keyboard corresponding to the language you chose appears. You can enter characters with it by clicking its buttons.

Mac windows versus Windows windows

This section refers to windows spelled with a lowercase *w* — those rectangular boxes on your computer's screen where all the action happens. Again, the basic idea in OS X is similar to what you're used to in the Microsoft operating system. You see a title bar at the top of each window, with colored buttons you can click. From left to right:

Keep it simple

You have oodles of ways to customize Mac OS X using system and application preferences, and you can download software that gives you even more possibilities. I recommend restraint. Don't customize OS X more than necessary, particularly when you're first getting used to working with it. The closer your Mac software is to its out-of-the-box configuration, the easier it is to get help when you have a problem, whether it's from this book, from Web sites, or from Apple customer service.

✔ **Red:** Closes the window

✔ **Orange:** Minimizes the window (it slurps down to the Dock)

✔ **Green:** Resizes the window to make better use of the screen

You move a window by clicking the title bar and dragging with the mouse. A scroll bar and slider appear on the right side. You can also adjust the window size by dragging a corner — only the lower-right corner on a Mac, but any corner in Windows.

May I See the Menu, Please?

As already mentioned, the menu bar in OS X is at the top of the screen, not in each window. The menu you see changes depending on which application's window is at the front. You change which application window is in front by either clicking a window that's behind the one in front or clicking the application's icon on the Dock.

You can see a summary of all open applications by holding down the Command key (⌘) and pressing the Tab key. As shown in Figure 5-2, you see a translucent bar with icons for each running application. Release the Command key, and the selected application comes to the front. Keep holding down the Command key and press the Tab key repeatedly to cycle through all applications. This feature is similar to the one performed by pressing Alt+Tab in Windows. If you hold down the Command key and press the accent-tilde key, `~ (just above the Tab key), OS X cycles through the open windows of the front application.

Figure 5-2:
The ⌘+Tab
display.

Apple menu

The leftmost menu is always the Apple menu, and it always offers the same set of choices, regardless of which applications are in use. Those choices are described in this list:

- **About This Mac:** Provides a quick summary of your computer's configuration, including memory, processor, and operating system release. Choose More Info for an excruciatingly complete rundown of everything in, on, or attached to your computer.

- **Software Update:** Updates your Mac to the latest versions of the software that came with it. Your Mac checks for updates every week automatically unless you change the setting, labeled, unsurprisingly, Software Update, in the System Preferences pane.

- **Mac OS X Software:** Opens the Apple Web site, where you can download neat stuff — some free, some not.

- **System Preferences:** Lets you see and change the numerous settings associated with OS X system software. It's the equivalent of Control Panel in Windows. Figure 5-3 shows the main window you see when you choose System Preferences, with all the icons you click to complete specific settings chores.

- **Dock:** Lets you control the size, location, and behavior of the Dock. Depending on your choices, the Dock can be your best friend or be truly annoying.

The option I like best is Turn Hiding On, which moves the Dock off the screen until you steer your cursor all the way to the bottom edge, at which time the Dock pops up, ready to do your bidding. Move the cursor away from the bottom of the screen, and the Dock hides itself again.

Figure 5-3:
The main
System
Preferences
window.

✔ **Recent Items:** Offers a quick way to return to the application, document, or server that you were just using. You can tell OS X how far back the Recent Items lists should go in the Appearance pane under System Preferences. The default is ten items.

✔ **Force Quit:** Lets you kill any application that isn't responding to commands (see Figure 5-4). Yes, Mac applications freeze, just as Windows applications do. Commit to memory the Force Quit keyboard shortcut: Option+⌘+Esc. You may need it if you can't open the menu for some reason. It's the Mac equivalent of the Windows "three-finger salute": Ctrl+Alt+Delete.

✔ **Sleep, Restart, Shut Down, and Log Out:** These commands perform the same tasks as they do in Windows. Apple provides only one sleep option; there's no separate hibernate nonsense. You control the sleep settings in the Energy Saver pane of System Preferences.

Figure 5-4:
The Force
Quit
window.

Application menu

The menu to the right of the Apple menu has the same name as whichever application is in front, and looking at the menu is the easiest way to find out just which application is active, if more than one is open. As with the Apple menu, this menu's contents are essentially the same from application to application. The top item displays the About screen for the application, which gives the application's version number and copyright notice and any other information that the application's developers want to tell you.

Other menu choices to expect are described in this list:

✔ **Hide and Hide Others:** These items (and their keyboard shortcuts) are handy to keep in mind when your screen becomes cluttered. Keep pressing ⌘+H until the application you want is in front; press Option+⌘+H to hide the rest.

- ✔ **Preferences:** Choose this menu item to change the application's settings. It's one of the most important menu items to know about for PC-to-Mac switchers.

- ✔ **Quit (and its shortcut, ⌘+Q):** Tells the program to terminate; it's equivalent to Exit in Windows.

- ✔ **Show All:** Brings all windows for this application ahead of any other applications' windows you may have open.

The Finder's application menu is where you empty the Trash.

File and Edit menus

In most applications, the two menus just to the right of the Apple menu are the File and Edit menus. These two closely resemble their Windows counterparts.

One big difference is that the Quit command isn't on the File menu; instead, it's on the application menu, to the left. This is one of the more annoying differences between Windows and OS X. Just remember the ⌘+Q shortcut and avoid the aggravation. Also, Preferences, the OS X equivalent of Settings in Windows, isn't on the Edit menu. It's on the application menu. It has a shortcut, too: ⌘+, (command comma).

When you save a new document for the first time or choose Open or Save As from the File menu, you see a dialog much as you would see in Windows XP or Vista when doing the same things. Figure 5-5 shows many of the navigation features of this window, including the sidebar with your favorite destinations and the option to select among Icon, List, and Column views. Note also the disclosure triangle in the upper-right corner.

Figure 5-5:
The Save
As dialog.

If you see the shortened version of the Save As dialog, shown in Figure 5-6, rather than the full version (refer to Figure 5-5), click the little disclosure triangle button to the right of the filename text field toward the top of the dialog to bring back the full dialog.

Figure 5-6:
The stunted
Save As
dialog box.

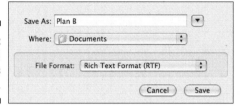

Help and Window menus

The Help menu is located to the right of the menus associated with the application, just as in Windows. To the Help menu's left, you usually find a Window menu, similar to the one found in many Microsoft Windows applications. The Window menu lists which windows the application has open and lets you bring the one you want to the front. You can also press ⌘+~ (tilde) to cycle through an application's open windows.

Applications typically have several other menus between the Edit and Window menus; these other menus are usually organized in ways that should be familiar to Windows users.

Filing Away in OS X

Files in OS X are similar to files in Windows or any other operating system, with one exception that you probably don't need to know about. So skip the next paragraph unless you're curious.

In most operating systems, a *file* is just a bucket of bits — 1s and 0s that programs can interpret as a text document, photograph, music, or whatever. The operating system is responsible for storing the file accurately and copying or deleting it if asked to, but that's it. Macs may add the resource fork to this notion of what a file is supposed to be. (*Fork* is used here in the sense of a fork in the road, not a fork in the steak.) The resource fork contains additional information about what's in the file that the application can use. The good news is that you probably don't have to worry about this issue. Resource forks are less common in newer applications, and OS X handles the forks automatically. The files you bring over from Windows don't have resource forks, anyway.

File types

Many of the file types you're used to on the PC are supported directly by OS X: documents in Microsoft Word format, photographs in JPEG format, and music MP3s, for example. Others require additional software. Still others, particularly music files purchased under one of the proprietary Microsoft formats, such as for the Zune music player, may not be usable, except, of course, when you're running Windows on your Mac. I give you the gory details about moving files from your PC to your Mac in Chapter 6.

Filenames

Filenames in Mac OS X can be as long as 255 characters, and you can use any characters you like except the colon (:). Windows doesn't allow any of these special characters in filenames:

: \ / | * ? " < >

If you're planning to move files back and forth between your PC and Mac, follow the more restrictive Windows naming rules so that filenames don't get mangled.

Extensions

In the Windows world, filenames have *extensions:* a period (.) and a few cryptic letters that are added to the end of a filename — for example, `Chapter5.doc`. The file extension tells the operating system which type of file it is so that the OS knows which program should open it. OS X uses file extensions in the same way, but it also has a separate way to know the file's creator, using a special four-character code that is assigned to each application and is stored with the file's directory entry.

Pathnames

A file is stored in a folder, which may be in another folder, which may be in another folder, and so on. Operating systems keep track of all that hierarchy by using a *pathname,* which lists all the folders you have to visit in turn to find your file. The names are separated by a special character. In Windows, this character is the backslash (\). For Macs — and in Unix, in Linux, and on the Internet — the forward slash (/), sometimes called the front slash, is used. You can make nice patterns stringing them together, like so: \/\/\/\/\/\/\/\/\/\/ — but this has nothing to do with what I'm talking about.

Disks and volumes

Disk drives appear on the desktop just as files do, but with distinctive icons (see Figure 5-7). The main hard drive icon looks like the real hard drive in your computer. Unfortunately, most people have never taken apart a computer and don't have a clue what a hard drive looks like. External hard drive icons resemble an external drive, with either a FireWire or USB logo on it, indicating the manner of connection. Optical disc icons look like, well, optical discs. Flash drives usually look like an old external floppy drive, as do virtual volumes that appear whenever you open a disk image file (which has a .dmg extension).

The Mac way to eject or dismount one of these disk volumes is to drag the volume to the Trash. This peculiar idiom goes back to the earliest Macs. You aren't deleting any information when you do this, and the Trash Can changes to an Eject icon (⏏) when you're dragging a disk or volume, to emphasize that nothing is being trashed. If dragging disks to the Trash seems too weird — you've become a true Mac person when it makes sense — right-click the disk or volume icon and select Eject from the menu that appears. All ejectable volumes also appear in Finder window sidebars and have Eject symbols (⏏) next to them that you can click.

Figure 5-7:
An OS X desktop displaying several disk volumes.

Aliases

Maybe you used shortcuts in Windows. A *shortcut* is an icon that points to another file, program, or disk drive. Macs have a similar feature, *alias,* which is quite handy. You can create an alias by clicking the name or icon of the file, program, or disk volume you want to alias and then choosing Make Alias from the Finder's File menu. It's worth remembering the keyboard incantation for making aliases: ⌘+L. Just as in Windows, the alias icon appears with a little arrow in its lower-left corner, and you can move the alias anywhere you want. You can even move it to the Trash if you no longer need it; the original file doesn't go away. Mac OS X has one big improvement over this Windows feature, however: In Windows, if you move the original file to another folder or change its name, Windows becomes unhappy and doesn't know where to find the file any more. OS X keeps track of where the file went, and the alias still works as long as the file stays on the same drive. Of course, if you delete the original file or eject the drive it's on, there's not much OS X can do.

Watch out for aliases when you want to copy files to another medium, such as an external hard drive, CD-R, or flash drive. If you drag an alias, only the alias is copied, not the file. To copy the file or folder that the alias points to, click the alias and choose File⇨Show Original, or just press ⌘+R.

The Finder Is Your Friend

When you first start your computer, you find yourself in a special program that Apple calls the Finder. The Finder is somewhat like Windows Explorer, but it's an even more basic tool on the Mac than Explorer is in Windows. You use it all the time.

You can reach the Finder by clicking anywhere on the desktop or selecting its icon from the Dock. Pressing ⌘+F3 makes all other windows go away, and you see only the desktop and the Finder. Press ⌘+F3 again to bring everything back.

Moving around with Finder windows

You use Finder windows to move around among folders. You see a window when you double-click a folder or choose File⇨New Finder Window from the Finder.

As shown in Figure 5-8, the name of the folder is at the top of the Finder window. The icon to its left is live; you can click it and drag it to wherever you want, just as you would drag the folder's icon in its parent folder or on the desktop.

Figure 5-8:
A Finder
window in
Cover-Flow
view.

Finder windows have a sidebar on the left with a list of available storage
volumes at the top and selected folders at the bottom. You can customize
them by dragging folders into or out of the list area. Each Finder window has a
toolbar at the top. You can select from four different ways to view files: by
icon, list, column, or cover-flow. List view includes details such as when the
file was last modified, its size, and its kind (Word document or picture, for
example). Folders have small triangles next to them. If you click one, the folder
expands. You can expand and manipulate more than one folder this way.
Column view shows you the contents of the current folder and the folder that
contains it, along with, optionally, a preview of any file you select. Widen
columns by dragging the II icon below the scroll bars. You can customize the
contents of the file view by choosing Finder⇨View⇨Customize View Options.

Cool Cover-Flow view is based on the way iTunes and iPods display album
covers to help you find the music you want, but in the Finder, Cover-Flow
view shows a preview of file contents. Click the Quick Look "eye" icon at the
top of the window (or press the spacebar), and you see a readable, scrollable
preview of the center file. Click the double-arrow icon at the bottom of that
view and you see a full-screen version. Quick Look supports text files, PDFs,
movies, Keynote presentations, and Microsoft Word and Excel files — no
need to open files in an application just to see what's inside.

The Finder window toolbar also has backward and forward arrow buttons
that are initially grayed out. As you open and close folders, these buttons
let you return to a previous view, in much the same way as you would with
buttons in an Internet Web browser. The Finder window toolbar also has
an action menu with a gear icon that lets you choose options that are also
available on the Finder menu. You can even customize the toolbar from the
Finder's View menu and add icons. I find the Path icon particularly useful
because it shows all the folders that include the current one and lets you pop

back to any one of them. You can also drag files and folders to the Finder window toolbar and the item then appears in all Finder windows. Right-click the icon to remove it from the toolbar. A temporary (Temp) folder can be handy when you're rearranging files, for example.

The text at the bottom of each Finder window tells you how much space remains on the disk drive or storage volume on which the folder is located. This is the easiest way to find out how much disk space you have available.

Getting info

Click an icon on the desktop or in a Finder window and press ⌘+I. A window appears with everything you always wanted to know about that file but were afraid to ask, including what kind of file it is, how big it is, where it's located, and when it was created and last modified. You can find much more if you click the little triangles next to other items in the Get Info window, such as Name & Extension, Open With (which lets you pick the application to open this file or all files of this type), Preview, and Ownership & Permissions. This last section lets you control who can read and who can change the file or folder. See Chapter 19, the section about understanding file permission basics, for more info on permissions.

Looking at optical drives: CDs and DVDs

All new Macs (except the MacBook Air) can read and write *(burn)* CDs and DVDs. An optional external SuperDrive is available for the Air.

Most Macs come with slot-loading optical drives that work with only full-size CDs and DVDs. Full-size discs are about 4³/₄ inches in diameter (120 mm, to be exact). Don't even think of trying to insert a smaller disk or one of those cute CD thingies the size of a credit card. If you need to read or create smaller-format discs, get a tray-loading external drive that supports them and is Mac compatible.

Singing the Blu-ray blues

As the time this book went to press, Apple didn't offer a drive that can read Blu-ray discs. These discs are the same size as CDs and DVDs, but hold much more data — up to 50GB — and are used to distribute high-definition (HD) movies. You can buy Blu-ray drives from MCEtech.com that you can install in a Mac Pro. MCE also sells external Blu-ray drives that work with other

Macs, and it will even install one to replace your Mac's internal SuperDrive. (It reads and writes CDs and DVDs, too.) You can use the Blu-ray drive to back up files and, if you buy the extra software, create HD movies that you can play on standard Blu-ray players.

The one thing you *can't* do is play commercial Blu-ray movies on your Mac under OS X. (You can do that if you boot under Windows.) Apple isn't happy with the Blu-ray license terms — Steve Jobs called them "a world of hurt." Maybe things will be worked out by the time you read this chapter. Then again, Apple distributes HD movies via the iTunes store, so adding Blu-ray may not be on the top of Apple's priority list.

Providing accessibility

Mac OS X has a range of features designed to improve accessibility for users with disabilities. These features include ways to make the mouse easier to use (including making the cursor bigger) and to operate the computer by using only the keyboard; the speech recognition technology, which lets OS X respond to spoken commands; and the ability to attach some assistive technology devices. You find the settings for most of these features by choosing System Preferences from the Apple menu and then selecting either Universal Access or Speech. See Chapter 17 for more on accessibility.

Installing software

When you try to install software on your Mac, OS X asks you for a password. If more than one user has an account on the computer, only those with *administrative privileges* can install software. Chapter 10 has more on setting up accounts; also, see the section "Setting up additional accounts," later in this chapter. If you give your kids an account, don't give them admin status. That way, you can control what software they load.

After you give a valid password, installing software on your Mac is simple. In most cases, the downloaded file or installation disc opens as a window, such as the one shown in Figure 5-9. You then just drag the icon or folder that contains the application into the Applications folder, which normally is in the sidebar of all Finder windows. Some applications come with install scripts. For those, you just double-click the install icon and follow the instructions. You may be given an option to *customize* your installation. Unless you're absolutely sure that you know what you want, installing the default configuration recommended by the software's publisher is best.

Figure 5-9:
A software
installation
screen.

If you're new to the Mac and are buying only new software, you aren't likely to run into software written for the older PowerPC processors that Apple used to use. But it's worth knowing that your Intel Mac can run software written for older PowerPC Macs as long as that software is designed for OS X. Apple uses some fancy Rosetta technology to do this. You have to install Rosetta first; it's in the Optional Installs folder on the Restore disk that comes with your Mac. Mac OS X on Intel Macs isn't designed to run software written for Mac OS 9 and older editions — the so-called classic Mac software. Ways exist to work around this limitation, but they aren't easy or fully functional. I describe some in the bonus chapter at www.dummies.com/go/switchingtoamacfd2e.

Uninstalling software

You uninstall software in OS X by moving into the Trash the folder or icon you originally installed. If you don't know where the program icon is, right-click any of its aliases, including the one on the Dock. Then select Show in Finder from the menu you see. If the program icon looks like a package, drag it to the Trash. If the icon is contained in a folder associated with the software, drag the folder to the Trash. In either case, don't empty the Trash until you're sure that everything else is working properly.

Printing on the Mac

Printers are the Bermuda Triangle of personal computing: Setting them up strikes fear in the hearts of most geeks. Apple has done a lot to simplify the process. It has introduced the Bonjour technology, which many printer manufacturers have adopted. Bonjour automates all the messy stuff. Also, OS X comes with drivers for dozens of printer models. So, if you have a fairly new printer, everything should go smoothly.

To set up your printer and do a test print, follow these steps:

1. **Make sure that the printer has power and is connected to your Mac.**

   If it's a USB printer, plug it into one of your USB ports. If it's an Ethernet printer, make sure that it's connected to the same network as your Mac. If it's a Wi-Fi printer, make sure that AirPort is on. Bluetooth printers may take some extra steps; check the printer's manual for instructions.

2. **Turn on the printer.**

3. **Open a short document or create one using TextEdit.**

4. **Choose Print from the File menu. Your printer's name should appear in the Print dialog. Select it and off you go.**

If your printer doesn't appear, try these steps:

1. **Choose System Preferences⇨Print & Fax and click the plus (+) icon.**

2. **Wait half a minute.**

3. **If your printer still doesn't appear in the list, click the More Printers button and select the type of printer you're using from the list at the top.**

4. **If nothing seems to work, go to the printer manufacturer's support Web site for the printer you're using and see whether you can find software for Mac OS X to download.**

   See Chapter 20 for more printer troubleshooting tips.

Setting up additional accounts

If more than one person will be using the computer, you should give each person her own account. To do so, follow these steps:

1. **On the Apple menu, choose System Preferences⇨Accounts.**

2. **In the Accounts pane, click the plus sign (+) under the list of accounts.**

   If the list is grayed out, click the lock icon beneath it to unlock it. You may have to enter your password to complete this step.

3. **For each new account you create, when prompted, enter the account holder's name, a short name that is the name of the account holder's home directory, and the password chosen for the account.**

   The account holder can change her password later, if she wants.

4. **(Optional) Select a picture for the account holder.**

5. **(Optional) Specify which programs will start up automatically for that account.**

6. **(Optional) Set up parental controls if this account is for a child.**

   Read Chapter 17 *before* setting up the account; I have lots of tips about the best way to set up an account for a child.

Backing up

The most important thing to remember about backing up is to swivel your head to look in all directions before putting the car in gear — do not rely on the rearview mirror. Wait, that's not the right advice for this book. The most important thing to remember about backing up your computer is to *do it*. Regularly. Most people don't back up their data even once a month, and that isn't often enough.

National Public Radio once ran a story about a woman who worked for a company that recovers data from defunct hard drives. The company charges lots of money for this service, but it isn't successful for all customers. The woman was trained as a grief counselor, and the company hired her to break the bad news to those unfortunate customers that their precious data was gone forever.

Time Machine and Time Capsule

Fortunately, the OS X feature Time Machine makes backing up your computer easier than backing up your car. Plug an external drive into your Mac, and Time Machine asks whether you want to use it as your backup device. Agree, and Time Machine takes over, backing everything up. It works in the background so that you can carry on with whatever you're doing with your Mac. You want a big external drive, 250GB or more. The Apple Time Capsule includes a large hard drive and a Wi-Fi router that lets all Macs running at least OS X version 10.5 to back up using Time Machine.

Time Machine awakens every night at midnight and backs up everything that has changed since the last backup. You can change the time, of course, and your Mac must be on or sleeping, not shut down. Time Machine organizes the backup files by date and presents the data as a series of Finder windows stacked up behind each other, stretching into the past. You can easily cycle back to the time you want and restore the version of the file you want. If you have stuff you'd rather not back up — and I won't speculate on what those items might be — you can tell Time Machine to skip them. You can also tell Time Machine to back up to a server on your network, if you prefer: Just click the Time Machine icon in System Preferences to make all these choices. And, if you're planning to back up out of your driveway, make sure that no toys, kids, or pets are behind your car before you get in.

Optical discs

Time Machine is truly cool, but I still like to burn important files to CD-ROMs or DVD-ROMs every now and then and keep them in a location that's separate from where I keep the computer. I like having data on something I can touch and know won't be reused for something else.

Portable media

For short-term backup, you can't beat USB flash drives. They're tiny and inexpensive, and many can hold many gigabytes of data. Having all the projects you're working on in your pocket feels good and lets you work on other computers when you need to.

The information superhighway

A number of services on the Internet offer large amounts of storage that you can use to back up files. Free services include Google Gmail and Adrive.com. The $99-per-year Apple MobileMe service includes storage space. These plans offer the following advantages:

- ✔ They provide off-site backup — your files are safe even if your house burns down.

- ✔ The companies that provide these plans generally back up their servers, so you have an additional layer of protection.

If you're concerned about what's left of our privacy in the information age, you should be aware that, in the United States at least, your data enjoys far fewer legal protections when it is stored outside your premises.

Enjoying the Difference

So far in this chapter, I concentrate on what you need to get comfortable with Mac OS X, but there is much more to know. The following sections offer a quick rundown on some of the cooler features. I cover others in later chapters.

Dashboard

Press F4 (the key with the meter symbol) and a whole new window of small applications appears as the screens you were viewing fade into the background. Welcome to Dashboard. You see, out of the box, only a few programs — Apple calls them *widgets:* a calculator, an analog clock, a desk calendar, and a weather forecast. Move the cursor over the lower-right corner of the analog clock. A little *i* appears. Click it. The clock flips over so that you can change its settings. Try the same trick on other widgets. Press F4 a second time and Dashboard goes away, letting you resume your other work.

You can download thousands more Dashboard widgets, and many for free. Just choose ☀⇨Mac OS X Software or go to `www.apple.com/downloads/macosx`. Some of my favorites include

- ✔ **iStat Pro:** System monitor
- ✔ **Kennedy Space Center:** Video feed
- ✔ **Quotes.com:** Stock-price service
- ✔ **Systran:** Language translator (as in French and German, not C++ and Python)

You can even make your own widgets; see Chapter 15, the section about adding handy widgets to the Dashboard, for more info.

Exposé

Exposé is a handy set of functions that Apple assigned to these function keys:

- ✔ **F3:** Separates all open windows on your display so that you can pick the one you want. (Check the symbol on the F3 key for a depiction.) When you have lots of windows open, the images that pressing F3 presents can become tiny. If you hover the cursor over an image, its title is displayed legibly. Click an image and it becomes the front window.

- ✔ **Control+F3:** Does the same trick as F3 but only for the application in front.

- ✔ **⌘+F3:** Makes all open windows scurry to the edges of the screen so that you can see the desktop. Click in the empty desktop space to see the Finder.

Pressing any of these keys a second time restores your original view of the screen.

If you have a laptop with the Apple Multi-Touch trackpad, you can access Exposé with four-finger swipes. You can set up Mighty Mouse, if you have one, to do this as well. See "Pointing the way — the mouse and trackpad" and "Gesturing with Multi-Touch," earlier in this chapter.

Front Row

You filled your Mac with music, photos, and videos. It's time to kick back and let your Mac entertain you. That's where the tiny, simple, optional Apple Remote takes over. Click its menu button and your messy work screen dissolves into a simple screen that lets you choose which media to play, in much the same way as you pick songs on the iPod. This feature, Front Row, is something you *can* take lying down.

Spotlight

Spotlight is the Apple search tool for Mac OS X. Its icon, a magnifying glass, is located on the menu bar in the upper-right corner of your screen. Its keyboard shortcut is ⌘+spacebar. Mac OS X maintains an indexed database of keywords and updates it as new files are added, so searches are fast. Spotlight starts displaying stuff as you type, so you often don't even have to finish typing the word you're searching for. Here are some tips on using Spotlight:

- ✔ **If you type more than one word:** Spotlight searches for items that match both words.

- ✔ **If you want searches to match either item:** Place a vertical bar (|) between them.

- ✔ **If you want Spotlight to exclude a word:** Precede the word with a hyphen. For example, you might search for *dogs|cats –lions –pitbulls*.

You also find a Spotlight search box in the upper-right corner of each Finder window. If you click the Save button under the search box, OS X saves the results of a search in a *smart folder,* which updates automatically as you add, change, and delete files. You can also tell Spotlight to ignore certain files by using its pane in System Preferences.

Sometimes you just want to search for an old-fashioned filename. In that case, in the Finder, choose File➪Find (or press ⌘+F) and select your options.

Is Windows 7 a copy of OS X?

The computer industry wouldn't be where it is today if companies didn't build on the good ideas of others. Still, some features of the new Microsoft Windows 7 operating system seem awfully close to a slavish copy of features in OS X. Windows 7 has a facility that looks very much like Dashboard, but the programs are called gadgets rather than widgets. The Windows 7 search box is in the lower-left corner of the screen rather than in the upper-right, its OS X hangout. The Windows 7 color schemes seem awfully familiar to users of older versions of OS X.

The good news is that learning to use OS X helps prepare you for Windows 7. The bad news is that

Microsoft's ability to innovate seems to be faltering. In the five years it took Microsoft to develop Vista, Apple released three major operating system upgrades — Jaguar, Panther, and Tiger — with a fourth, Leopard (OS X 10.5) released a couple of months after Vista Home Edition. Snow Leopard and Windows 7 came out at approximately the same time (second half of 2009). Some analysts are speculating that Windows 7 may be Microsoft's last personal computer operating system, though I think that's unlikely. Microsoft will have to keep catching up with Apple.

Screen saver and desktop background

Leave it to Apple to turn the boring screen saver into a killer app. Choose System Preferences➪Desktop & Screen Saver. The Desktop tab that appears lets you select a background pattern or photo for your screen when you're working. Make your pick and then click the Screen Saver tab. The screen saver kicks in after your computer has been idle for a few minutes. (You can tell it how many minutes with the slider you see.)

Apple provides several artistic displays to choose from (I like Cosmos), but the choice I like best is the Pictures folder. The screen saver randomly selects and animates pictures from your collection. You can also limit its choices to a folder or slide show. If you enjoy taking pictures but rarely get to look at them, using this screen saver will bring tears to your eyes.

Apple has gone one step further, however. You can set things up so that you can send pictures to *someone else's* Mac over the Internet. It's a helpful way to let grandparents keep up with what's happening with their grandkids. See Chapter 17 for more details.

Chapter 6

Moving Files from Your PC to the Mac

● ●

In This Chapter

▶ Backing up your PC to the Mac

▶ Recovering files from a trashed PC

▶ Handling common file types

▶ Purging files before getting rid of your hard drive

● ●

*Y*ou have your Mac up and running and you played around with OS X a bit, so you at least know how to start programs and make folders. You're ready to take the plunge and begin using your Mac for the bulk of your work. It's time to move those files off that PC and onto your Mac.

Backing Up and Movin' On

I hate to be a nag, but when was the last time you backed up your PC? If you're like most users, it has been awhile. Even if you're planning to keep using your PC, it's worth moving your files to the Mac just to have another backup. The next PC virus could be your last.

I subscribe to the belt-and-suspenders approach to backing up. You should back up everything to your Mac *and* make copies of your most important files to permanent, write-once CDs or DVDs.

If you made an inventory of your PC's files, as I suggest in Chapter 3, look over the inventory and add anything you may have missed. If not, now would be a good time to make an inventory. One important question your inventory should answer is how much data you need to back up. If you save mostly word processing documents and e-mail, you may well have less than the 700MB that a single CD-R optical disc can hold. If you take some digital pictures and occasionally download music, all your files may fit on a 4.7 GB DVD-R or an 8 GB flash drive. If you're an avid photographer, videographer, or music collector, you're better off using an external hard drive.

The good news is that you have many different methods by which to accomplish this moving job. I describe a bunch of ways, but you don't need to read them all. Pick one that sounds as though it might work for you and give it a try.

External hard drive

High-capacity external hard drives are quite affordable these days. You can buy a 1 terabyte (TB) drive for less than $150. A *terabyte* equals a trillion bytes or 1,000 gigabytes or the equivalent of 700,000 floppy disks — a stack over a mile high. You probably don't need that much space, but drives half that size (500GB) sell for less than $100.

Be sure to buy an external drive labeled "for Mac and PC." These drives are usually formatted using the Microsoft FAT32 format, which both Macs and PCs handle well. If your drive is formatted in the newer Microsoft NTFS format, your Mac should be able to read it, although writing to it may be a problem. You can reformat the drive with the OS X Disk Utility after you finish transferring your data.

Here's how transferring files with an external drive works:

1. **Plug the external drive's USB cable into your PC and copy your files to the drive.**

2. **After everything is copied, shut down Windows and unplug the hard drive's data cable from the PC.**

3. **Plug the cable into your Mac.**

   The drive's letter or name should appear on your Mac's desktop.

4. **Double-click the drive icon.**

5. **Copy your files from the external drive to your Mac.**

   Either copy everything to the Mac (make a folder for all the files), or just copy the files you need and keep the rest on the external drive. Remember that you can use the Finder to navigate to your Documents folder, Pictures folder, and others.

Flash memory and iPods

USB flash drives are handy for moving modest amounts of data — as much as 32GB. Follow the same procedure for an external hard drive, as outlined in the preceding section. You can also use an iPod in disk drive mode to transfer data. The larger models hold 120 gigabytes, enough to back up most older PCs. In either case, you can again follow the same procedure as for an external hard drive. Go to `apple.com/macosx/switch/howto/ipod.html` for tips on using an iPod to transfer files.

Optical media — burn, baby, burn

If your PC has a CD burner or, even better, a DVD burner, you can move files by burning discs on your PC and reading them on the Mac. Use ISO format and avoid "sessions" or "packet write." This approach has the added advantage that your files will be stored on a separate medium that you can put away for safekeeping. I like read-only media, such as CD-Rs and DVD-Rs, better than read-write (R/W) media because I'm not tempted to reuse it for something else. Read-only media tends to last longer, too. One source of free CD and DVD writing software is `cdburnerxp.se`.

Ethernet or Wi-Fi at your service

If your PC has an Ethernet port or a Wi-Fi wireless connection, you can network your PC to the Mac, set up your PC as a file server, and then copy over everything you need. This process has five steps:

1. **Connect the Mac and PC to the same network.**

2. **Enable file sharing on the PC.**

3. **Make sharable the files and folders you want to transfer.**

4. **Access the shared folders from your Mac.**

5. **Move the files.**

When it works, networking is the easiest way to transfer your files. But some settings can easily be messed up along the way, and you might find it hard to figure out what the obstacle is when networking becomes *not*working. You also need enough free disk space on the Mac to hold all your files. When you're all done transferring the files, you still should make a backup copy of everything. These are the reasons I recommend using an external hard drive in most cases.

I talk more about networking in Chapter 9, but here's a quick approach to setting up your PC for file sharing:

1. **If your home network doesn't have Wi-Fi, you need an Ethernet cable. Plug the Mac into your Ethernet router or, even better, just run an Ethernet cable between the Mac and the PC.**

   You can borrow the cable that connects your PC to your high-speed Internet modem, if you have one. Don't forget to put it back when you're done.

2. **Determine whether your Mac has already detected your PC on the network. In the Finder, choose Go⇨Network. Then click the various icons in the Network browser that appears, to see whether your PC's icon is among them.**

3. **If you don't see your PC from the Mac, choose Start⇨Control Panel on the PC and double-click the Network Setup Wizard icon. Follow its instructions.**

   Make a note in the margin of the name you give your computer and the workgroup name that's assigned.

4. **After you set up file sharing, drag to the Shared Folder on the PC desktop the folders on the PC that you want to access on your Mac.**

   Alternatively, you can right-click any folder you want to share and select Properties from the menu that appears. Click the Sharing tab and select the Share This Folder on the Network check box (see Figure 6-1).

Figure 6-1:
The Folder
Properties
Sharing tab.

5. **On the Mac side, choose Go⇨Network and look for icons with the names you just assigned. Double-click those icons.**

   You should see your PC folders appear on the Mac desktop.

6. **From the Finder menu, choose New Folder. Name the folder** My PC files **or whatever you want.**

7. **Drag all the files you want to this folder.**

   For extra neatness points, make separate folders for each folder you bring over from the PC, such as My Documents, My Pictures, and My Movies, matching the names you used on your PC. After your files and folders are safely on the Mac, you won't regret spending some quality time organizing them. When you're done, move them all to your Mac's Documents folder.

Commercial solutions

Moving files isn't that hard, but if you'd rather leave this task to someone else, some folks would be happy to help for a modest fee.

Apple ProCare

Perhaps the easiest way to move your files is to sign up for the $99 Apple ProCare premium service plan when you buy your Mac at an Apple retail store. As part of the ProCare plan, the folks at the Apple store move your files for you. You have to bring them your PC within a limited time after you buy the Mac. Ask at the store for current details.

Apple offers additional suggestions on moving files at www.apple.com/lae/switch/howto.

Move2Mac

Move2Mac is a commercial file-transfer product from Detto.com that costs about $75, though it's often discounted. It comes with a special cable that you must use to transfer the files. Detto offers two types of cables. Both have a USB connector at one end that you plug into your Mac. If your PC has USB ports, you should buy the cable with a second USB connector. If the PC has a parallel printer port and is an older model, with no USB ports, or is running Windows 95 (which doesn't support USB), you can use the cable that Detto offers with a USB connector at one end and a parallel printer port plug at the other.

You have to install Move2Mac software on both machines, so the PC must be in good enough shape to do this. Just in case it isn't, I explain other approaches later in this chapter.

You cannot use a standard USB cable for installing Move2Mac software. USB is intended only to connect slave devices to an active computer, so the connector at the other end of a standard USB cable doesn't plug into a computer. Detto cables have a blivit (a "something") in the middle with a chip in it that lets the connection be made. The cables are for use only with Move2Mac software. You can't use the Detto cable for any other purpose, such as hooking up a printer or networking two computers.

A big advantage of using the commercial solution is that providers of these services have worked through many more moving scenarios than I have space to tell you about. Move2Mac claims to handle documents, spreadsheets, photos, music, files, folders, IE favorites, an IE home page, graphics, databases, an address book, and backgrounds.

Move2Mac doesn't try to convert application data files from PC format to Mac format. I discuss those issues later in this chapter. If your life is on the PC, a commercial solution may be worth the money.

Clone your PC on your Mac, virtually speaking

If you're thinking about running Windows on your Mac, consider using one of the third-party virtual hosting solutions — Parallels or VMWare — described in Chapter 16. Both allow you to copy your entire PC, operating system, applications, files, and settings to your Macintosh. Of course, you need to have enough hard drive space on your Mac to hold everything that's now on the PC and still leave plenty of room for all the Mac stuff you want to add. And, you have to determine what the licenses you have for Windows and your application packages permit. In all likelihood, you need to remove all purchased software from the PC after you successfully make the transition. Make sure that you have a complete backup of everything before erasing the PC's hard drive. See Chapter 22 for suggestions on what you might do with the erased PC.

In some ways, this solution is ideal. You have your complete PC environment on the Mac — files, applications, and all your settings. On the other hand, you haven't yet transitioned to OS X; you merely have a new PC. Still, this approach allows you to take things gradually, moving one set of applications and files at a time as you're ready. Meanwhile, you can surf the Internet in safety from the OS X side of your computer.

Files on floppies, Zip disks, magnetic tape, and other media

If you have a collection of files on floppy disks, Zip disks, magnetic tape, or other obsolescent removable media, the simplest solution is to read them all onto your PC's hard drive and then move them to the Mac with your other files. If you have too many disks or tapes for this strategy to be practical, or if you have only a few disks you really need but you're not sure which ones, a few possibilities exist. You can also buy Zip drives with a USB interface from Iomega (`www.iomega.com`). For 3½-inch floppy disks, Iomega (and others) sell a USB floppy drive that can read PC floppies. For other media, such as 5¼-inch floppies or magnetic tapes, some companies can transfer your files for a fee, but you may be better off hanging on to your old PC until you're sure that you no longer need any of the older files.

Before sending out removable media for conversion, or working on them yourself, open the write-protect tab on the media to reduce the likelihood of accidental erasure.

Recovering Data from a Damaged PC

We all know the safe computing rules by heart: Use a good antivirus program, never open e-mail attachments you weren't expecting, and back up your files regularly. Most of us aren't so careful. Or, maybe your kids figured out how to get around whatever security system you set up. Anyway, your PC is barely working, if it even boots. What do you do?

This problem has a number of solutions; a whole industry is devoted to it, in fact. The following sections cover a couple of these solutions.

Try accessing your PC from the Mac

If your PC boots, try accessing it from your Mac using an Ethernet cable, as described previously in this chapter. Even if the PC is barely responding, the server software may still be fully functional.

If your PC is so trashed that the mouse no longer works, you may still be able to control it using the Windows accessibility tools. To do so, follow these steps:

1. **Press the Windows key on your PC's keyboard to open the Start menu.**

2. **Use the arrow keys to highlight the Control Panel option, and then press Enter.**

3. **Use the arrow keys to highlight the Accessibility Options option; then press Enter.**

4. **Press Shift+Tab and then the right-arrow key to select the Mouse tab.**

5. **Press Alt+M to select the Use Mouse Keys check box; then press Enter.**

6. **Press Num Lock to turn on the numeric keypad.**

   You should now be able to use the numeric keypad to move the cursor around without using the mouse. The 5 key is the mouse button. Press – (the minus key) for right-clicking and press / (the division sign) to get back to left-clicking. Press Insert to hold down the mouse button for dragging, and press Delete to stop dragging.

If you mess up at some point, remember that pressing Esc activates the Cancel button in dialog boxes in Windows — and in OS X.

Use the Windows System Restore program

The *System Restore* tool in Windows lets you roll the operating system back to a kinder, gentler time, before all the nasties got into it. To use it, follow these steps:

1. **Save any open files.**

2. **Choose Start⇨All Programs.**

3. **Choose Accessories⇨System Tools⇨System Restore.**

4. **Select the Restore My Computer to an Earlier Time option and then click the Next button.**

5. **Select a date far enough back when you dimly remember that your computer was working well; then click the Next button.**

   If this restore date works, transfer your files and perform a backup as described earlier in this chapter. If the date you chose doesn't work, you can try other dates, earlier or later.

Knoppix to the rescue

The complete PC operating system *Knoppix* fits on a single CD-R optical disc and can automatically boot up most PCs. It isn't Windows or OS X, however; Knoppix is a version of the Linux operating system. That's the bad news and the good news:

> ✔ **The bad news:** You have enough of a challenge on your hands getting
> used to OS X without being introduced to a third system.
>
> ✔ **The good news:** Linux isn't affected by whatever cooties your computer
> has. Also, you need to deal with only a few Linux commands.

You can make a Knoppix disc on your Mac that should boot in your PC,
assuming that the PC hardware isn't broken and its peripheral devices are
fairly standard. Knoppix can detect and use most common peripherals.
However, if your PC's hard drive is encrypted, Knoppix can't read it.

To make the Knoppix disc, you need a blank CD-R disc. Here's the recipe:

1. **Go to** www.knoppix.org **and click the English flag in the upper-left
   corner, assuming that *Sie sprechen kein Deutsches.***

2. **Click the Order button and find a company in your country that sells
   Knoppix on CD for a nominal fee. Or, click the Download button and
   select a download server located on your continent.**

   You're asked to concur with a "use at your own risk" agreement. (You
   expect a warranty with free software?)

   If you accept the agreement, you see a list of available downloads. You
   normally want the latest English version, which will have a filename
   that looks something like KNOPPIX_V6.0.1CD-2009-02-08-EN.iso,
   where 6.0 is the version number, EN means it's an English version, and
   .iso means it's a disc image. You also can download files with similar
   names but with the extensions .md5 and .sha1. These cryptographic
   signatures enable you to verify that the files are authentic. For extra
   credit, download them as well. They're very short, and you might as well
   act as though you're interested. The .iso file, on the other hand, is big —
   about 700MB. It just fits on a CD-R. The size isn't a big deal if you have a
   broadband connection, but plan on an overnight download if you use a
   dialup connection.

3. **Download the files you selected by dragging them to the desktop; do
   the short ones first.**

   When you have the .iso file on your Mac's desktop, you're ready to
   burn it to the blank CD-R disc.

4. **Open the Application folder and then the Utilities folder.**

5. **Double-click the Disk Utility icon, and when the Disk Utility window
   opens, click the Burn button in the upper-left corner.**

6. **In the Select Image to Burn dialog, find the .iso file, click it, and
   click the Burn button.**

7. **Pop in a blank CD-R and let 'er rip.**

Chill.

When the CD-R is all cooked, you see a message saying whether the burn was successful; if it wasn't, try again on a fresh CD-R. After you complete a successful burn, eject the CD by right-clicking its icon and choosing Eject from the context menu. Label the CD with a soft marking pen.

Now you can put your new Knoppix disc into the PC's CD reader and restart your PC. Knoppix takes a couple of minutes to boot, and lots of text flashes by as it does its thing, but when it's done, you should see a nice welcome screen. On the left side of the screen, you see icons for all the drives that Knoppix found as it booted up. You should see an icon for your PC's hard drive if it's working. It's labeled something like hda1. Double-click that icon. You should see the contents of your PC's hard drive. With your PC contents on display, you can gather your files in one of the following ways:

- ✔ **If you have one, connect a portable hard drive or a flash drive to the PC.** Its icon should appear on the Knoppix desktop. You can now drag files from the PC to the device you plugged in.

   When you're done transferring files, right-click the removable drive's icon and select Unmount. Or, you can just shut down Knoppix by selecting Log Out from the K menu in the lower-left portion of the Knoppix taskbar.

- ✔ **If you have an Internet e-mail account, such as Yahoo! or Gmail, you can email the files to yourself.** Log on to your account using Konqueror, the Knoppix Web browser and file manager, and mail yourself files as attachments.

- ✔ **If your PC hardware has a second optical drive that can burn optical discs, you can also write your files to a CD or DVD using Knoppix.** Right-click in an open directory window, choose Action⇨Create Data CD with K3b, and follow the instructions.

Knoppix can do a lot more, including repairing a damaged Windows file system and networking directly with your Mac, but these topics are too complex to cover here. Take a look at *Knoppix For Dummies*, by Paul G. Sery (Wiley Publishing), if you want to do more with this powerful tool.

Should you run antivirus software before transferring your files?

PC viruses don't hurt OS X, but they could cause problems if you plan to run Windows on your Mac or exchange files with Windows users. So, updating and running your antivirus program before transferring your files is probably a wise move. However, if your PC is truly on the edge, you probably should move your important files off before running any programs. In that case, I suggest doing the file transfer twice, before and after an antivirus run. If the latter transfer goes smoothly, the first set of files can be erased.

More extreme measures

If none of the above measures work, consider removing the drive and putting it in an external drive enclosure to mount on your Mac. It's a bit tricky — you have to determine what type of hard drive you have to get the right enclosure — and more often than not in a bad PC it's the disk that's shot. If you're not experienced in doing work on your computer's insides, get a technician or repair shop to do this. Get an enclosure that's designed to work with Macs as well as with PCs. Units that employ the Oxford chipset generally do. Putting your PC hard drive into a portable enclosure gives you another usable backup of your old files. It makes more sense if the hard drive is 20GB or more because it can later serve as a useful accessory to your Mac. Note that disks formatted in Windows NTFS open on OS X as read-only. When your Mac offers to reformat the drive, don't allow the reformat unless you're satisfied that all data is safely transferred and backed up. Then you can use the OS X Disk Utility to reformat the drive (which *deletes* all your files but doesn't *erase* them fully) and use it as you want. Disk Utility can also erase the drive after you format it. Click the Erase tab and then click the Erase Free Space button.

If truly valuable (more than $1,000) files are on your hard drive, look for a hard drive data recovery firm. Visit www.myharddrivedied.com for interesting presentations on the process. They suggest some things you can do yourself if you're willing to risk doing more damage.

Dealing with Common File Types

Most PC file types can be used with appropriate programs on the Mac. The following sections describe some of these file types.

Portable document format (.pdf)

The popular portable document format, originally developed by Adobe.com, is the standard display mode on OS X. The Preview program that comes with the Mac conveniently displays PDF documents. OS X can also create PDF files; it's an option you find by choosing File➪Print for most programs. You don't need to download or buy software to work with PDF files, although Adobe Acrobat offers additional capabilities beyond what OS X provides.

JPEG photos (.jpg)

JPEG stands for Joint Photographic Experts Group, the name of the committee that pulled together the format. Macs love JPEGs. The OS X Preview application displays them, and the iPhoto program stores them, organizes them, slices them, dices them, and spits out slide shows and coffee table books. Both programs come with every Mac sold. I discuss iPhoto more in Chapter 12, but the quick way to get your photos into iPhoto is to move the files to your Pictures folder, open iPhoto, and choose File➪Import to Library.

MPEG movies (.mpg)

The Motion Picture Experts Group came up with this family of standards for moving images. Apple QuickTime, which comes with each new Mac and is available free for Windows, is happy to screen MPEG-1 and MPEG-4 files for your viewing pleasure. Apple offers an MPEG-2 Playback Component that you can download for about $20 from www.apple.com/quicktime/mpeg2.

A free open source alternative media player, VLC, handles all MPEG formats and a whole lot more. It's available from www.videolan.org.

If you're into video editing, see the discussion of iMovie in Chapter 13.

Music (.mp3, .aiff, .wma, and others)

The iTunes program in Windows is compatible with iTunes on the Mac, so if you're using iTunes on your PC, you can transfer all the music, video, audiobooks, and podcasts you have accumulated. One exception is .wma files — Macs don't play them without additional software. Inexpensive solutions you can download are available from Flip4mac.com and easywma.com. You can also import any music or other sound files that are in .mp3 format (MP3). You can also import files in .aiff or .wav format. However, your Mac cannot play files in Microsoft PlaysForSure (.pfs) or Zune format. These files use a digital rights management technique that isn't compatible with the Apple FairPlay system.

You have a number of ways to transfer your iTunes music library from a PC to a Mac. You can simply copy all the files from the Music\iTunes folder on your PC over to the Music folder on the Mac and then choose File➪Import within iTunes. Apple recommends that you use the Backup to Disc feature in iTunes. You need a CD burner or, better yet, a DVD burner on your PC. See support.apple.com/kb/HT1382 for details.

Digital rights management — curse or blessing?

A popular form of entertainment on the Internet is *trolling,* or mentioning a hot-button topic in a discussion group and watching the heated controversy erupt. Few topics are more effective as troll bait than digital rights management (DRM), which is seen as either an enabling technology that allows music and movies to be enjoyed by way of the Internet, or as an evil, dangerous technology that allows all information to be centrally controlled by powerful interests. Both viewpoints have merit.

The rights that DRM manages are the rights that copyright law gives to content owners. When it works, DRM encrypts content and then allows decryption only on the computer or player that the copyright holder authorizes. DRM can also restrict the number and quality of copies made and the number of times content can be viewed. Providers of Blu-ray high-definition video are insisting that all computers that will show such content implement strict DRM.

Anti-DRM activists are concerned that the technology gives content creators too much power. Apple has switched from its own DRM system, FairPlay, which was relatively benign, to selling DRM-free music on its iTunes music store. (Apple calls DRM-free music iTunes *Plus.*) You can even unlock past purchases for a small fee. But movies and iPhone applications still use DRM.

Apple president Steve Jobs called for an end to DRM music in February 2007, saying "Imagine a world where every online store sells DRM-free music encoded in open licensable formats. In such a world, any player can play music purchased from any store, and any store can sell music which is playable on all players. This is clearly the best alternative for consumers, and Apple would embrace it in a heartbeat." Check out the rest of his comments at www.apple.com/hotnews/thoughtsonmusic.

ASCII text (.txt) and rich text format (.rtf) files

Text files are supposed to be as simple as anything gets in computers. They're just a bunch of characters in American Standard Code for Information Interchange (ASCII) encoding. Unfortunately, even these files aren't so simple. The three different operating system families — Windows, Unix, and Mac OS — use different conventions for ending a line, or paragraph, of text. Unix uses a line-feed (LF) character, Mac OS 9 used a carriage return (CR), and Windows uses both (CR+LF).

The TextEdit program that comes with OS X reads text files created by Windows, Unix, and Mac OS. However, by default, it saves files in rich text format (.rtf), which, among other things, preserves basic formatting of text. You can change the default settings to text format in the TextEdit Preferences.

Transferring your e-mail address book

If you're using an online e-mail service such as Yahoo! or Gmail, you don't need to do anything — your address book is stored on the mail service's servers and you can access it just as well from your Mac.

If you're using Outlook Express, you can transfer the addresses by using vCard records. To do this, prepare a new folder on your external hard drive or flash drive. You can call it Outlook Addresses. Start Outlook Express and choose Tools⇨Address Book. Choose Edit⇨Select All. Drag all addresses to the folder you created. You can then import them into the Apple Mail program (see Chapter 8). I discuss moving your AOL address book in Chapter 8.

Purging Your Files Before Disposing of the Disk

When you're satisfied that you have all your files safely moved to your Mac and backed up, it's time to remove from your PC hard drive any data that you may not want others to see. It can include e-mail, personal correspondence, proprietary work documents, and financial information. Sensitive information, including credit card numbers and passwords, may be stored in your computer without your knowing about it, in the form of temporary cache files and cookies. *Cookies* are blocks of information that your Internet browser often stores so that Web sites you revisit know about your past usage.

The simplest solution is to erase everything on the PC's hard drive. Doing so makes your computer much less usable if you decide to sell or donate it, however. If you still have the original discs that came with the computer, you can restore the operating system after you erase. You can also restore any applications you own.

Alternatively, you can just erase the data files you're concerned about. The My Documents folder is an obvious candidate, but you must also check to see where other files may be stored. This approach is more risky, and I recommend it only if you're planning to give the computer to another family member or someone else you trust.

Removing the hard drive

A third approach, and perhaps the safest one, is to simply remove the hard drive before you dispose of your PC. This is relatively easy for a tower PC, but more tricky for a laptop. You can pay a technician at a computer store to do this for you. Of course, the computer will be much less usable without a hard drive, although it can still be used with a Knoppix CD, as previously described. If the machine is reasonably current, it may be worth it for the next owner to install a new, perhaps larger, hard drive. These drives are relatively inexpensive.

You can simply keep the old hard drive in a safe place, or you can ask the technician who removes it from your PC to install it in a portable hard drive enclosure. See "More extreme measures," earlier in this chapter.

Wiping data off your hard drive

Safely removing files from your PC isn't just a simple matter of deleting them. When Microsoft Windows deletes files, it only removes information about those files from its file directory and makes the space on the hard drive available for reuse. It doesn't erase the data itself. Programs are available that can often recover deleted files if they haven't been erased. Even if a file has been erased once on older hard drives of less that 15GB capacity, it's sometimes possible to recover data by using highly specialized equipment. However, according to the U.S. National Institute of Science and Technology, "most of today's media can be effectively cleared by one overwrite." You can use the following programs to overwrite your data one or more times:

- ✔ **SDelete:** Microsoft suggests using this free command-line program. You can see instructions and a download link at

  ```
  www.microsoft.com/technet/sysinternals/utilities/
          SDelete.mspx
  ```

- ✔ **Eraser:** This program is also free, although a donation is suggested to help support the author. You can download it at

  ```
  www.heidi.ie/eraser
  ```

- ✔ **Darik's Boot And Nuke:** You burn this free program to a self-contained boot disk. It also works with Macs. You can download it at `www.dban.org`.

Mac OS X has a built-in file-wiping utility. When you drag files to the Trash, you can choose Secure Empty Trash from the Finder menu. In addition, the OS X Disk Utility can erase all your free space, so you can get rid of any files you didn't securely erase.

Safely destroying your PC hard drive

Perhaps you don't want to or can't reuse your PC's hard drive but simply want to destroy it. Maybe it's so far gone that you can't access it with any program but you know it contains sensitive data that someone with the right tool and a big budget could still get at. You have a bit of a problem. It's hard to dispose of it in a truly safe and environmentally friendly way. The most widely recommended ways include melting, incineration, crushing, or shredding — yes, shredding. Some companies offer this service.

Perhaps the simplest solution is to erase it as best you can, remove it from the PC, and take it apart. You need some small screwdrivers, and often a screw or two is hidden under a label. The process is instructive, though, and you find some neat, powerful magnets inside. Simply bending the disks renders them essentially unreadable. (Some newer disks — generally more than 50GB — are made of glass and may shatter, so pick a safe location and wear eye protection.) Figure 6-2 shows a disassembled hard drive with an ordinary claw hammer used to bend the platters. The super magnets are in the upper-left corner of the hard drive case. Be careful with them; they're strong enough to pinch.

Figure 6-2:
Dis-
assembled
hard drive
with bent
disks.

Chapter 7

Switching Applications

● ●

In This Chapter

▶ Introducing iLife

▶ Identifying office productivity applications

▶ Switching to graphics, design, and personal finance software for the Mac

▶ Settling for Windows-based applications when necessary

▶ Adding functionality to your Mac with recommended downloads

● ●

*T*he Mac OS X, from Apple, comes with an amazing collection of software programs to help you create and enjoy what Apple refers to as your *digital life:* music, photos, home movies, and Web content. They're so useful that I devote Chapters 11 through 14 to telling you more about them. I also cover the quite capable word processor TextEdit later in this chapter. The programs in the iLife suite and the chapters that cover them are described in this list in the order I cover them:

✓ **iTunes:** Manages your music and videos, syncs with your iPod, and talks to the online iTunes Store. (See Chapter 11.)

✓ **iPhoto:** Takes care of everything associated with digital photography, including retrieving images from your digital camera, performing basic editing, organizing images into slide shows and albums, and printing albums. (See Chapter 12.)

✓ **iMovie:** Lets you import and edit all those home movies you took of your vacations and kids (but never watch) and turn them into professional-looking mini-biopics that won't bore your guests. They might even garner 15 minutes of fame on YouTube. In your work life, you can produce video clips that compellingly present your ideas. (See Chapter 13.)

✓ **iDVD:** Burns those edited iMovie shorts and epics (along with iPhoto slide shows) to DVDs that you can play on almost any DVD player or computer with a DVD reader. Make the grandparents very happy. (See Chapter 13.)

✔ **GarageBand:** Helps you put together the original score for the home video epic or just fan your long-suppressed creative musical talents. Also use it to record podcasts and learn to play guitar or piano. (See Chapter 13.)

✔ **iWeb:** Builds all this creative output into spectacular Web pages. (See Chapter 14.)

Because all these programs are built by Apple, using the OS X toolbox, they all work well together. You can use an iTunes playlist as a background for your iPhoto slide show. You can integrate iPhoto images into your iMovie, animating the images by using cinematographic techniques popularized by Ken Burns. Your creations can also extend beyond your Mac. You can carry your digital works on your iPod and iPhone or show them on your home entertainment center using Apple TV.

Although Apple emphasizes the personal use of these products, they have obvious business uses as well: organizing slide shows for presentations, presenting sales and training videos, and creating less-boring Web sites.

You don't need to worry about installing iLife. It's on your Mac already, in your Applications folder, with shortcuts on the Dock. There's nothing extra to do. Sorry.

Although iLife covers many needs, you may have applications on your PC that you use regularly or need occasionally that don't have direct equivalents among the programs included with OS X. In the rest of this chapter, I guide you through the more common situations and point you to additional resources for others.

Keeping Your Appointments with iCal

OS X comes with the sophisticated calendar program iCal. You find it on the Dock, represented by an icon that looks like a desk calendar open to today's date. (Does anyone even remember what a desk calendar looked like?) It supports multiple calendars (for example, work, personal, and rule-the-world conspiracy) and offers daily, weekly, and monthly views of your schedule. Apple iCal is based on the iCalendar standard, which is supported by many other calendaring systems, including Microsoft Outlook.

You can move your Outlook calendar to your Mac by following these steps:

1. **Export your Outlook calendar in iCalendar format using the free tool available at `outlook2ical.sourceforge.net`.**

2. **Move the resulting `.ics` file to your Mac.**

Chapter 6 explains all sorts of ways to move files from your PC to your Mac.

3. **Import your Outlook calendar into iCal by selecting File⇨Import.**

Synchronizing with Entourage is also supported, as is using the older `.vcs` files. If you have a MobileMe account, you can keep your calendars constantly in sync with all your Apple toys and with your desktop, laptop, iPhone, iPod touch, and even your PC.

iCal works with other calendaring systems that support the CalDAV standard to let you check your colleagues' availability, arrange meetings with them, and book a conference room with a projector and party hats. You send everyone meeting material by simply dragging the document icon or icons to the event in the iCal window.

Processing Words and Numbers

Once upon a time, in the dim ages of the past century, people who wanted to produce a written document for other people to read sat down in front of a mechanical contraption, called a *typewriter,* that was filled with levers connected to keys arranged in much the same way as the keys on a computer keyboard. Writers checked their spelling by looking up words in a paper book.

Today, it would be considered a form of abuse to make someone write without the aid of a good word processor. If you're working with other people in most organizations, you're pretty much expected to read and produce documents in a format compatible with Microsoft Office — particularly Microsoft Word.

The need for Microsoft Office compatibility complicates what would otherwise be a clean, bare-knuckle-competitive relationship between Apple and Microsoft. Apple needs Office, and Microsoft makes good money selling it to Mac users. Bill Gates once half-joked that he made more money when Apple sold a Mac than when a Windows PC was sold, because Mac users were more likely to buy Office.

Many word processing solutions work with a Macintosh, ranging from the software that comes free with OS X to the full Microsoft Office for Mac suite to a number of other possibilities.

Although most word processing programs can open documents in certain older formats, if you have documents that have been around a long time or were created using obsolete applications, you may not be able to read them directly from the standard Mac office suites that I describe in the following sections. MacLinkPlus, found at `www.dataviz.com`, converts numerous older types of documents (it goes back as far as WordPerfect DOS 5.0) to modern formats. See the DataViz Web site for a complete list: `www.dataviz.com`.

TextEdit

The humble word processor included with OS X, TextEdit, is quite powerful, with many more features than its Windows equivalent, Notepad. You find TextEdit in the Applications folder. In particular, TextEdit can read and save documents produced by Microsoft Word 97, 2003, and 2007. Although TextEdit reads ASCII text files generated in Windows, UNIX, Linux, and Mac OS, unless you change its preferences, it doesn't save files in ASCII text format, for reasons discussed in the previous chapter. Instead, TextEdit normally saves files in rich text format, .rtf, a relatively simple format for styled documents that was introduced by Microsoft in 1987. TextEdit can also read and save documents in HyperText Markup Language (HTML), Microsoft Word (.doc), Microsoft Extensible Markup Language (XML), Open Office XML, and OpenDocument formats. It can also produce PDF documents by using its Print command.

TextEdit supports character formatting and the inclusion of graphics and multimedia images. Some of its more powerful features can be a little hard to find. For example, to make and edit tables, you choose Format⇨Text⇨Table. Choose Format⇨Text to find more list management features. TextEdit allows sophisticated control of letter spacing and even speaks text aloud, but it doesn't support multicolumn documents. Its simple editing screen, shown in Figure 7-1, understates its capabilities.

Figure 7-1:
The simple
TextEdit
editing
screen.

This is the OS X TextEdit window.

TextEdit has full support for *Unicode,* a computer industry standard character set that includes the written characters of most of the languages now used in the world — and a few ancient ones, such as *Linear B.* (See Chapter 5 for more information on keying in special characters and other languages.) A committee is studying the addition of Egyptian hieroglyphs to Unicode. In the meantime, you can purchase the glyph processor MacScribe 2.1 at www.macscribe.com. The site is in French, but if you understand Egyptian hieroglyphics, you probably speak French, too.

If you want to edit HTML files in TextEdit, choose TextEdit⇨Preferences and select the Ignore Rich Text Commands in HTML Files check box. You also see this option for a particular file when you choose File⇨Open.

Word and Office from Microsoft

Microsoft Word and the other Microsoft Office applications (Excel for spreadsheets and PowerPoint for presentations) are the most widely used standards in most workplaces and schools. Microsoft sells versions of these programs for the Mac. If you frequently need to use files created by these programs, buying Word or the entire Office suite may be a wise investment. Microsoft Office 2008 is file-compatible with Office 2007 for Windows.

You can buy Microsoft Word, shown in Figure 7-2, by itself, or you can buy the entire Office suite, which includes Word, Excel, PowerPoint, and Entourage, a Mac program similar to Outlook in Windows but with somewhat different features. I discuss Entourage a bit more in Chapter 8.

Microsoft Office is pricey, especially if you aren't upgrading from a previous version and don't qualify for the Home & Student version. As mentioned previously, TextEdit, which comes with OS X, can open files in Microsoft Word (.doc) format. You have other alternatives if you want full independence from the Redmond empire.

If you're planning to install Microsoft Windows on your Mac and you need to work with Office documents only occasionally, one approach is to install the Windows version of Office in Windows and use it there. If you use the virtual technologies for installing Windows, the Office applications can be used alongside Mac applications. You can also use the CrossOver Mac program from CodeWeavers.com (www.codeweavers.com). It runs the Windows versions of Office 97, Office 2000, and Office 2003 on your Mac without installing Windows. The CodeWeaver approach isn't always perfect, however. See Chapter 16 for more on all these options. But if you're planning heavy use of Office, you'll be happier installing the Mac version. Get with the program, program.

Note that Microsoft Office 2008 doesn't support Visual Basic for Applications (VBA). If your life depends on VBA, you might want to get hold of a copy of the older Office 2004 (try eBay). A version of Basic that runs on the Mac is available from www.realbasic.com, or you can use AppleScript, which Office 2008 supports. OpenOffice.org 3.0, which I'm about to tell you about, has limited support for VBA and runs many Office macros.

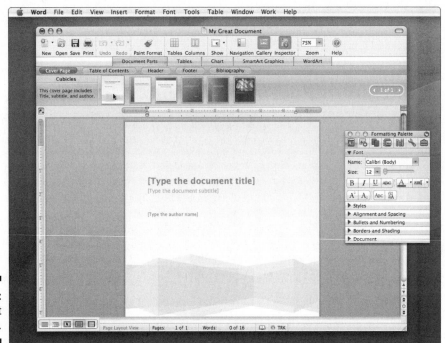

Figure 7-2:
Microsoft
Word.

OpenOffice.org

OpenOffice.org is a suite of office applications developed by the open source community that largely parallels the capabilities of Microsoft Office. The program can generally read and write files in the various Microsoft formats, but is most comfortable with OpenDocument format. Oh, and it's open source and free.

OpenOffice.org says that it appends the `.org` suffix to its name because someone else owns the OpenOffice trademark. The program can be used on a variety of computing platforms besides the Macintosh, including Windows, Linux, and most other forms of Unix. OpenOffice.org consists of these components:

✔ **Base:** A relational database management system

✔ **Calc:** A spreadsheet

✔ **Draw:** A vector graphics drawing program

✔ **Impress:** A presentation program, similar to PowerPoint

✔ **Write:** A word processor

OpenOffice.org 3.0 runs on the Mac using the normal OS X user interface. (Earlier versions employed X11, a windowing system developed years ago at MIT.) To install it, follow these steps:

1. **Point your Web browser to** `http://download.openoffice.org` **and click the Download Openoffice.org link.**

2. **While the installation image is being downloaded, OpenOffice asks you for a voluntary donation.**

   Be nice and give up some money — the software is quite a good deal. You can also look at the large library of available extensions and try versions of OpenOffice still under development, though I suggest that you stay away from the latter. Downloading experimental software voids the warranty on this book — oh, right, we're not offering a warranty.

3. **After the installation image has downloaded, double-click it (it's in your Downloads folder) and drag the OpenOffice.org icon into the Applications folder.**

   A screen shot of OpenOffice.org displaying a draft of this chapter, stored as a Microsoft Word document, is shown in Figure 7-3.

All in all, OpenOffice.org is a powerful program. In the previous edition of this book, which covered the older, X11 version of OpenOffice.org, I said it was an excellent example of both the strengths and weaknesses of open source software. I'm not sure that the new Mac-friendly version exhibits many weaknesses.

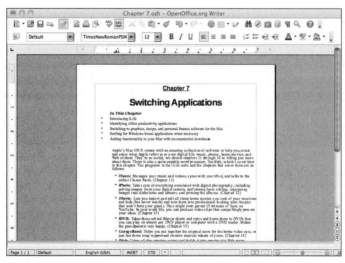

Figure 7-3: OpenOffice.org at work.

iWork

The Apple program iWork includes Pages, a word processing program; Numbers, a spreadsheet program; and Keynote, a presentation program. All are quite impressive.

Pages

Pages incorporates many of the features of a page-layout program. You don't just type and format text with pages — you create finished documents ready for printing or display on the World Wide Web or as PDF files. For example, check out these features:

- **Charts:** Pages has three-dimensional charting capabilities, with the ability to rotate the chart image in 3D mode to create exactly the effect you want.

- **Image editing and page layout:** You can edit images in Pages; you don't need to jump back and forth to an image editor for image adjustments. You can crop images to arbitrary shapes that you create in Pages and flow text around them. And, Pages comes with a set of templates that Apple has designed to give your documents a professional look.

  Nearly everything can be edited in real time.

- **Mailings:** Pages can do mail merges, even using your address book or a spreadsheet table in Numbers to create personalized mailings and newsletters.

- **Organizational tools:** Outline mode lets you create a multilevel outline that you can quickly reorganize by dragging and dropping. To help with long documents, Pages shows detailed color thumbnail images for every page in the left sidebar of your screen.

- **Tables and calculations:** Pages can create tables that perform simple calculations, such as addition, multiplication, and averaging.

Pages can read and export Microsoft Word, HTML, RTF, and text-only files from the Mac or PC. It even supports Apple's older AppleWorks format. Pages does a good job of retaining the formatting of documents it imports, including Word revision tracking. It also works with the popular MathType and EndNote programs for adding math equations and bibliographic references, though you need to buy the latest Mac versions of these programs.

Numbers

The world runs on spreadsheets, but they're kind of boring. Apple adds pizzazz with a flexible canvas on which you can place intelligent tables, 3D charts and graphs, text, pictures, and whatever. Canned templates and lots of small touches, such as one-click formulas and Formula List view, make Numbers easy for non-bean-counters to use. Don't worry: It can read and write most Excel files.

Keynote

Keynote is Apple's attempt to one-up Microsoft PowerPoint, which has become the primary means of business communications in the 21st century. In a joke about two kidnapped businesspeople about to be executed who are offered a last request, the first person **asks** whether he can finally give the presentation he had been working on before his capture. The second person asks to be killed first so that he doesn't have to sit through one more PowerPoint presentation.

Keynote is designed to make it easy to create killer presentations that don't bore the audience to death. Apple president Steve Jobs claims that he is Keynote's prime customer, and that he demands ever-improved features for his numerous presentations. Keynote has a dizzying array of special effects, transitions, slide builds, animation tools, and templates. It also calls on tools from Pages and the iLife suite to simplify slide creation so that you can have tables that update when you change the numbers and 3D charts that you can rotate. You can also export Keynote presentations in PowerPoint format (`.ppt`), but some of the cooler effects may not translate fully.

Always be sure to preview your presentation on the computer, the program, the projector, and, if possible, the room you will use when your audience shows up. Put your presentation on automatic play and sit in the back of the room to see how legible those slides are from that vantage.

Web-based office applications

In a major new trend in computing, Web sites are offering software applications, either free or for a subscription fee. All you need to use them is a computer with a reasonably modern Web browser. You don't have to download any software. You sign up for the service and access the document and the programs you need to create and then edit them over the Internet. It works a lot like Web-based e-mail, and it's no surprise that one of the foremost vendors of this type of service is Google, but others have gotten in the act as well. Here's a quick looks at the pros and cons of Web-based apps:

- ✔ **The upside:** A special advantage is that you can access documents stored on the Web site from any computer, anywhere you find an Internet connection. Your documents are password-protected, of course, but most sites have a way for you to share documents with colleagues and work on them collaboratively.

✔ **The downside:** Obviously, you cannot work when you're out of range of an Internet connection — say, when traveling with your laptop. Also, you need to have a fast Internet connection, and even then, response times can be slow compared to desktop programs.

Google Docs & Spreadsheets

Google offerings include a word processor and a spreadsheet. If you have a Google account and password for Gmail, groups, or another Google service, you simply log on to use Docs & Spreadsheets. Otherwise, you can register for a new account with little effort. All Google requires is your e-mail address. Even your full name is optional. Docs & Spreadsheets lets you

✔ **Create or upload documents:** They're stored on Google's servers. You can also upload documents in Microsoft Office `.doc` and `.xls` formats, as well as `.rtf`, OpenDocument, and of course, plain-text formats.

✔ **Share a document with other people:** Enter someone's e-mail address and that person receives an e-mail invitation and can see and edit your document as soon as sign-in is complete. Multiple people can view and edit a document at the same time. The spreadsheet program even has a chat window, allowing all the editors to discuss what they're up to.

✔ **Track changes to a document:** You can see who made changes, when the changes were made, and what was changed.

✔ **Store, download, or post the final document:** When you're done, you can leave the document on the Google server. You can also download the document to your Mac in a variety of formats, including `.csv`, `.doc`, `.html`, `.ods`, `.odt`, `.pdf`, `.rtf`, and `.xls`. You can also publish your document on the Web in `.html` format.

Figure 7-4 shows Google Docs displaying a draft of this chapter, which was uploaded to Google in Microsoft Word `.doc` format. Figure 7-5 shows a simple Google spreadsheet.

Other online office applications

A number of other Web sites are offering online office applications; this list describes a few:

✔ **EditGrid:** This online spreadsheet program has strong collaboration features. It's free for personal use and requires a monthly fee for businesses. See whether you can guess its Web address.

✔ **ThinkFree:** ThinkFree.com (`www.thinkfree.com`) offers Write, for word processing; Calc, a spreadsheet program; and Show, for presentations.

✔ **Zoho:** Zoho Virtual Office includes word processing, spreadsheets, and presentations. It's available free for individuals at `www.zohox.com`. Business users pay a small monthly fee and get a few additional features.

Figure 7-4:
Google
Docs at
work.

Figure 7-5:
A Google
spread-
sheet.

Personal finance

If you use Quicken or QuickBooks in Windows, you'll be glad to know that versions of these programs are available for the Mac from Intuit.com. It's possible to transfer records between the Windows and Mac versions of these programs, but the process isn't perfect and some types of data don't get converted. You can find full information at www.intuit.com/support. Select the product you are interested and enter "converting to Mac" in the search box. I'd advise waiting until the end of your accounting year to change from the PC version of a program you depend on to the Mac version, or just keep running the PC version you already use under Windows on your Mac. (See Chapter 16.)

MYOB sells another popular line of accounting packages that work on both platforms. (www.myob-us.com) You'll find other business and finance applications for your Mac at www.apple.com/downloads/macosx/business_finance.

Accessing Databases

The only major application missing from Microsoft Office for the Macintosh is Access, the Office database component. Not only is Access not supported on the Mac, but Microsoft also doesn't make it easy to transfer Access databases to other systems. Your simplest option is to export Access tables as Excel files on your PC and then import those data tables into whichever database solution you choose on the Mac. You have to reconstruct any relations, forms, or queries on the Mac side. The following sections describe the main database alternatives available on the Mac, from simple to more complex and esoteric.

Bento

Bento is an inexpensive ($49) consumer- and small business-oriented database program from FileMaker, Inc., a wholly owned subsidiary of Apple. Its name alludes to the tidy, compartmented bento boxes used to serve assortments of Japanese delicacies (yum). Bento is well integrated with standard OS X applications, such as Address Book, iCal, and Mail as well as Numbers and Microsoft Excel. And there's a $5 version of Bento for the iPhone and iPod touch that syncs with the Mac version. Although you can easily configure Bento to your own database needs (if they're not too complex), it comes with a wide variety of preformatted and themed database templates — from Animal Stats to Wine Collection. Small-office templates include Customers, Inventory, Issue Tracking, and Time Billing. No programming or configuring needed; just enter your data.

FileMaker

FileMaker is a full-featured, commercial database program, also (duh) from FileMaker, Inc. Considered one of the better database programs out there, it has a loyal following. It's easy to use (for a database) and has many powerful features. FileMaker is also available in a Windows version, and the two versions can be networked, allowing databases to be shared between users employing both platforms. The .fp7 database format is the same on both platforms, but differing fonts can sometimes cause problems if you don't stick to OpenType fonts or the Windows TrueType fonts on both platforms. FileMaker is suitable for a range of applications from small and simple to large and complex, with Web-based access. If you add ODBC-compliant drivers, it can interact with Microsoft Access data. A strong community of FileMaker developers exists. FileMaker Pro costs about $300, and numerous add-ons are available, including

FileMaker Server, FileMaker Advanced, and FileMaker Server Advanced. A server version is even available for Linux. FileMaker provides the following white paper that compares its database to Access:

```
www.filemaker.com/downloads/pdf/fm_access_comparison.pdf
```

MySQL

This multiuser, Web-oriented database powers some of the most famous sites on the Internet, such as Craigslist.org classified ads, Flickr.com photo sharing, and the Wikipedia.org free online encyclopedia. The Mac OS X server edition comes with MySQL built in. Using MySQL requires programming skills and is significantly beyond the level of Microsoft Access. For more info on this powerful tool, see *PHP & MySQL For Dummies,* 3rd Edition, by Janet Valade (Wiley Publishing).

OpenOffice Base

The Base component of OpenOffice.org is a relational database written in the Java programming language. Its look and feel mimic Access, but it has limited ability to import and export database files, and then only in the Windows version. See the following Web page for details:

```
wiki.services.openoffice.org/wiki/Connecting_to_Microsoft_
                Access
```

Base, a relatively new open source project, is still being improved. It's free with the rest of the OpenOffice.org suite. It's worth playing with or trying out on small projects. Future releases may be more suitable for mission-critical stuff.

Finding Graphics and Design Programs

Many people use graphics and design programs for personal and professional uses, and the market leaders in each category have versions for both Windows and the Mac, with good compatibility between them. For the most part, all that's involved in switching is getting hold of a Mac version of the program in question. Check with each vendor to see whether switching to the Mac version entitles you to the upgrade price or other discounts.

Graphics editing

Basic graphics editing capabilities are built into the Apple iLife suite (see Chapter 12), including the ability to crop images, adjust brightness and contrast, and remove the red-eye effect that sometimes appears when taking pictures of people while using flash illumination. Apple's Aperture (see Chapter 12), a professional photographer's program, provides still more. Still, these programs don't match the capabilities of top-of-the-line graphics editors.

The **Adobe Photoshop** graphics editor has altered the meaning of photography from being a way to capture reality to a way to make an image of anything imaginable. My favorite example of the sophistication of this program is a wrinkle-removal feature that includes a slider so that you can adjust how many wrinkles to remove. It lets you make a portrait subject look just a bit younger — but not so much as to strain credulity. Photoshop is available in Mac and Windows editions that share underlying .psd file types. The CS3 and CS4 versions of Photoshop have native support of Intel.

Photoshop Elements, Photoshop's less expensive sibling, also has file compatible versions for both platforms, as do most of the members of the Adobe family. Although not as capable as Photoshop, Elements can meet the needs of many amateur photographers and is much less expensive than Photoshop. It is often included free with products such as scanners.

The GNU Image Manipulation Program (GIMP) is a free, open source graphics-editing program with many, but not all, of the capabilities of Photoshop. GIMP requires the X11 window manager, which comes with OS X. (A limited version named Seashore, at seashore.sourceforge.net, which uses the OS X window manager, is available). Because it runs under X11, the GIMP user interface, shown in Figure 7-6, is more Windows-like than Mac-like. In particular, menus are associated with each window, and keyboard shortcuts use the Control key rather than the ⌘ key that you expect with OS X native programs So, in Gimp, Ctrl-X means "cut" and Ctrl-V means "paste," for example,.

GIMP is one of the most mature open source programs, with a wide following and much Internet support. For example, visit www.ghuj.com for a large collection of GIMP tutorials. GIMP handles a wide variety of image formats and allows editing by layers and individual color channels. If your budget is limited and you need more image-manipulation capabilities than the iLife suite provides, GIMP is worth a try before you spend lots of money on brand P (Photoshop). You can find more info at www.gimp.org. If you want to give it a try, download the Mac application bundle for GIMP, available at gimp-app.sourceforge.net. Open the disk image for the application bundle and drag GIMP to your Applications folder. When you start GIMP, it automatically starts the X11 window system. When you quit Gimp, you still must separately quit the X11 system.

Figure 7-6:
A photo of
the family
dog touched
up using
GIMP's
powerful
image-
editing tools.

GraphicConverter, found at `www.lemkesoft.com`, is an extremely handy shareware program that has long been a part of the Macintosh universe. It includes a number of image-editing tools, and even accepts many Photoshop-compatible plug-ins, allowing a variety of special effects. But its best attribute is its ability to import some 200 different file formats and save in 80 formats. It's well worth the $35 shareware fee.

Page-layout programs

Desktop publishing was born on the Macintosh, taking advantage of Apple's introduction to the industry of a high-resolution, what-you-see-is-what-you-get (WYSIWYG) display, a graphical interface, and laser printing. Even in corporations that have standardized on the Windows operating system, Macs are plentiful in the graphics design department. As mentioned previously, Apple's Pages program provides many tools for high-quality page layout and may be all you need if you're not a professional designer. But Pages is no threat to the top two programs the industry uses: Adobe InDesign and QuarkXPress. Both programs have a long and strong association with the Mac platform. QuarkXPress started on the Mac, and InDesign traces its lineage to PageMaker, also a Mac-first program. Both are strongly supported on the Mac, and file transfer is generally straightforward. In fact, Quark uses the same application on both platforms.

Adobe also sells the document-processing program FrameMaker, often used for high-end technical documentation. However, the current version isn't available for OS X, so if you need it, run it in Windows on your Mac.

Replacing Specialized Programs

Some software categories still exist for which the market leader doesn't offer an equivalent program that runs on Macs. Also, some companies expect their employees to use programs developed by that company's information technology (IT) department that run only in Microsoft Windows. The simple answer to these situations is to install Windows on your Mac, a process I discuss in detail in Chapter 16. In some of these software categories, you find some quality Mac programs that are worth switching to. And, more IT departments are replacing their internal applications with software that can be accessed from any Web browser.

Computer-aided design

In the early 1970s, when industry first began to use computer-aided design (CAD) systems to replace old-fashioned drafting boards, the software ran on 16-bit mini-computers with $\frac{1}{1000}$ the speed and $\frac{1}{10,000}$ the memory of a low-end Mac. Those systems cost a couple hundred thousand dollars per seat, back when a single family home cost less than $50,000. Modern CAD programs run on standard personal computers but are still pricey, often costing more than the computers they run on. The most popular CAD program now on the market is probably AutoCAD, from Autodesk. Autodesk doesn't sell a Mac version of AutoCAD.

However, several CAD programs for the Mac are well reviewed and can exchange .dwg files with AutoCAD. Some players in this field include ArchiCAD, BOA, CADintosh, CADtools, DenebaCAD, MacDraft, PowerCADD, TurboCAD, VectorWorks, and Vellum Draft.

In addition, Google offers Google SketchUp (sketchup.google.com), which can meet many design needs. Check out *Google SketchUp 7 For Dummies,* by Aidan Chopra (Wiley Publishing) for help getting started with this program. Another option is OmniGraffle from www.omnigroup.com — it's a really nice alternative to Visio. The Web site www.architosh.com has reviews and other information for people, especially architects, who want to work with CAD on the Mac.

Share the wealth

Many of the most creative ideas in personal computers come for individual developers who distribute their products as shareware. Most let you try their program for free, simply asking for a modest payment if you choose to keep using the program. Some distribute programs as freeware, possibly asking for a donation from those so motivated. So do the right thing and pay up when these programs save your butt!

GPS navigation

The global positioning system (GPS) has revolutionized navigation. Adding GPS to a laptop can enable any number of innovative applications, from vehicle navigation (cars, boats, planes, and even balloons) to collecting survey data. For a long time, GPS receiver manufacturers supported only the PC. In 2006, Garmin, a leading brand, announced plans to fully support Mac users. Mac GPS software is also available at www.gpsy.com and www.macgpspro.com.

You also need a GPS receiver. Many GPS units communicate using a serial protocol. This can often be accommodated using a serial-to-USB adapter, but it typically means keeping track of two cables. Newer GPS receivers use USB or even Bluetooth. Both are better for Mac use, and Bluetooth is ideal because no cable is required.

Voice dictation

"Take a letter." In days of old, an executive would utter those words and a secretary would enter the office with a notepad in hand, ready to take down the boss's words in shorthand, for later transcription on the newfangled typewriter.

These days, good software is available for personal computers that converts your speech into text and that you can edit and use with a word processor. The current top-rated product is Dragon NaturallySpeaking for Windows, from Nuance.com. Fortunately, a version of the Dragon speech-recognition engine, MacSpeech Dictate, is now available for OS X from MacSpeech (www.macspeech.com). The package includes, for best performance, a headset with a certified, noise-canceling microphone. MacSpeech Dictate can also control your Mac by using voice commands. Of course, you can run the Nuance product under Windows on your Mac, if you already own it.

OS X has built-in speech recognition that allows you to verbally order the operating system around. It also has the ability to go the other way, to turn text into speech. I talk more about these features in Chapter 17.

Adding Functionality As You Need It

Oodles of shareware and freeware programs are out there that you can download to add functionality to your Mac. I recommend that you take it easy at first and work with your Mac pretty much as it comes out of its box. Explore this rich world of add-ons when you've grown more used to your Mac and have an easier time detecting when something isn't quite right after a program is installed. Still, I recommend making a few downloads sooner rather than later because they have particular relevance to easing the switching experience. I already mentioned GraphicConverter, the excellent Swiss Army knife for image formats by Lemkesoft, earlier in this chapter. The following sections describe a few more you might keep in mind.

Adobe Flash Player and RealPlayer

Flash and Real are two other popular multimedia formats. Both have free players available for OS X. Adobe Flash used to be Macromedia Flash, and Real used to be RealAudio. Companies like to change their names because it cuts down on those nasty profits by confusing consumers, so they end up paying less in taxes. You can download the free players from www.adobe.com and www.real.com, respectively. Adobe has two versions, one for Intel Macs and the other for the older PowerPC Macs. RealPlayer can also play QuickTime files and offers to take over for QuickTime Player, if you let it.

Flip4Mac

Quite a bit of content on the Internet is available only as Windows Media files (.wma and .wmv). With Windows Media Components for QuickTime, by Flip4Mac, you can play these files directly in QuickTime Player as long as they don't have digital rights management (DRM) restrictions. Flip4Mac also lets you view Windows Media content on the Internet from your Web browser. A free version is available from the Microsoft Mac site, www.microsoft.com/mac (click the Other Products link), or you can look for the link to the free version at flip4mac.com.

StuffIt Expander

OS X can open a variety of compressed files and archives and can do Zip compression (you right-click a file or folder and choose Compress <filename>). StuffIt Expander (www.stuffit.com), from Smith Micro Software, can open many more formats, including some older Mac formats such as .sit and .hqx. It comes free from the Web site, but you have to navigate past offers for more capable programs that aren't free.

Part III
Connecting Hither and Yon

The 5th Wave   By Rich Tennant

"Wow, I didn't know OS X could redirect an e-mail message like that."

In this part . . .

Likely the first things you want to do after your Mac is set up are get online and check your e-mail. Apple software makes it easy to accomplish these tasks — most of the time. But connection scenarios vary and hiccups happen. In this part I help you get on the air quickly. Then I take a closer look at the various ways you can network a Mac. In Chapter 10, I deal with security. Hassle-free safe surfing is one of the great benefits of switching to a Mac, but you can do some simple things to make Mac use even safer.

If you're browsing in the bookstore and have no intention of buying a Mac or this book, at least read what I have to say about security in Chapter 10. The advice there can reduce security problems with your Windows and Internet use, and that's in everyone's interest.

Chapter 8

Getting Your Mac Online

· ·

· ·

*G*etting a Mac online is like teaching a duck to swim: It usually comes naturally. If you answered all the questions during the setup process outlined in Chapter 4, you're probably already online and working away. But if you have a problem, the solution may not be obvious.

Using Your Current Internet Account

If you have Internet service that you like, you can probably stick with it. Most Internet service providers (ISPs) support Macintosh users, and Macs can generally connect anyway with the few that say they don't. The first thing is to see whether your Internet connection works. If you have a high-speed modem — cable, DSL, or satellite — you should be all set.

If you run into a glitch, the fixes depend on whether you're using an Ethernet or a wireless connection for high-speed service. Also, if you're using dialup or a service at work or school, you have different items to check. The following sections have the details.

If you're looking to upgrade to cable, DSL, or satellite high-speed service, see the section "Upgrading Your Internet Service," later in this chapter.

Checking wires on an Ethernet connection

A wired Ethernet connection uses an Ethernet networking cable that plugs into your computer. Ethernet cables have plastic plugs that look like the plugs used on telephones in North America, only fatter. (But don't try to use a phone cable.) The following tips can help if you have this type of connection:

- ✔ **If your high-speed modem is connected to an Ethernet router,** see whether the router has an extra Ethernet port and run an Ethernet cable from it to the Ethernet port on your Mac.

  If you don't have a router or switch, you should get one; they're cheap enough. In the meantime, you can unplug the Ethernet cable from your PC and plug it into your Mac to get started.

- ✔ **If your PC is connected to your high-speed modem by a USB cable —** a rectangular metal plug — you may not be able to use that cable with your Mac, even though the Mac has USB ports. Check with the modem manufacturer to see whether it supports USB connections to OS X. If not, you must use an Ethernet cable.

  Most modems that support USB connections also have Ethernet jacks, but with many, you can only use one or the other, not both together. If you want to use the PC and your Mac but your PC doesn't have an Ethernet port, you need a combined USB and Ethernet router.

Picking up Wi-Fi signals at home

If you will be using wireless Internet with your computer, life is even easier. Most new Macs include built-in AirPort, the name Apple uses for Wi-Fi. Another common name is 802.11, Wi-Fi's very own IEEE standard number. The number 802.11 is followed by a letter that indicates the speed and frequency band supported. Macs handle them all.

All you need to use an existing Wi-Fi service is a password, and not even that if security isn't enabled. See Chapter 9 for more about Wi-Fi security, including what to do if you forget the password you initially set up.

If you don't already have Wi-Fi and have or plan to get an Apple laptop, consider buying a Wi-Fi router. It offers these benefits:

- ✔ Having one lets you use your laptop anywhere you choose to work, as long as it's within range of the router's signal.

- ✔ If your desktop installation isn't near a phone or cable TV jack, the wireless capability means that you don't need to run cables everywhere.

Apple sells a Wi-Fi router combined with a backup hard drive named Time Capsule. It has many cool features that make it worth considering as your first Wi-Fi base station. You can find out more about Time Capsule in Chapter 9, too.

Setting up dialup service

If you're connecting to the Internet using an old-fashioned dialup connection — the kind that makes "beep-boop-beeep-wahh-wahhh" noises (often called *whale songs*) every time you connect — you need a USB dialup modem to continue using that connection with your Mac. New Macs don't have built-in modems. Apple sells a tiny USB + dialup modem for about $50. Other USB dialup modems may work. Again, check with the manufacturer.

To get your dialup service to work on your new Mac, you need certain information, such as your account name, password, and the phone number your computer must dial to get connected. If you don't have this information handy, and you've been using your PC to access your dialup account, follow these steps on your PC to find the information you need:

1. **Choose Start⇨Control Panel and double-click the Network Connections icon.**

2. **Right-click your ISP's icon in the dialup area and select Properties from the context menu.**

3. **Write down the setting info you see.**

Alternatively, just give your ISP a call and ask the folks which settings you need. In either case, save the paper with the dialup setting info along with your Mac's manuals or write the settings in the margin here.

When you have the needed information, follow these steps to set up your modem on your Mac:

1. **Plug your modem into a USB port and then plug the phone cable into the modem.**

2. **Select System Preferences from the Apple menu.**

3. **Click the Network icon.**

4. **Click the modem line in the sidebar.**

5. **Fill in the requested information.**

Connecting at school, work, or elsewhere

If you plan to use your Mac at work or school, you will likely connect using that organization's Internet service:

- ✔ **If Wi-Fi is available,** try selecting the school's or company's signal under the Wi-Fi icon on your Mac's menu bar and then open your Web browser. A page will likely open with instructions for logging in.

- ✔ **If you will be using wired Internet,** look for instructions on your organization's Web page or intranet from another computer, or visit your system administrator. Fresh-baked cookies are always welcome.

Surfing the Wi-Fi cloud

Many people who operate a Wi-Fi access point or router don't turn on *any* security. Because the usable range of a Wi-Fi signal can be a couple of hundred feet, someone outside the premises of the router owner can see the access point in his list of available connections and may be able to connect by using it. Your computer may connect to another available access point without much warning if the access point you normally use isn't available. In densely populated urban areas, several open signals can be available from many locations.

A Wi-Fi connection is open because its owner didn't take the extra steps necessary to turn on one of the encryption features included in all Wi-Fi access points. That can happen because the owner didn't know how to turn on encryption, didn't want to be bothered, or deliberately chose to leave it off, thereby inviting others to use it. I go over the steps necessary to secure your Wi-Fi connection in Chapter 9.

Open Wi-Fi access points raise questions of security, ethics, and legality:

- ✔ **Security:** If your computer is well locked down, and you use secure sites for activities like online banking, you have relatively little risk that an intruder will access your

files through an open Wi-Fi signal — yours or someone else's.

- ✔ **Ethics:** Advocates of open access argue that turning on encryption is simple enough that any open access point is an implicit invitation for use.

- ✔ **Legality:** Someone could use your connection for a nefarious purpose and you might have some explaining to do to the authorities. Sharing your Wi-Fi connection with others may violate your ISP's terms of service, and many jurisdictions have laws against unauthorized access to someone else's computer.

Quite a few locales offer free Wi-Fi hotspots, and some municipalities have free Wi-Fi in certain neighborhoods. OS X conveniently shows you which access points are open in the list that drops down when you click the Wi-Fi icon in the menu bar — they're the ones without lock icons. A quick check of your e-mail or being able to find directions to a restaurant from any street corner or coffeehouse is certainly handy, and it's neighborly to allow that. The use of open Wi-Fi access is growing despite the many concerns raised.

Upgrading Your Internet Service

When you buy your new Mac, you may find that it's a good time to upgrade your Internet service. If you're still using dialup, check out DSL, cable, or satellite service. Or, maybe you just got a MacBook and want the ability to go online wherever you go. Whatever your reasons, the following sections help you get started with common Internet service upgrades.

Speeding up with DSL or cable service

If you're using dialup or you aren't satisfied with the service you're using, now may be a good time to upgrade. If you live in an urban area, you probably have a choice of getting high-speed Internet service from your telephone company or from your cable television provider. The telephone company service is usually DSL (digital subscriber line), but you may encounter the older term *asymmetric DSL* (ADSL). Both cable and DSL can work quite well, so it's worth checking what pricing plans and special features each one offers. Here are some things to remember:

- ✔ High-speed service can be more expensive than dialup, but you can share it with several computers and it doesn't tie up your landline voice service.

- ✔ The speeds quoted by service providers are best-case speeds. Things can run slower at peak times of the day or when a news event draws many people to the Net. Also, speeds for downloading data may be much faster than those for uploading, such as when you send messages with large attachments.

- ✔ Top cable speeds are generally higher than those for DSL, but cable prices are usually higher as well.

- ✔ You may not be able to get DSL service if you're too far from the telephone company's switching equipment.

- ✔ Some phone companies are installing fiber-optic lines to homes and businesses. These allow very high-speed connections.

- ✔ You may have a choice of buying the high-speed modem you need or renting it from the service provider. Find out the difference in price, and figure out how long it will take to pay for the modem in higher fees. Also consider that rented modems usually include free service if the unit dies, which isn't uncommon.

- ✔ Check for package deals that bundle Internet access, television, and even phone service. These can be significantly cheaper than buying the services individually, but watch out for promotional prices that are only good for six months or a year. Ask what the rates will be after the promotion expires.

✔ Ask whether your service provider has a phone number you can call for dialup access when you're traveling.

✔ Ask your neighbors which Internet provider they're using, whether they like it, and what their customer service experiences have been like.

✔ Back up your data before your installation appointment and disconnect the backup device. The service provider's personnel aren't necessarily computer experts and can cause unexpected problems.

Mobile Internet: Taking your connection with you

If you use your Mac when traveling, you can choose from a number of ways to access the Internet. Some involve little expense. Look for hotels that offer free Internet access when making travel reservations. Coffeehouses and public libraries often offer free Wi-Fi connections. You can also take advantage of the Wi-Fi cloud, described in the nearby sidebar, "Surfing the Wi-Fi cloud." If you need something more dependable, you can try using a wide-area network (WAN) or using your cellphone as a modem.

In this section, you just skim the surface of connecting to the mobile Internet with your Mac. If you're curious about all the mobile Internet has to offer businesspeople or the whole family, check out *Mobile Internet For Dummies,* by Michael J. O'Farrell, John R. Levine, Jostein Algroy, James Pearce, and Daniel Appelquist (Wiley Publishing). Also, check out free articles and videos that can help you get started at Dummies.com.

The Mac road-warrior kit

If you're on the road a lot with your Mac portable, consider creating a travel kit that's always ready to go. Here are some items you should include:

✔ A short (3-foot) Ethernet cable

✔ A cheap three-way extension cord — to share power outlets at airports and lamp sockets in hotel rooms

✔ An airplane MagSafe power adapter (available at the Apple store)

✔ International power adapters (use Radio Shack Model 273-1405 or visit the Apple store)

✔ USB flash drive loaded with backup copies of files you need

✔ Apple Ethernet adapter if you use a MackBook Air

✔ A couple of blank CD-Rs or DVD-Rs or a spare flash drive

✔ A checklist for other items you want to take, including your laptop and cellphone chargers and the serial number of your laptop

Where am I on the Internet?

The Internet has two ways of referring to a computer hooked up to it: A *domain name* is has several snippets of text separated by dots, as in www.dummies.com. The last snippet (.com, in this case) is the *top-level domain (TLD)*. Other common TLDs include .edu for schools; .gov, reserved for the U.S. government because it invented the Internet; and .org, usually for not-for-profits. Two-letter TLDs are country codes: .us for the United States, .uk for the United Kingdom, .bk for Burkina Faso, and so on. You can find a complete list of TLDs at www.iana.org/root-whois.

To find a computer, the inner guts of the Internet use a bunch of numbers known as the *IP address*. When you type a domain name into your browser's address bar, the name is sent to special computers on the Internet, *domain name servers,* that look up the corresponding IP address in their databases. The common form of IP address (IPv4) consists of four numbers separated by dots, such as 123.4.56.78. Each number is between 0 and 255. A computer with full status on the Internet has a permanently assigned IP address. Most individuals that connect through an Internet service provider are assigned one "leased" IP address for their entire home network. That number may change from time to time. Special blocks of IP addresses are reserved for private networks and are never transmitted on the public Internet — your router uses them for local computers. A newer form of IP addressing, known as IPv6, has lots more numbers, so every computer, cellphone, and refrigerator can have its own IP address. Macs can handle IPv6, but the system has yet to be widely adopted.

Going first class

Many cellphone service providers offer wireless wide-area networking (WWAN) that communicates via radio signals using a special device that you plug into your laptop. Wide-area service is most often used by businesspeople. Although this service can be pricey, you typically get connect-anywhere service within the provider's coverage area. If you're considering this service, keep these points in mind:

- ✔ Some WWAN radios are in ExpressCard/34 format. For these, you need the MacBook Pro because it's now the only model that accepts these cards.

- ✔ Other WWAN radios plug into a USB port; you should be able to use them on any new Mac.

- ✔ Don't get a WWAN card in PC card, PCMCIA, or ExpressCard/54 format. It doesn't plug into in any Mac now sold — though you may be able to find a clumsy adapter that works.

- ✔ Make sure that the coverage area covers the areas you cover.

Putting your cellphone to work as a Bluetooth modem

Some cellphones can connect your Mac to the Internet — a feature called *tethering.* You don't even need a special cable — the cellphone talks to your Mac using Bluetooth wireless networking. You need a cell phone with this capability and a cellular service provider that allows such use — some don't or require additional monthly fees.

Internet from space — satellite service

If you live far from a cable or DSL Internet service and want something better than dialup, consider getting Internet service via satellite. Compared to other high-speed services, satellite Internet service can have performance problems, particularly with online games and Voice over IP (VoIP) telephony, because of the relatively long time it takes for signals to reach a satellite in a geo-synchronous orbit and back down to Earth. Also, upload speeds are slower than download speeds. Despite the drawbacks, high-speed Internet service can make rural living feel a lot less isolated, and satellite service may well be worth the money if no other high-speed services are available.

The following tips can help you get started:

- ✔ A couple of variations exist, but you should look for two-way satellite service. It's relatively expensive, with a high initial cost for equipment and high monthly usage fees.

- ✔ Professional installation is generally required at an added cost. A small dish antenna is mounted outside your home.

- ✔ The installer needs to place the dish in a spot with an unobstructed view of the southern sky — assuming that you live in the Northern Hemisphere.

- ✔ One satellite ISP that explicitly supports Macintosh customers is Skycasters.com. A Google search can find others.

Starting Up Your Web Browser

To surf the Internet, you need a browser. Most people use Internet Explorer as their PC browser, but you may have switched to an alternative browser, such as Firefox or Safari. In this section, you find out what your browser options are and find a quick introduction to Safari, the browser included in Mac OS X.

Picking a browser

In addition to Apple's own browser, Safari, you can use Mac versions of several other popular browsers, including Firefox. You can download the following browsers for free and use with your Mac:

- ✔ **Camino:** www.caminobrowser.org
- ✔ **Chrome:** www.google.com/chrome
- ✔ **Firefox:** www.mozilla.com
- ✔ **OmniWeb:** www.omnigroup.com/applications/omniweb
- ✔ **Opera:** www.opera.com
- ✔ **Shiira:** www.shiira.jp

For the most part, the choice of browser is a matter of taste. Various Mac browsers interpret Internet standards in different ways. As a result, some Web sites don't work with Safari but work with Firefox, for example. Opera has strong support of accessibility — you can use it without a mouse. Camino boasts speed and elegance. Shiira has excellent Japanese support.

I suggest that you start off using Safari, unless you already use and like the PC version of one of the other browsers previously listed. Consider downloading and installing Firefox too. It's a chance to practice installing a Mac program, and you'll have it handy if you run into a Web site that doesn't work with Safari. The Firefox screen is shown in Figure 8-1.

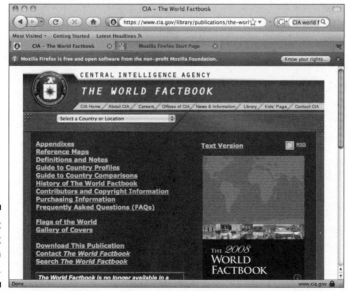

Figure 8-1:
The Firefox
Web
browser.

Some Web sites and corporate intranets require Internet Explorer for Windows. The most common reason is that they use *ActiveX controls,* which are available only in Windows. If you need to access a Web site that depends on ActiveX controls, you can run Windows on your Mac or use your old Windows machine.

Introducing Safari

Safari is a full-featured Web browser with good support for numerous Web standards. It includes these features:

- ✓ Tabbed browsing
- ✓ Bookmarks set up to match the popular iTunes interface
- ✓ Built-in Google search box
- ✓ Password management using Keychain, a well-respected security system built into OS X
- ✓ Automatic form filler
- ✓ Pop-up ad blocker and anti-phishing feature

Safari, shown in Figure 8-2 displaying the Alliance for the Prudent Use of Antibiotics page, is built on WebKit, an open source Web-rendering engine. This computer program knows how to display the various multimedia formats that the Web is built on. Apple has added much functionality to WebKit, and it's being used by several other open source projects. Safari is built into the iPhone, and a free version is available for Windows.

Figure 8-2:
Safari Web browser.

Courtesy of the Alliance for the Prudent Use of Antibiotics

Setting up Safari

Safari is ready to go out of the box. You might want to adjust these settings to suit your needs:

1. **Select Preferences from the Safari menu.**

2. **If you don't see the General preferences pane, shown in Figure 8-3, click the General icon in the upper-left corner and select the options you prefer.**

   The General pane lets you specify your home page and control where downloaded files are stored and how long they're kept. You can also change your default browser here.

   Note that tabbed browsing is off by default. Click the Tabs icon and select the Enable Tabbed Browsing check box if you want to try this feature.

   The Open Safe Files after Downloading check box is worth remembering. It's normally selected, allowing many types of multimedia to start up automatically after you download them. If you hear about viruses affecting these types of files on a Mac, deselect this check box for the duration of the security scare.

   Reach other Safari preference panes by clicking the icons at the top of the window.

3. **When you're done, close the preferences window.**

The Firefox Preferences settings are similar to Safari's.

Safari, Firefox, and most other browsers keep a history of the sites you've visited in the past few days. This can be handy when you want to go back to something interesting you saw, but it can compromise your privacy if others have access to your computer. The following items describe how to clear your history:

✔ In Safari, choose History⇨Clear History.

✔ In Firefox, choose Firefox⇨Preferences and click the Privacy icon. Then click the Clear button on the History line.

Figure 8-3:
Safari
General
preferences
window.

Switching Your E-Mail to Your Mac

These days, just about everyone has an e-mail address. A large part of getting your Mac online is transferring all your e-mail accounts and addresses.

Moving to Apple Mail

OS X comes with the good e-mail program *Mail.* Although other mail readers are available for OS X, Apple Mail has a couple of big advantages:

✔ It's free and already installed.

✔ Apple supports it, so no finger pointing takes place if you have a problem and call AppleCare.

✔ It's well integrated with OS X and applications that come with it, including Address Book, iChat, and iPhoto. You can search individual mail messages by using Spotlight, the OS X search tool, and you can easily include photos, resizing and cropping them as needed without leaving Mail.

I've long been a fan of plain-text e-mail. It's what nature intended e-mail to be. But the world has gone for a more multimedia e-mail experience. Apple Mail leads the way with stationery templates that let you include photos, artwork, and fancy backgrounds in every message. You can (and should) have separate stationery for different purposes: personal messages, business correspondence, love letters, party invitations, marriage proposals, press releases, breakups, birth announcements, subpoenas, sympathy cards, classified documents, extortion notes, book proposals — the list is endless. Apple supplies a set of professionally designed templates to get you started. Figure 8-4 shows Apple Mail composing a templated message.

Figure 8-4:
Apple Mail with a template.

Another cute Mail feature lets you send messages to yourself. Called *notes,* these reminders are integrated with the Apple calendar program, iCal, so you can tack a note or to-do list to an appointment or another type of event.

I discuss how to get the information you need to set up an e-mail account in Chapter 4. If you entered that information when you first turned on your Mac, you may already be good to go. Otherwise, Mail guides you through the process when you first start it up. And, if that doesn't work, enter the information by selecting Preferences from the Mail menu and clicking the Accounts icon. See Figure 8-5.

Figure 8-5:
Mail
preferences.

You can move your collection of e-mail messages from your PC. Mail can import mailboxes created by a number of other mail systems, including Outlook Express, Eudora, and Mozilla Netscape.

Exchanging data with Microsoft Exchange

If you work for an organization that uses Microsoft Exchange e-mail and calendaring system, you should be all set. In Snow Leopard, support for Microsoft Exchange 2007 is built into OS-X Mail, Address Book, and iCal. Snow Leopard accesses your e-mail, contacts, and calendar on your organization's Exchange Server using the Microsoft Exchange Web Services protocol. Simply select Exchange 2007 from the Account type list when setting up your work mail account.

Choosing Entourage (from Microsoft)

A number of other mail readers work well in OS X. I have used Eudora for years and am happy with it. But if you're new to the Mac, you should stick with Apple's Mail. You might also consider Entourage, the Microsoft e-mail and personal organizer for the Mac. Entourage is included in Microsoft Office for the Mac and is the Mac equivalent of Outlook in Windows. If you really like Outlook or have to work with a Microsoft Exchange mail server at work, Entourage may be a better choice. The Mail program can work with Exchange server and is certainly worth a try, but the one-neck-to-wring philosophy works against Mail here. Using a Microsoft product to connect to a Microsoft server may get you better support from Microsoft and your company's IT department.

Using Address Book and iSync

In OS X, Address Book is a separate application. Mail and other OS X applications, including iChat, make use of the Address Book database of contacts. You can search it with Spotlight. You can sync your address book with cell phones via Bluetooth and with other Macs you own via MobileMe and the OS X iSync application. Apple's Address Book supports industry standards for contact information, including vCard and IMAP. You can even beam contacts from a Palm device to your Mac if it has an infrared port (all but the Pro and Xserve).

Some mobile devices require additional third-party software to sync with your Mac. For example, Pocketmac.com sells software that adds support for the BlackBerry and Windows Pocket PC devices. It can also link Entourage on your Mac with a wide variety of mobile devices. Markspace.com sells iSync software for Palm OS, Windows Mobile, and Sony PSP.

Transferring addresses from other mail services

You'll want to use the large collection of contact information you have accumulated over the years on your Mac. Different mail services often use proprietary formats for storing this information. Many tools are available on the Web that can assist you in moving your contacts.

Transferring your Outlook Express addresses

Fortunately, Outlook Express addresses are relatively easy to transfer. You start by grabbing your contacts from your PC:

1. **Plug a flash drive or external hard drive into your PC.**

2. **Create a new folder on that drive and name it — for example,** addresses to transfer.

3. **From your PC's Start menu, open Outlook Express.**

4. **Choose Tools⇨Address Book, and then choose Edit⇨Select All.**

5. **Drag the selected addresses to the** `addresses to transfer` **folder.**

6. **Click the Remove Hardware icon in the Windows system tray.**

7. **Click the Safely Remove Mass Storage Device line that matches your flash drive in the window that appears. Count to ten, and then unplug the drive.**

On your Mac, you then follow these steps:

1. **Open the OS X Address Book application.**

   The Address Book should be in the Dock; if not, it's in the Applications folder.

2. **Plug the drive into your Mac.**

3. **Double-click the drive icon and then the** `addresses to transfer` **folder.**

4. **From the Finder menu, choose Edit⇨Select All.**

5. **Drag the selected contacts to the Address Book window.**

6. **Right-click the drive icon and select Eject.**

Transferring your AOL address book

Of course, you can use your AOL address book if you continue to use the AOL mail service. However, you may want to switch to Apple's Mail or another service, or you might want to consolidate all your contacts in the Apple Address Book. If this is the case, you have a couple of options:

- ✔ AOL Sync (`aolsync.aol.com`) synchronizes your AOL address book with Outlook Express, and you can transfer from there to the Mac, as described in the previous section. You can also use AOL Sync to synchronize your AOL address book with an iPhone or iPod touch, if you have one. From there, you can sync to the OS X Address Book.

- ✔ Another option is the Windows program ePreserver, from Connectedsw. com. It can also transfer your AOL address book to Outlook Express.

- ✔ Other possible approaches don't require a PC, but they typically involve transferring data through several e-mail programs.

Opting for online mail services

If you use your PC Web browser to access one of the online mail services, such as Google Gmail, MSN Hotmail, or Yahoo! Mail, you can continue to do so using any of the Mac browsers. Just enter the URL you normally use in the Mac browser's address bar.

Gmail and Yahoo! Mail also allow you to download and read your mail on your computer, using a mail program such as Apple Mail. Both support the Post Office Protocol (POP). This feature is free in Gmail, but you must pay $20 per year to use it in Yahoo! Mail or Hotmail.

- ✔ For Gmail instructions, go to the Gmail Web site's Help page and click the POP Access link.

- ✔ To sign up for the Yahoo! Mail POP service, click the Mail Upgrades link in your Yahoo! Mail window and then click the Upgrade to Yahoo! Mail Plus button.

- ✔ Hotmail users should sign up for Hotmail Plus.

Hushmail.com, a secure e-mail service, supports OS X and is worth considering if mail confidentiality is a concern. Read the part in Chapter 10 on picking a strong pass phrase before signing up.

Handling common e-mail problems

The utility of e-mail has diminished in recent years because of the rise of a number of antisocial uses. The first was junk e-mail advertising, known as *spam*. The name comes from a skit on *Monty Python's Flying Circus*, the BBC television comedy series. A Google search for *Monty Python spam video* is likely to find a clip of the original sketch. Watch it.

Unsolicited commercial e-mail or spam

One big problem with spam is that it can drown out your real messages, wasting your time and possibly causing you to miss something important. Most of the better e-mail services use special software intended to filter out spam. They aren't completely effective, however. The Mail program has its own spam filter that you train by indicating messages you think should have been caught as spam. It learns some of your criteria as you do this. For example, it might realize you're happy with the size of your body parts and suppress messages offering to enlarge them.

You can reduce the amount of spam you receive by selecting an unusual e-mail address, either random letters or some initials your friends might remember but spammers wouldn't come up with, such as `agrfromnyc`. Avoid e-mail addresses that end in numbers, such as `sampark456`. And don't post e-mail on Web sites and mailing lists without a disguise, such as `reinhold{you know what to type here}theworld.com`.

The mail order virus

Another concern is the use of e-mail for distributing viruses, worms, and other malware. This issue is less prominent on Macs because few OS X viruses have been found in the wild.

Still, it's worth remembering the advice you have followed as a PC user: Don't open file attachments you weren't expecting. The Mac has an added twist because it asks for permission and a password when installing new software. If you get this type of request after opening an e-mail or its attachment, just say no. And, if you have other people with accounts on your Mac, particularly kids, don't give them administrative privileges. That way, they have to ask you before this type of installation takes place.

See Chapter 10 for more security tips.

419s and phishing

Most of us have been deluged with mail requesting assistance in handling a large sum of money, in return for which you receive a nice cut of the proceeds. If you reply, you're eventually asked to advance a modest sum of money for necessary fees — a trivial amount compared to your eventual cut. After the criminals have you on the hook, you see more requests for fees and perhaps an invitation to travel to a Third World country, where all sorts of mischief await. This type of e-mail is sometimes known as the *419 scam.* Reportedly, it violates Section 419 of the Nigerian penal code. (Nigeria is one country where running these confidence games is a major industry.) Never respond to one of these e-mails. Never. Period. The people who run them are experts at exploiting that tiny flicker of hope that, against all reason, the story is true. They can even make large sums of money appear in your bank account for a while. These disappear when the bank finds out that no funds are available to cover a transfer along the line. Don't respond. Ever.

Phishing is sending mail that pretends to be from one of your regular business contacts, a major bank, eBay, or PayPal, for example. You're asked to update your records, validate your credit card, or confirm a purchase you obviously didn't make. These messages often appear authentic, with corporate logos and valid links to the real company's Web site, such as links to the company's privacy policy or a Web page where you can report suspected fraud (always a nice touch). But they all contain an action link that takes you to a fake Web site that, again, looks like the real thing. There, you're asked to enter your password, credit card number, date of birth, mother's maiden name, and other details, such as an expiration date — everything a hard-working identity thief could want. Dealing with these e-mails is tricky. The messages describe situations that *could* be true — unlike that e-mail from the heartbroken spouse of an executed African dictator with $35 million in a frozen bank account who found you through a mutual friend.

If you think that a message from eBay, PayPal, your bank, or some other source you're familiar with isn't authentic, don't click any of its links, handy though that may seem. Instead, type the URL of the business, (`ebay.com`, for example) directly into your Web browser's address bar. Then navigate to your personal account and log on to see whether any such requests are pending. If you're still not sure, call the company, using a phone number from a recent bill or bank statement, not from the suspect e-mail.

The most dangerous button

One button on your computer screen can get you into no end of trouble. It's the Send button in your e-mail program. When you click it, your message is on its way, irretrievable. It's all too easy to click the Send button when you think you've finished your message, particularly if you're replying to something that ticked you off. E-mail correspondence is different from speaking to someone in person or on the phone. No tone of voice exists to clue you in to the underlying emotions, and e-mail lacks the instant feedback of objections, grunts, and even pauses. And, e-mails are written documents, easily preserved and searched for. Billion-dollar lawsuits and criminal trials have turned on a surfaced e-mail message.

E-mail may be the most powerful tool ever created for creating misunderstanding. Even if you think your message is levelheaded and couldn't possibly be taken the wrong way, it may contain typos and grammatical errors that change its meaning, or just create an impression of carelessness.

Get in the habit of clicking the Save As Draft button rather than the Send button. Go have a cup of coffee, and give yourself some time to think it over. Then read the e-mail aloud — even to an empty office — before you send it.

One of my favorite _Mary Tyler Moore Show_ moments was when Rhoda showed Mary a letter that Rhoda had written, professing undying love to a man she had just met. When asked for ways to improve the letter, Mary replied, "The important thing is that you don't send it." Sometimes, the best use of mail is to get your thoughts on paper and then just leave them in the Drafts folder.

Instant Messaging

You used to see ads in the New York subway for a stenography school that read "if u cn rd ths u cn gt a gd job." Nowadays, the ability to read that ad just means that you use text _instant messaging,_ or _IM._ The difference between IM and e-mail is that IM is live. You and the other person are both online at the same time. You type, the other person sees what you type, and he types something back.

Systems like this, and the same abbreviated argot, go back to the dawn of electronic communication, with Morse code telegraphers chatting with each other over hundreds of miles of wire. The deaf community has been using this type of communication for decades, under the name TDD. The early Internet introduced the system Internet Relay Chat (IRC), which was similar, but no permanently assigned names existed. It took commercial services, such as America Online, to add that important feature. Texting has since been added to cellphones, with the phone number serving as a unique identifier. Teens love it.

With your Mac and an Internet connection, you can take your pick of programs and services for reaching out to others. The following sections cover the more popular ones: iChat and other IM systems, Skype (the favorite program for free Internet phone calls), and social networking sites.

iChat

Unfortunately, the different commercial services rarely allow intercommunication among their systems. The Apple iChat program comes close to being a universal communicator for instant messaging, and it can do a lot more than "how r u?" text messaging. In iChat, you have these features at your disposal:

✔ You can chat on AOL Instant Messenger (AIM) as well as Apple's own MobileMe Mac.com system and Google Talk. iChat also supports Jabber, a new open standard for IM. Jabber, in turn, lets you connect to ICQ and Yahoo! Messenger. You can also chat directly with other OS X users on your local network by using Bonjour.

✔ iChat can support voice and live video communications. The latter requires you to have a suitable video camera — iMacs and Apple laptops have them built in. You can invite as many as nine other people for a voice conference or three other people for a videoconference. Video is transmitted using the ITU H.264 standard, which sends high-quality pictures over a limited bandwidth. You can videoconference with people on Windows computers as long as they have AOL Instant Messenger version 5.5 or later. It gets better:

  • **iChat Theater:** Lets you share a slide show or Keynote presentation with friends or business associates. They even see a live image of you as you give your presentation.

  • **iChat Screen Sharing:** Lets you and another person control a single computer desktop, making it easy to collaborate on a project or help someone with a computer problem.

  • **MobileMe:** Can automatically encrypt chats with other MobileMe members. You both must enable this option, and the encryption uses public key certificates generated by Apple, which means Apple or anyone who can serve Apple with a subpoena, can potentially read your chats.

  • **OS X Server:** Lets businesses set up private, secure iChat systems on their local networks. The internal system can include non-Mac computers.

✔ Finally, iChat includes parental controls that let you limit what your kids can do and whom they can chat with.

All you need to set up iChat are the account names and passwords for each chat account you use. If your Mac doesn't have a built-in camera, you can use a FireWire camera or any USB camera that's UVC (Universal Video Class) compliant. If you have an older USB camera, check out iUSBCam, from `www.ecamm.com/mac/iusbcam`. The inexpensive software might let you use the camera you already own.

Other IM systems

You can use your Mac to chat on other IM systems. Yahoo! Messenger and MSN Messenger both have OS X clients you can download for free:

- ✔ **Yahoo! Messenger:** `messenger.yahoo.com/mac.php`
- ✔ **Microsoft Messenger for Mac:** `www.microsoft.com/mac/products/messenger`
- ✔ **Mercury Messenger:** `www.mercury.to` (offers a Java-based MSN client that runs on OS X)

The MSN Messenger client is also included in Microsoft Office.

Certain tricks let you access MSN and Yahoo! IM using iChat via Jabber servers. They're not for the fainthearted, though. These links can get you started:

```
www.jabber.org.au/ichat
www.allforces.com/2005/05/06/ichat-to-msn-through-jabber
```

Still another alternative is Adium, a popular open source messaging client for OS X that supports AIM, Google, ICQ, Jabber, MSN, and Yahoo!. You can download it for free at `trac.adiumx.com`.

Internet telephony via Skype

Apple iChat has voice communications built in. Other systems allow voice communications over the Internet (VoIP), which are more like using a telephone. The Skype system, from `www.skype.com`, is an example and is free when you talk to other Skype-equipped computers. These can be Windows, Linux, and Pocket PC machines as well as Macs. Skype can also transfer files and do video, if you have a camera.

Skype offers a paid service that lets you call telephones all over the world for a small fee. Other paid services include inbound calls from telephones, voice mail, and SMS messages to and from cellphones.

Social networking sites

Social networking Web sites, such as Facebook, LinkedIn, MySpace, Twitter, and the like, operate over the World Wide Web, and your Safari browser connects you to them just fine. All you need are your passwords. Apple's iPhoto makes it easy to upload your photos to these sites. See Chapter 12. And see Chapter 14 for ways to make social networking sites even more fun and useful with your Mac.

Chapter 9

Networking the Mac Way

Computers without network connections are like fish without water except that they don't start to smell bad. And, Macs are great network swimmers. They can connect to just about anything.

Apple uses widely accepted standards such as Ethernet and Wi-Fi for digital communication between computers. Apple leads by integrating multiple networking technologies into its products and by fielding innovative ways to make networking easier to use. One example is Bonjour, a set of software tools that let your computer find other services, such as printers, on a local-area network, without your having to type magic incantations.

In this chapter, I cover the basics of Macintosh networking, including setting up wired and wireless networks. I also cover accessories such as keyboards, mice, and cellphones that network over short distances using Bluetooth technology. At the end of this chapter, you can also find out about unique ways of networking and about sharing files over your network.

Getting Wired with Ethernet

Important elements of the technology in Macintosh computers originated at the Xerox Palo Alto Research Center (PARC). The most famous example is the graphical user interface, but *Ethernet,* invented at PARC in the mid-1970s, was just as revolutionary. It let computers talk to each other without one being made a master of ceremonies that dictated which computer could talk and when. The key idea in Ethernet was teaching computers "manners" so that they kept their messages short and didn't interrupt another computer when it was talking. And if by chance two computers started talking at the same time, both would silence themselves for a random few microseconds, making it less likely that they would collide a second time.

All recent Macs have an Ethernet port, as do many PCs and quite a few printers and other devices, including the Apple TV. All you need to connect two such computers is an Ethernet cable. The cables are inexpensive, and you can find them in varying lengths at computer and electronics stores and many drugstores and supermarkets. With two devices connected via an Ethernet cable, you can create a local network that lets you transfer files easily.

Many offices have Ethernet jacks in the walls, allowing you to plug in to the corporate network. Check with your friendly IT staff before you do.

Although connecting two devices with a cable is easy, you most likely want a network that's a little more capable. For example, your home network can enable two or more computers to share a printer and an Internet connection. To complete that type of setup, you have a bit more work to do to set up an Ethernet network. The following sections walk you through the process.

Configuring Ethernet on your Mac

For the most part, Ethernet just works. If you need to configure its settings, follow these steps:

1. **Select ⇨System Preferences and then click the Network icon.**

   You see the System Preferences pane, shown in Figure 9-1.

Figure 9-1:
The System Preferences Ethernet pane.

2. **Select Built-in Ethernet from the sidebar.**

The pane you see tells you your Mac's IP address and the IP address of your router, assuming that it sees it. Write down your router's IP address on a sticky note or blank label and stick it on your router. You want it handy if you need to configure the router. You also see your address in the new, nobody-is-using-it-yet IPv6 addressing scheme.

3. **If you click the Advanced button, you see a pane, shown in Figure 9-2, with a row of buttons labeled TCP/IP, DNS, WINS, AppleTalk, 802.1X, Proxies, and Ethernet.**

If you aren't a networking guru, don't mess with any of them unless someone instructs you to do so, such as a tech support person from your Internet service provider (ISP) or office IT department. Because many of these support people have limited Mac training, it's good to know where to find these settings. You may click the Ethernet button to see the unique address assigned to your Macintosh's Ethernet. It's a Media Access Control (MAC) address (no relation to a Mac computer). You can also find it in the Hardware section of the About This Mac More Info display on the Apple (🍎) menu. The Ethernet Advanced pane also shows the local IP address of your Mac and the IP address of your router.

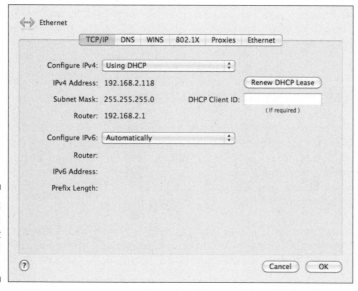

Figure 9-2:
The
Ethernet
Advanced
pane.

Understanding routers

If you want to connect more than two computers and hook them all up to the Internet, you need an Ethernet router. This small box has several Ethernet jacks so that you can plug in each computer. You use a special jack to connect the router to your high-speed Internet modem or to another router. Some routers also include a Wi-Fi access point. I get to that topic in the next section.

Your router has a small computer inside that knows how to send the right messages to the right computer attached to it. Most routers have blinking lights in front that clue you in to what's working and active. Routers include a number of capabilities, such as firewalls for increased security and parental controls. You configure a router using your Web browser — its setup screen appears as a Web site with a special address.

Devices on your Ethernet are automatically assigned IP addresses in one of the special ranges that are reserved for private networks. These never go out on the public Internet, so you and your neighbors can be using the same addresses on your respective home networks without a problem. These numbers are usually assigned automatically. From the outside, your local network is known by the globally unique IP address assigned to it by your Internet service provider. Your computers — you can network more than one — use their internal addresses, and your router converts those to the external address automatically as needed, a process known as Network Address Translation (NAT).

Hooking up your router

You may already have a router as part of your PC installation. If so, you just need to run an Ethernet cable from your Mac to an empty port on your router. If not, and if you want to share your Internet connection with multiple computers, you should purchase a router. Apple makes some nice ones, including Time Capsule, that also includes a large hard drive for over-the-network backup. See Chapter 2 for more information.

The exact procedure for setting up a router can vary for different models, so look over the instructions that come with it and then save them with the other papers that came with your Mac. The installation generally goes like this:

1. **Run an Ethernet cable from your high-speed modem to your router's WAN port.**

2. **Run an Ethernet cable from each computer you want to wire to the network to one of the router's LAN ports.**

   If you have a Wi-Fi router, you don't need to run a cable to a Wi-Fi-equipped computer, though you can if you want.

3. **Hook up power to your router.**

   Typically, you plug the power unit that came with the router into an outlet on the wall or a power strip and then plug the power unit's wire into your router.

Configuring your router

Your router sits on your network like any other computer. Most routers — but not Apple's, which I explain in a bit — put up their own Web site on your local network that you access with any Web browser, such as Safari. You configure the router through this Web site. Don't confuse this Web site with the router manufacturer's Web site, such as www.linksys.com. The one you use to change settings is literally inside your router and is accessible only from computers on your local network.

Your router keeps one internal IP address for itself, and you need to know that numeric address to access the browser's Web site. The default address your browser uses is in its manual. In case you lost it, here are the IP addresses most often used by popular manufacturers, though the one used for your model may vary:

- ✔ **D-Link:** 192.168.0.1
- ✔ **Linksys:** 192.168.1.1
- ✔ **Netgear:** 192.168.0.1
- ✔ **SMC:** 192.168.2.1
- ✔ **USRobotics:** 192.168.123.254

With the IP address in hand, you can set up your router as follows:

1. **Open your Web browser and type your router's IP address on the address bar.**

   For most SMC routers, you type **192.168.2.1** in your browser's address bar to access the router's Web page.

2. **When the router's logon screen appears and asks for a password and, on many models, a username, enter the information that's requested.**

If you assigned a password and forgot it, the simplest thing to do is to reset the router. However, you lose any configuration information, such as game ports, you had previously set up. You might first try one of the common default passwords: `admin`, `password`, `1234`, `12345`, and none (that is, leave the password field blank).

If all else fails, reset your router. You can often press a small button hidden behind a hole in back of the case. The standard method is to use a toothpick or straightened paper clip. After it resets, your router accepts a default username and password. Again, check your manual. If you don't know your router's default password, try the ones listed previously or check the booklet that came with the router. If you can't find it, check the manufacturer's Web site. It helps to know the router's model number, too. Also, this Web site compiles default usernames and passwords for routers: `www.phenoelit-us.org/dpl/dpl.html`.

3. **After you get past the router's logon screen, you see what looks like a miniature Web site with many pages you can navigate to change settings.**

   Figure 9-3 shows a typical router configuration page.

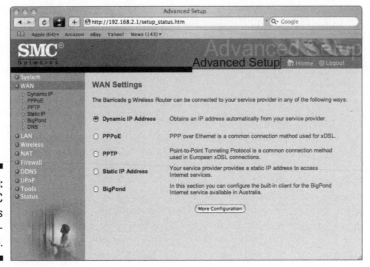

Figure 9-3: An SMC router's configuration screen.

Exactly what you can do varies by model, but common capabilities include these actions:

- Set a new username and password.

- Configure how your router connects to your high-speed Internet modem.

- Turn on or off a built-in firewall that helps protect computers on your local network from attacks over the Internet. To do this, you block most *ports*, which are special code numbers your computer can respond to.

- Allow certain ports to be visible through the firewall, a capability needed for many online games.

- Set parental controls, such as limiting Internet use on certain computers to certain hours. (See Chapter 17.)

4. **When you're done, follow the prompts to save your settings, if needed, and exit your router's internal configuration page.**

Networking Wirelessly

Apple didn't invent Wi-Fi wireless networking, but it was the first company to popularize its use, under the brand name *AirPort*. A geekier name for the same thing is its Institute of Electrical and Electronics Engineers spec number, IEEE 802.11. Most new Macs, including all laptops, come with Wi-Fi built in and ready to go. The MacPro just needs to have an AirPort card installed to be on the air.

Ethernet has a geek name, too: IEEE 802.3. And, as the numbers suggest, Wi-Fi is related to Ethernet. But rather than send short messages over wires, Wi-Fi sends them by way of radio signals. The Wi-Fi protocol is more complicated than Ethernet's because radio signals can fade in and out as laptops move around, and you can move from one access point to another automatically.

Understanding access points

The heart of a Wi-Fi network is an *access point* that supervises the communications. An access point may be built into your Ethernet router, or it may be a stand-alone unit. Each access point has a limited range, up to about 300 feet, or 100 meters; however, you can have more than one access point, and they can talk to each other. To let Wi-Fi computers within range access the Internet, at least one access point has to connect to your Internet modem, usually with an Ethernet cable.

Wi-Fi comes in several flavors, denoted by lowercase letters attached to the geek name. They are 802.11a, 802.11b, 802.11g, and 802.11n. The 802.11b was the first version that Apple introduced. It's also the slowest: nominally, 11 Mbps (megabits per second). The 802.11g version came later and can operate at 54 Mbps. The *a* version is as fast as *g* but operates on a different frequency band. The latest version is 802.11n. It's as much as five times as fast as *g* and can use both frequency bands. New Macs support all four standards.

The speeds listed for the various versions are maximum speeds. The speed you see depends on many factors, and it's usually no more than half the maximum. A big advantage of the faster speeds is the ability to stream media files between computers and to your home entertainment center's Apple TV. If you're connecting to the Internet using Wi-Fi, you're also limited by the speed of your Internet connection, which, even with high-speed cable or DSL service, is often slower than even 802.11b. Be aware that a Wi-Fi network automatically throttles down to the speed of its slowest member, so if you have an older laptop that only knows how to speak 802.11b, you might want to turn it off or shut down Wi-Fi on it when it's not in use.

Dealing with Wi-Fi security

Another issue Wi-Fi has to deal with is security. Ethernet signals are pretty much confined to the wire, so unless a snoop enters your premises and taps in, your communications stay private. Wi-Fi is radio and can go beyond your walls. A snoop could park on your street and possibly pick up your Wi-Fi signal with a laptop, or receive it from miles away with a high-gain directional antenna. (Instructions are available on the Internet for making a good antenna out of a Pringles potato chip can.) So the Wi-Fi folks added an encryption option, which evolved into these two options:

- ✔ **WEP (Wired Equivalent Privacy):** The first form of encryption, WEP was meant to offer the same level of security you enjoy with wired Ethernet. Researchers soon found gaping holes in its design; using WEP is like posting a Keep Out sign on your property. Honest people respect it; crooks don't.

- ✔ **WPA (Wireless Protected Access) and WPA2:** These two newer security standards were added in response to the problems with WEP. The latter, WPA2, has the geek name of IEEE 802.11i. WPA and WPA2 provide protection more like a high chain-link fence (WPA2 adds barbed wire on top). But a fence isn't worth much if the gate has a lock that's easy to pick. To take full advantage of WPA and WPA2, you need to set a strong, cryptovariable-grade password or pass phrase when you set them up. I tell you how to pick strong passwords in Chapter 10.

If you have to use WEP for some reason, be especially careful to check whether Web sites are secure — look for the closed-lock icon — before entering passwords and other personal information. If you need to access corporate or other sensitive sites, see whether they support a virtual private network (VPN). VPNs use "end-to-end" encryption, so data intercepted by a wireless snoop is meaningless to them.

Setting up your Wi-Fi hardware

Most of the heavy lifting needed to set up a Wi-Fi network takes place at the access point or base station. In the sections that follow, you find out how to set up Wi-Fi connections in a number of different ways. I start by explaining the Apple access point and other access points. But this isn't your only option. Depending on your setup, you may want to make your Mac an access point or just network several computers wirelessly. Read on for details.

Apple's Time Capsule base station

If you already have a Wi-Fi router or access point, you can use it with your Mac. (See the next section in this chapter.) But if you don't have one or want to move up to the faster 802.11n standard or just want more coverage in your home or office, consider getting the combined Apple Wi-Fi base station and backup disc, Time Capsule. Chapter 2 offers a quick overview of what Time Capsule offers as I write this book. One cool trick worth noting here is that Time Capsule can stream content — such as music, movies, and slide shows — to an Apple TV in your home entertainment center. The streamed content can come from your Mac or the shared disk. Everything plays together. Welcome to the future.

If you don't want the backup drive, Apple sells a similar product without one: *AirPort Extreme*. It has the same connection ports as Time Capsule, including the USB port, so you can add an external backup drive if you want. To set up your Time Capsule or AirPort Extreme from OS X, you run the AirPort Setup Assistant program. It's in the Utilities folder that's inside your Applications folder. If you want to access the shared printer and hard drive from your PC, you load on your PC the Bonjour for Windows software that comes with the base station. You need to be running at least Windows XP with Service Pack 2.

Configuring other base stations

Most non-Apple Wi-Fi base stations are built into a router and are configured using your Web browser, as described in the section "Configuring your router," earlier in this chapter. When you enter the browser's IP address, username, and password, you see the usual router Web page, such as the one shown earlier, in Figure 9-3, with router configuration options plus additional ones for wireless, which include options for these tasks:

✔ Turn on Wi-Fi so that your hardware is enabled. This is also the place where you can turn off Wi-Fi if the need arises.

✔ Specify which Wi-Fi modes are allowed — your old friends *a, b, g,* and *n.*

✔ Give your network a name, or *service set identifier (SSID)*. Avoid using a name that reveals your identity, such as thereinholds. Be creative.

✔ Decide whether to broadcast that name. Turning off SSID broadcast makes it a little harder for snoops to find you, but it's also harder for you to find your own network.

✔ Decide whether to turn on security and, if you do, decide which mode to use: WEP, WPA, or WPA2. If you know that all the computers and other Wi-Fi devices you're using are relatively new and support WPA2, that's the security mode to use. Otherwise, I suggest WPA, which works with most stuff out there except for some game controllers. WEP is a last resort, to be avoided if possible.

See the section "Dealing with Wi-Fi security," earlier in this chapter, for details.

✔ Decide what password to use for wireless security. The password you're asked to enter has nothing to do with your computer's logon password and should be different. WPA and WPA2 are both quite strong encryption schemes, as long as you use a WPA password that's hard to crack. WPA uses its password as a cryptographic key, and that key can be broken if the password is too simple. I discuss picking strong passwords in Chapter 10. But the bottom line is to use 16 or more random letters. Write them down and keep them somewhere safe. Yeah, I know, someone told you never to do that. I don't agree. You can read my reasons in Chapter 10. If you forget your Wi-Fi security password, reset the unit as described in the section "Configuring your router," earlier in this chapter, and create a new password.

Making your Mac a Wi-Fi access point

If you have a Wi-Fi–equipped Mac connected to the Internet by a wired Ethernet connection or even a dialup modem, you can turn that Mac into a Wi-Fi access point and share the connection with other Wi-Fi-equipped Macs and even PCs.

A RADIUS you can ignore

When you set up an access point (other than AirPort), you may see configuration options for RADIUS or 802.11x. They're generally used by enterprise-scale installations that have computer servers set up to manage user authentication. Wi-Fi access points can be set up to communicate with these Remote Authentication Dial-In User Service (RADIUS) servers to get their cryptographic keys, and so on. It's good stuff, but probably not something you need for a home or small office. If you work in a large enterprise that uses RADIUS, the IT staff can clue you in on what to do. If you *are* the IT staff, try reading a different book.

To do this, follow these steps on the computer that has the Internet connection:

1. **Select ⇨System Preferences or click its Dock icon, and then click the Sharing icon.**

2. **Click the Internet tab.**

3. **From the Share Your Connection From pop-up menu, select the way this computer is connected to the Internet: It's typically Ethernet, Modem, or Bluetooth.**

4. **In the To Computers Using section, select the AirPort check box.**

5. **Click the AirPort Options button.**

6. **Assign your new network a name.**

7. **Turn on encryption, if you like (icky WEP is the only option) and enter a password.**

8. **Click the OK button.**

9. **Back in the Sharing pane, click the Start button in the Internet Sharing section.**

Your other computers should now see your new Wi-Fi network. When you no longer want your Mac to serve as an access point, go back to the System Preferences Sharing pane and click the Stop button in the Internet Sharing section.

Creating a network with no base station

If you just want to network with a bunch of other Wi-Fi-equipped computers, you don't need no stinkin' base station. Just follow these steps:

1. **Select Create Network from the Wireless icon list.**

2. **Give your network a name.**

3. **Turn on wimpy WEP encryption if you like — that's all Apple offers, so don't use this mode for sensitive information.**

   For some added protection, be sure to use 128-bit mode with a random password that you change frequently. See `diceware.com/airport. html`.

   You're on the air.

Windows can do this trick, too, and you can join each other's networks. These computer-to-computer networks show up in a separate section of the Wireless icon list.

Connecting with Wi-Fi

After you set up your hardware, you're ready to connect to your network. Turn on AirPort — the Apple name for Wi-Fi — by following these steps:

1. **Click the Wireless icon at the top of your screen (see Figure 9-4).**

Figure 9-4:
You have lots of Wi-Fi networks to choose from, including one that's open.

2. **Click the Wireless icon again, just once.**

   Be patient. Count to five.

3. **In a couple of seconds, a list of wireless networks that your Mac can hear appears (refer to the list shown in Figure 9-4).**

   Hopefully, yours is on the list.

   Beware of Wi-Fi phishing! In public places, such as airports (the kind with runways) and computer trade shows, you commonly see computer-to-computer networks with names like Open Hot Spot or Free Internet Access. The people who set up these networks usually don't have your best interests at heart. Windows users who log on to these sites often receive a free virus sampler for their efforts, and Mac viruses may show up one of these days. So stay away from computer-to-computer networks you don't know about, and definitely don't give out personal information, such as a credit card number or even a home address — criminals pay for information such as "the Smith family is waiting to board a plane to Europe."

4. **Select the network and enter your password when asked, assuming that you set one.**

   If you're joining a network that doesn't broadcast its name for the world to see, select Other from the Wireless icon list. You're then prompted for the name of the network (spelling counts), the type of security used, and the password, if any.

Figure 9-5 shows the AirPort pane of the System Preferences Network window. Be sure to select the Show AirPort Status in Menu Bar check box. The Advanced button shows you the Airport networks that your Mac considers preferred and the order in which it tries to connect, while giving you the option to change that information.

Figure 9-5:
The System
Preferences
AirPort
pane.

Fixing interference problems

The performance you enjoy can also be reduced by interference from other radio signals. The *b* and *g* versions of Wi-Fi operate on a radio band, 2.4 GHz, where licensed operation is permitted. This band is shared with other users, including Bluetooth hardware, cordless telephones, microwave ovens, and amateur radio, not to mention your neighbor's Wi-Fi network. The *a* version operates at 5 GHz, also unlicensed, but at a less-cluttered spot on your microwave dial. Wi-Fi can use several different channels in each band — the number varies by country — so a fair amount of band sharing is possible.

Somewhere in the back of your computer's manual with all the other legal notices, you should see this notice:

> *This device complies with Part 15 of the FCC Rules. Operation is subject to the following two conditions: (1) This device may not cause harmful interference, and (2) this device must accept any interference received, including interference that may cause undesired operation.*

Of course, this legalese applies within the United States, but other countries have similar rules. If you have interference, you're usually on your own.

You can take the following steps to combat interference and other signal problems:

- **Move your laptop.** Closer to the access point is usually better, but any change in position and orientation can help, even a few inches. (One-quarter wavelength at 2.4 GHz is about an inch-and-a-quarter — that can be the difference between a signal null and a hot spot.)

- **Move the access point.** Put it in a more central location, hang it high on a wall, or move it away from a known source of interference, such as a cordless phone base station or a microwave oven. Experiment.

- **Adjust the access point's antenna.** Try small increments. If it has two antennas, have them point in different directions, at right angles to each other.

- **Turn off your cordless phone and unplug the base station.** If that reduces the interference, move your cordless phone and base station farther from the access point and from your laptop. Plug the base station into a different outlet. If those steps don't help, replace your cordless phone with a model that operates on a different frequency band (the band is usually marked on the package), or just go back to wired phones. (You probably carry a cellphone anyway.)

- **Get a new microwave oven.** You can easily tell whether your microwave oven causes network problems — the problems happen only when it's cooking. If the microwave is used infrequently, you might just live with the interference, but if it's used a lot, say, in a small office at lunchtime, consider buying a newer model. It's cheap and you can return the new one if it's no better. Also, make sure that the microwave is on a different electrical circuit from your laptop and access points.

- **Buy a Wi-Fi repeater.** These units plug into a wall outlet and retransmit Wi-Fi signals from your access point for greater coverage. Having a second signal source may reduce interference problems.

Getting Personal with Bluetooth

The mission of the Bluetooth wireless technology differs from Wi-Fi's. Wi-Fi connects the computers and other devices within a home or place of business to create a local-area network. Bluetooth has a much shorter range, about 30 feet. It's designed to create a personal network around an individual. The most familiar example is the Bluetooth headset — a friend calls them *Borg implants,* after the evil Star Trek cyborgs. These units fit over your ear and connect wirelessly to Bluetooth-equipped cellphones. They let the wearer talk hands-free. Bluetooth can also be used to connect a keyboard and mouse to your Mac without wires. Nintendo uses Bluetooth in its Wii game controllers. Bluetooth can link your Mac to your iPhone and other cellphones, allowing address book updates to be shared among all devices, in the process known as *synchronizing*.

Bluetooth was the nickname of a tenth-century Danish king, Harald I, who unified many warring tribes. Like its namesake, Bluetooth networking can unify may disparate devices to create your own, personal computing empire. Next-generation Bluetooth will let small devices talk to each other without an intervening personal computer.

Pairing before sharing

Two Bluetooth devices can't talk with each other until they have been formally introduced, a process called *pairing*. You can easily understand why this is necessary. You don't want your Bluetooth cellphone chitchatting with the cellphone of the person sitting next to you on the bus — unless that person is cute. You might wonder how to get them to pair if they can't talk to each other. The answer is that you have to put one of them in the special state known as *discoverable*. How this is done differs for each device. In some cases, you press a special button or hold down a regular button longer, or you must navigate through a cellphone menu maze. The details are in each device's manual. This leads me to state the following law:

King Harald's First Law of Bluetooth: *Never throw out the instruction booklet supplied with a Bluetooth device.* In Chapter 4, I suggest that you find a place to keep all the manuals and discs that come with your computer and accessories — one you won't forget about. You can keep cellphone and Bluetooth papers there, too. If you do lose the booklet, check the device manufacturer's Web site. Most have instructions online for recent models.

Configuring Bluetooth

You configure Bluetooth on the Mac side by clicking the Bluetooth icon at the top of your Mac's screen. The list you see includes options to turn Bluetooth on and off, make your Mac discoverable by other Bluetooth devices, and browse for files on Bluetooth devices. You can also open the Bluetooth preferences screen, shown in Figure 9-6, which is also available from System Preferences.

Figure 9-6:
The
Bluetooth
preferences
screen.

Networking in Other Ways

Ethernet, Wi-Fi, and Bluetooth are the main ways to network Macs, but the following other tricks may come in handy:

- **FireWire:** You can connect a FireWire cable between two Macs that have FireWire ports, and OS X can use that cable as a network connection. FireWire shows up in the System Preferences Network pane's pop-up menu list, just like Ethernet or AirPort. You simply select it and configure it, if necessary, the same way you would configure Ethernet.

- **FireWire disk mode:** Another way to use FireWire to transfer data between two FireWire-equipped Macs is to reboot one of them (not both) while holding down the *T* key. That Mac starts up in what Apple calls FireWire disk mode. You see a large FireWire logo dancing around your computer's screen. If you then plug the other end of the FireWire cable into the Mac you didn't reboot, the first Mac's hard drive appears on the second Mac's desktop as just another hard drive. You can then move files to it or transfer files out of it, just like on any external hard drive.

- **MobileMe:** The Apple MobileMe service lets subscribers share access to their iDisks. You can even synchronize files, contacts, and appointments between two Macs. Space is limited, however.

- **Sneakernet:** The ultimate fallback networking scheme is to use a USB flash drive to transfer data from one computer to another. A flash drive can easily fit in your pocket, and most incorporate a loop so that you can attach them to a key chain. Some people hang theirs around their neck on a lanyard. Wearing sneakers is optional.

Sharing Files over Your Network

Regardless of how you establish your network, you probably want to use it to share files with other connected computers.

Sharing files from your Mac

You can tell your Mac to make files available to other computers on your local network, or even over the Internet. From an administrator account, follow these steps:

1. **Select ⇨System Preferences or click its Dock icon, and click the Sharing icon.**

   You see the Sharing pane, shown in Figure 9-7.

Figure 9-7: The System Preferences Sharing pane.

2. **Select the check boxes next to the sharing modes you want to use.**

   Personal File Sharing allows other Macs to access files on this machine. To let your PC see your Mac files, click the Options button and then select the Share Files and Folders Using SMB check box. You then have to specify which accounts on your Mac can use Windows sharing. Normally, only the Public folder is shared, but you can specify other folders to be shared.

   You can select more than one sharing mode, but because each one has potential security risks, don't select more modes than you plan to use.

Sharing files from your PC

I cover setting up PC file sharing from Windows XP in Chapter 6. (You right-click a folder you want to share, choose Properties, and select the Share This Folder on the Network check box.) File sharing from Windows Vista is controlled from the Network and Sharing Center Control Panel. You select the check boxes next to the modes you want to enable. It works much like the process in OS X, except that Vista shares files only in a Shared folder, and you have to promise Vista you won't share anything bad.

Seeing the files you shared

To see shared files from your Mac, follow these steps:

1. **Select Connect to Server from the Finder's Go menu, and then click the Browse button.**

   Or, you can click the Network icon in the sidebar of an open Finder window.

2. **Click the Servers line.**

   You see the Network browser, shown in Figure 9-8.

3. **Click the server you want to access and log on.**

   You need a password for the other machine, if one has been set.

Figure 9-8: The OS X Network browser.

The procedure from a PC is quite similar. Click the Network Neighborhood icon or select Start⇨My Network Places.

Chapter 10

Staying Secure in a Connected World

A s you most likely know, the convenience of hopping on the Internet has its downside: viruses, spyware, identity theft, and more. You're better equipped to avoid these hassles if you have at least a basic understanding of what they are and how to keep them at bay. One reason you may be switching to a Mac is precisely because you're looking for better security.

In this chapter, Mac security features are in the spotlight. You find out not only what Mac OS X does behind the scenes to keep the gunk away from your computer but also how to take advantage of features and techniques that improve on its already good defenses — namely, strong passwords and file encryption tools.

What Makes a Mac More Secure?

Macs have a reputation for security on the Internet, and for the most part, it's well deserved. Critics say Macs have such a small share of the overall computer market that computer criminals and hacker hobbyists don't consider them worth the time to mount an attack. That may indeed be part of the story, but Mac users aren't complaining about being ignored. Popularity isn't always a good thing.

However, there is much more to Mac security. Apple built OS X on top of the operating system Unix, which AT&T developed for its internal use, back when it was the telephone monopoly in the United States. UNIX had good security tools, and Apple added more.

Modern operating systems, such as OS X and Microsoft Windows, assign different levels of privilege to different programs. Operating systems are the gatekeepers of a computer, deciding which programs are allowed to run and what they're allowed to do. Intruders have two goals: to be able to run their evil programs on your computer and to get maximum privileges for their programs. After they get that gold pass, the programs can install themselves in the innards of the operating system in ways that are hard to detect. The maximum permission level on many operating systems is the *root* level, and hacker tools that can penetrate to this level are *rootkits*.

Windows XP lets many programs run at a maximum privilege level. If an attacker can subvert one of these programs — and he often can — the hacker is home free. OS X is more careful with the privileges it doles out. You can tell Windows to be more careful too, but doing so can cause problems for legitimate programs that were designed to operate at a high privilege level. OS X has always restricted application program privileges, so all Mac applications are cool with those restrictions.

Just as in Windows, users can adjust security settings up or down in Mac OS X, but because OS X is shipped with security set at a high level to begin with, and most people never mess with the settings, Mac viruses are hard to spread. Epidemiologists have learned that they don't have to inoculate an entire population with a vaccine to stop an epidemic. As long as a large enough fraction of the population is immune, the disease stops spreading. It works the same for computers. Having most Macs set at a high security level makes it difficult for any Mac virus to propagate.

Protecting Yourself with Passwords

Never write down your password. Eat five servings of fruits and vegetables every day. Use a different password for every account. Get 30 minutes of aerobic exercise four times a week. Always select passwords with uppercase and lowercase letters, numbers, and special characters. Every time you're with that special someone, be sure to use a — well, you get the idea. We're constantly bombarded with good advice — advice that we know we should listen to — but most of us fall short.

As computers and Internet technology have crept into more and more aspects of our daily lives, our use of passwords has exploded. E-mail, instant messaging, online banking, brokerage accounts, automated teller machines, computers,

Internet routers, multiplayer games, social networking Web sites — they all ask for passwords. And then we need a bunch more at work and school. The average computer user accesses dozens of different password-protected thingies. And the consequences of forgetting a password or having one fall into the wrong hands range from inconvenience to disaster.

Following a proper personal password policy

Your Mac isn't an island, and no amount of fiddling with its security settings can protect you if you don't use passwords wisely. But advice that made sense when most people had one or two passwords to remember becomes impossible to follow when people have 20 or 30 to keep track of. Increasingly, computer security experts are realizing that the traditional password policy is unrealistic at best and counterproductive at worst. So, in the following sections, I present some suggestions for using passwords that you can actually follow and that can make your computer far more secure than the vast majority out there.

Use a common password for unimportant accounts

If someone figures out the password for your newspaper subscriptions and other informational Web sites that demand registration for no good reason, it's not the end of the world. So it's reasonable to use one password for all those accounts. For extra credit, you might have two common passwords: one for stuff you *really* don't care about and a second for sites that feature social networks or instant messaging, for example, where you have no big risk of financial loss but you want to maintain some privacy.

Use separate, stronger passwords for important work accounts and for personal accounts, such as online banking, where real potential exists for misuse that can cost you money or enable identity theft.

Write down your passwords

Most people can't memorize as many passwords as they need for optimal security. You can too easily to forget the ones you don't use daily. Instead, they just keep recycling one or two easily remembered passwords. If software at work makes them pick a password with mixed cases and special characters, they add the minimum needed to get past the password police.

You're more likely to pick strong passwords if you know that they're written down someplace so that you run no risk of forgetting them. The trick is to keep the list safe. The classic Post-it note stuck to your monitor isn't what I have in mind. Good choices include the following places:

✔ **Your wallet:** You have other valuable information in there already, such as your credit cards and driver's license. You're careful with it by habit. If you lose it, you quickly notice it's gone and you can change the passwords on your computer accounts at the same time you're canceling your charge accounts.

✔ **A clever hiding place at home:** Use your ingenuity. A slip of paper doesn't take up much space. You probably have lots of nooks and crannies. But be sure to pick a location you'll remember. The first place you think of is one you'll likely remember again.

✔ **A safe-deposit box:** Although it's awkward when you need to add new accounts, it can be a good place for your master list. Keep recent changes in your wallet. If you plan ahead, your next of kin will have a much easier time dealing with your estate if someone can acquire a list of your passwords after you're gone. If you want to take some secrets to the grave, use a separate password and leave it off this list.

✔ **A password manager program:** These applications keep all your passwords in an encrypted file. All you need to remember is one master password. And, most of these programs offer to generate strong, random passwords for you when you open new accounts.

Mac OS X has the built-in password manager Keychain. OS X automatically uses Keychain to store the passwords it needs, such as for Wi-Fi, networks, and accessing various Web sites. You can see the passwords it stores, and add more entries if you want, by opening Keychain Access in the folder that opens when you choose Applications⇨Utilities. You need to enter your login password to see the stored passwords. Figure 10-1 shows the Keychain Access displaying a stored password. To add a new password, click the plus sign icon (+) in the lower-left corner of the window.

Figure 10-1:
Keychain
Access.

Quite a few password manager applications ([...] for the iPhone and iPod touch. Some are free [...] ten dollars, relatively expensive, as iPhone ap [...] category of application is that you have no ea [...] one application to another. You generally hav [...] a real pain if you have lots of passwords. So tr [...] while before you enter all your data.

None of the iPhone password managers I've fo [...] impossible to check how well the encryption a [...] features are implemented. Some allow only a n [...] data — that's not secure enough. I've been usir [...] a Mac or PC if you purchase the more expensiv [...] platforms.

The following good password managers are ava [...] ... Mac OS X and Palm OS:

> ✔ Mac programs include only the Java version of Password Safe
> (passwordsafe.sourceforge.net) and Password Gorilla
> (www.fpx.de/fp/Software/Gorilla). Both are free and open source
> and are compatible with each other and with their Windows and Linux
> versions.

> ✔ For Palm OS, I suggest Keyring (gnukeyring.sourceforge.net), also
> free and open source. It's a handy program, but note that although you
> can back up your password file to your Mac during a HotSync operation,
> you can read the password file only on a Palm OS device.

Change your passwords only when you have a good reason

I know, the password police say to change passwords every few months.
Some companies configure their software to require periodic changes. I find
this advice dubious at best for most people. A miscreant who gets hold of
your password is likely to use it promptly. And, people forced to change
passwords soon learn the minimum change they need to make to get past
the password-change program. Attackers know those tricks, too. The time
to change passwords is when you think they may be compromised, such as
when you have to give someone else a password — never a good thing to
do, but it happens — or when a trusted employee quits or is fired. Using a
sensitive password at a cybercafé is another occasion for a change.

#12 06-04-2014 12:15PM
Item(s) checked out to p14646109

TITLE: Switching to a Mac for Dummies
BARCODE: 3111502131135
DUE DATE: 06-26-14

Assessing risk

Security doesn't exist in a vacuum. You have to consider the risks you face. For computer security, risks fall into two major categories: outside and inside. Outside risks refer to things bad guys can do without entering your premises: sniff your Wi-Fi signal from your parking lot, capture your data as it makes its way through the Internet, or just steal your laptop, for example. Inside risks cover things that can be done by guests, family members, fellow employees, and the cleaning people.

By using passwords, you make outside risks generally easier to protect against than inside risks. A determined insider has too many ways to capture your password, ranging from installing keystroke-capture software on your computer to placing a concealed video camera above your desk. (With tiny, inexpensive wireless cameras, this is now alarmingly easy to do.)

The best practice for large organizations that demand strong internal security requires *two-factor authentication.* Users demonstrate who they are to the computer by knowing a password or PIN *and* by having in their possession a small device called a *token.* Some tokens plug into the computer; others display a number that changes frequently. The user types the number into the computer along with the password during logon. At least one vendor, Cryptocard.com, supports two-factor authentication on Macs.

Picking powerful passwords

Passwords are like medicine: If all you have is a common cold, you might pick up whichever remedy catches your eye on the drugstore shelves. But if you have a serious condition, you want prescription drugs that are tested and known to work. Picking passwords is similar. If you're protecting stuff that doesn't matter all that much, most any password will do. But if your password is guarding information that could do real harm if the wrong people got hold of it — harm to yourself, your family, your business, or your clients — you need a method of picking passwords whose quality is measurable.

You find lots of advice on how to create a password, and much of it is negative. Don't pick a single word in a dictionary. Don't use a password shorter than eight characters. Don't use passwords that people who know you might easily guess, such as the name of your kid, pet, or significant other. The positive advice mostly asks you to do something clever, like think of a famous quote, lyric, or title and then abbreviate it; for example, `2bornot2b`, `0saycanuc`, or `S2Mac4D`. The problem is that people who write password-cracking programs know all these tricks and have built them into their programs. And, those password-cracking programs and dictionaries are widely available on the Internet.

The amazing power of random

Few silver bullets in life exist, but one is available for picking passwords. If you pick the letters or symbols of your password at random and make it long enough, the odds of someone guessing it become astronomically low.

Most security experts don't push random passwords, out of concern that most users won't accept them. The passwords seem ugly and hard to remember. Because it's possible that you've now read several chapters of a computer-advice book, I think you're exceptional and might be willing to put in the little bit of effort needed to get the best security you can.

One reason I take a contrarian view on some standard password maxims is that they encourage less secure behavior. Asking people to have separate passwords for every account, telling them to never write down passwords, and forcing them to change passwords regularly absolutely guarantees that they will find ways to circumvent the process. The ways most users do that are all too predictable. I think it's better to write down a random password than to memorize an easy one that won't stop an attacker anyway.

Another old saw asks people to include a mix of uppercase and lowercase letters, digits, and special characters in their passwords. The well-intentioned idea is to make their passwords more random. But most people simply add a digit or special character to their favorite password. And, they typically do that in predictable ways. Security expert Bruce Schneier recently found that the most commonly used password on MySpace.com was `password1`.

Scoring a password

One nice thing about random passwords is that you can measure their strength. You can easily assign a point score that says how hard they are to guess. Each additional point means that it's twice as hard to guess the password.

The way you figure the score is quite simple: Each character or symbol in the password scores a certain number of points, and you just add them up. The number of points per character depends on how many possibilities you choose from. If you pick a character at random from the 26 letters *a* to *z*, it receives 4.7 points. If the possibilities include the 26 letters and the 10 digits 0 to 9, you receive 5.1 points per character. Pick at random from any of the 94 possible characters on a standard U.S. computer keyboard — lowercase and uppercase letters, digits, and special characters — and you score 6.5 points per character.

The thing to note is that the fancy passwords score more, but not that many more, points per character. An 11-character password of single-case letters *a* through *z* has the same strength as an 8-character password made up of all

94 possible keyboard characters: about 52 points. Which password style you choose is mostly a matter of taste. Both are equally secure. If you use your password a lot, saving three characters may be worth the trouble. On the other hand, if you travel to other countries and plan to use local computers there to log on to your accounts, you may have trouble. Some of the special characters in your password may not be on the keyboards you find there, and the ones that are present may be in unfamiliar locations on the local keyboards. And, typing special characters on handheld devices, such as the iPhone, can be a pain.

Making passwords memorable

Remembering passwords that contain special characters can be easier if you use short nicknames for the special characters. Table 10-1 offers some suggestions.

Table 10-1	Nicknaming Special Characters		
Character	*Name*	*Character*	*Name*
`	Ding	{	Sneer
~	Twiddle	}	Smirk
!	Bang	[	Uh
@	At	]	Duh
#	Hash	|	Pole
$	Bucks	\	Back
%	Ears	:	Eyes
^	Hat	;	Wink
&	And	"	Quote
*	Star	'	My
(	Frown	<	Mouth
)	Smile	>	Nose
_	Under	,	Tear
-	Dash	.	Dot
+	Plus	?	Huh?
=	Equals	/	Slash

The true meaning of password points

You may be wondering what these points I keep talking about represent. Or not — in which case, feel free to skip this sidebar. The points I'm using refer to the concept of entropy, and in the technical literature, the points are bits. *Entropy* measures how random things are; the concept goes back to the 19th century, when scientists were trying to figure out how to make better steam engines. One bit or point is the amount of randomness introduced by flipping a fair coin. The formula I use to assign points to passwords was discovered by the great physicist Ludwig Boltzmann and is carved on his tombstone.

Tell me a story

One way to memorize a random password is to make up a story that goes with the letters and symbols. For example, to remember the following password

```
1!30c;tF
```

you might make up a story about hearing one bang when you were 30 and seeing a winking tall fighter. I have a Google spreadsheet online that converts ten random letters into a memorable sentence. For example, `twpxjrufhc` converts to "Tom's wild peacocks expertly join rude uncles finding happy comfort." The sentence is just to aid memory. You use the ten characters as your password. You'll find a link to the spreadsheet at DitchMyPC.com.

Permitting Password Assistant to assist

The phrase *pick at random* is easier said than done. Computers are designed to do the same thing every time you run a program. Most computer programming languages include "random number generator" functions that aren't truly random. Better operating systems, including OS X and Windows, have ways of making things truly random, measuring exactly how long it takes hard drive arms to move, for example. Unfortunately, many programs on the Internet that claim to make random passwords don't use these tools.

OS X includes its own password generator: Password Assistant. It's designed to help you pick passwords for your Mac OS X accounts, but you can use it for other purposes. Here's one way to do that:

1. **Open Keychain Access; it's in the Utilities folder, inside the Applications folder.**

2. **Click the plus sign near the bottom to create a new entry.**

   You don't have to save your new password in Keychain, but you can if you want. This is just one way to reach Password Assistant.

3. **Click the Key icon next to the Password field.**

   The Password Assistant window appears, as shown in Figure 10-2.

Figure 10-2:
OS X
Password
Assistant.

	Password Assistant
Type:	Random
Suggestion:	a2JFb"((;t
Length:	10
Quality:	
Tips:	

4. **From the Type pop-up menu, select Random to create a password.**

   For an explanation of the other options, see the nearby sidebar "Ordering up passwords from Password Assistant."

5. **If you want your password to be a particular length, move the Length slider.**

   See the section "How long does it have to be?" later in this chapter, for details about how password length affects security.

6. **After you select the password you want from the Suggestion field, write it down or save it in Keychain — or both.**

7. **To save your new password in Keychain, fill out the Keychain Item Name and Account Name fields and click the Add button. Otherwise, click the Cancel button.**

If you use computers a lot, you'll face the need to come up with a new password from time to time, often in situations when you're in a bit of a hurry. If you click the arrow next to the Suggestion field, Password Assistant shows you a list of candidate passwords. Write down a bunch on a slip of paper and carry it in your wallet so that you always have a few handy.

Ordering up passwords from Password Assistant

Password Assistant truly excels when you need a secure random password, but if you've just plain had it in thinking up your own passwords, Assistant offers many more options:

✔ **Memorable** offers passwords made up of two dictionary words separated by a number and a special character; for example, `rig25{laden`. They're good for medium-level security with a strength in the 40- to 45-point range. Longer passwords of this type aren't much stronger, so pick one about 12 characters long.

✔ **Letters & Numbers** mixes uppercase and lowercase letters and digits; for example, `io5ItCqm8N`. Used that way, the passwords are worth almost 6 points per letter. If you don't want to mess with the Shift key, make all the letters the same case, in which case their worth drops to 5.2 points per letter. This number isn't much of a loss,

but remember to type your single-case version: `io5itcqm8n`. Don't cut and paste from Password Assistant.

✔ **Numbers only** is handy for picking new personal identification numbers (PINs) for credit cards and so on, but you need a long number for a strong password. Digits are worth 3.3 points each.

✔ **Random** uses all characters on the keyboard and produces passwords that look like `G!0chN6-j2`. Score 6.5 points per character.

✔ **FIPS-181 compliant** makes up letter-only passwords that are relatively easy to pronounce, such as `voofyaidia`. The method used is specified in a U.S. government Federal Information Processing Specification; hence the name. FIPS-181 passwords are worth 4 points per letter.

Finding other ways to pick random passwords

Be leery of password-picking programs you find while perusing the Internet. Many are poorly written, and it's hard to tell which ones do an acceptable job. The password managers I mention earlier in this chapter are good. Here's a link to a password generator I wrote and trust: `www.theworld.com/~reinhold/passgen.html`.

One way to guarantee that your password is random is to select the letters one at a time, using ordinary, six-sided dice:

1. Throw the pair of dice.

2. **Use the two numbers you roll to pick a character from Table 10-2.**

   Use the die that lands to the left to pick the row and use the other die to pick the column. (Yes, *die* is the singular of dice.) So, rolling a 3, 5 adds the letter *q* to your password.

3. **Keep rolling and picking letters or numbers from the table until the password is the length you're looking for.**

   See the next section in this chapter for details.

Table 10-2		Generating Passwords by Rolling Dice			
	1	**2**	**3**	**4**	**5**	**6**
1	a	b	c	d	e	f
2	g	h	i	j	k	l
3	m	n	o	p	q	r
4	s	t	u	v	w	x
5	y	z	0	1	2	3
6	4	5	6	7	8	9

How long does it have to be?

Your password, that is. As with other size questions, this one generates much controversy. Here are some guidelines I think are reasonable for most users:

- ✔ **Low security** doesn't require much to achieve. An 8-character Password Assistant Memorable password does fine. Or, you can recycle an old, inactive password you remember well, as long as you haven't used it in a while and it isn't similar to others you use.

- ✔ **Medium security** doesn't stop a determined and skilled attacker, but the attacker will probably go pick on someone else who's an easier mark. I suggest at least 46 points, a 7-character Password Assistant Random password, 10 random letters, or a 12-character FIPS-181 pronounceable password — breaking it into two words may make it easier to remember. (If you're unsure what the points mean, see the section "Scoring a password," earlier in this chapter.)

- ✔ **High security** is an open-ended concept, but I suggest at least 56 points, a 9-character Password Assistant Random password, or 11 random letters and numbers.

✔ **Cryptovariable passwords** are for programs that turn your password into an encryption key. Most applications that employ passwords use them as gatekeepers. Know the password, and you're allowed access to the computer or program in question. But some passwords work harder. They're used as the key or cryptovariable in an encryption algorithm. Examples of passwords that need cryptovariable strength include

- WPA and WPA2 wireless network passwords
- Your OS X master password
- FileVault passwords
- Passwords for encrypted e-mail
- Passwords of other disk-encryption schemes

For cryptovariable applications, people often use *passphrases* rather than passwords. A passphrase is longer and often made up of words selected at random, on the theory that a sequence of words is easier to memorize than a long sequence of letters. See www.diceware.com for suggestions for picking a strong but memorable passphrase using dice.

Cryptovariable passwords should have at least 65 points. This requirement can be met with a 10-character Password Assistant Random password, 14 random letters, or a 5-word Diceware passphrase.

✔ **Windows passwords:** If you continue to use your Windows computer along with your Mac, know that a longstanding security flaw exists in Windows XP and earlier versions of Windows, having to do with support for the old network standard LAN Manager. You can turn off LAN Manager (and it's a good idea), but you can avoid the problem entirely by using passwords that are at least 15 characters long.

Hardening OS X

Out of the box, OS X offers good security. But you can do a number of things — besides picking good passwords — to make it even stronger. Read on for details about using FileVault, making encrypted volumes, and using other security tricks and tips.

Locking up your data with FileVault

With FileVault, OS X can encrypt each user account. All the data associated with that user is scrambled using the widely accepted AES-128 cipher.

Using FileVault is an excellent idea if you store sensitive data and you travel with a laptop, or if many people have access to your computer. Microsoft has a similar feature, BitLocker, but it's available only in the more expensive versions of Vista and Windows 7.

Encryption slows hard drive access somewhat and may affect tasks that involve a lot of data, such as movie editing or Photoshop work, and it makes restoring files backed up by Time Machine more awkward. One compromise is to have two user accounts — one with FileVault for sensitive work and the other without FileVault protection for work where processing speed matters.

To turn on FileVault for a user, follow these steps:

1. **Log on as that user.**

   If you like, you can turn on FileVault while creating a new account — you see a check box to select. See the section on setting up additional accounts in Chapter5.

2. **Select ➪System Preferences and click the Security icon.**

3. **Click the FileVault tab at the top, if it isn't already highlighted.**

   You see the FileVault setup window, shown in Figure 10-3.

Figure 10-3: The FileVault setup window.

4. If you haven't already done so, set a master password for your Mac by clicking the Set Master Password button.

   This step allows you to recover data for any FileVault user who has forgotten his password. Knowing the master password also lets you reset any user's login password.

5. **Choose a cryptovariable-level password, as described in the section "How long does it have to be?" earlier in this chapter, and write down that password.**

   You can call up Password Assistant to help you choose this password by clicking the Key icon next to the password entry field.

6. **Because FileVault encrypts your home directory by using your login password, your account should have a high-security-level password. If you need to change your login password, select ⌘⇨System Preferences and click the Accounts icon.**

7. **Change your login password. Log out and log back in to make sure that everything is working.**

8. **After you have a master password set and you like your login password, return to the System Preferences Security pane and click the Turn On FileVault button.**

   Depending on how much data is in your home directory, the initial encryption process can take awhile. If you're working on your laptop, plug in the charger. If you already have sensitive info stored in your account, select the Secure Erase check box to ensure that OS X obliterates the unencrypted data when it's done encrypting.

When you log out of a FileVault account, OS X often asks your permission to tidy up and recover some unused space. Say Yes only if you have time and battery power for the operation to complete. Otherwise, tell OS X to wait.

Making an encrypted volume

If you have some data you want to protect but don't want to go to the bother of encrypting your entire user directory, you have another option: Create an encrypted disk image. This file looks like a disk volume when you open it. It looks much like the volume typically created when you download an application program. It even has the same .dmg extension, but you need a password to open it.

To create an encrypted volume, follow these steps:

1. **Go to the Utilities folder in your Applications folder and open Disk Utility.**

2. **Choose File⇨New⇨New Blank Image.**

3. **Pick a size for your volume that's large enough for everything you plan to store in it, with room to spare.**

If you keep the volume size below 700MB, the encrypted volume fits on a CD-R, in case you choose to back it up that way; 4.38GB can fit on a DVD-R.

 4. **Give the volume a name, such as** Super Secret War Plans **or** Recipes.

 5. **Select AES-128 Encryption.**

 6. **Click the Create button.**

 7. **When prompted, enter a password.**

    If you click the small Key icon, Password Assistant appears and offers suggestions. See the sidebar "Ordering up passwords from Password Assistant," earlier in this chapter, for more on using this feature and for password selection in general.

 8. **If you don't want OS X to store the password in Keychain, deselect the Remember Password check box.**

Advanced Encryption Standard (AES)

The security features in OS X use an algorithm, the Advanced Encryption Standard (AES), for scrambling data. AES was selected by the U.S. National Institute of Standards and Technology (NIST) in 2001 after a lengthy public competition. The winning design was submitted by two Belgian researchers, Vincent Rijmen and Joan Daemen. AES is a *block cipher:* It takes data in 128-bit chunks and scrambles it into another 128 bits. The exact way it scrambles the data is determined by another block of digital data, called a *key* or *cryptovariable.* AES comes in three flavors, with 128-, 192-, or 256-bit keys. Apple uses the 128-bit version. Although it didn't participate in the original design and selection, the U.S. National Security Agency has stated that the AES cipher can be used to protect classified information; the 128-bit version, which Apple uses, is approved for

information at the Secret level. That doesn't mean that you can use Macs to take home classified documents. The NSA has a stringent approval process for devices used to store and transmit such data — you must consider a lot more than the strength of the codes. But it's a strong vote of confidence in AES.

A stronger version of AES doesn't add security if you're using a password as a key, unless the password has a comparable number of bits. Here's what a 192 bit-strength password looks like:

```
erdl ubym 09ie u9fj lbg9 f4dd 7s1t
            zwmi 6iyd0
```

If you're not willing to use such a long password, don't expect more "bits" in the cipher to add security.

Enhancing your Mac's security

Besides choosing good passwords, you can do a number of things to make your Mac even more secure.

Setting safer settings

Select System Preferences. Click the Security icon and then click the System tab. You see the window shown in Figure 10-4. You can select several check boxes to enhance your Mac's security, usually at the price of some minor added inconvenience in operation. Here's a rundown of the check boxes and what they mean for your security:

Figure 10-4:
The OS X Security settings window.

 Require Password X Minutes after Sleep or Screen Saver Kicks In: A common security problem is the unattended machine: You go get a cup of cappuccino and someone sits down at your computer and does as she pleases. Selecting this check box and, perhaps, the Log Out after *xx* Minutes of Inactivity check box can help prevent this situation, but you have to type your password *a lot.*

 Disable Automatic Login: Select this check box if you care about security. If you don't select it, the computer automatically logs on to the primary account without asking for a password every time you (or anyone else) restarts it.

✔ **Require Password to Unlock Each System Preferences Pane:** If many people share your computer (your kids, in particular) and you want to retain strict control, select this check box. Otherwise, don't bother.

✔ **Use Secure Virtual Memory:** If you plan to use FileVault, select this check box. Your Mac sometimes writes temporary information to disk to free more of its main memory. Because this temporary information can contain sensitive information, you want it encrypted, too. This option slows things down a bit.

✔ **Disable Remote Control Infrared Receiver:** Someone with a remote could have your computer display images you'd rather not share. If this prospect frightens you, select this check box.

Keeping up to date with Software Update

Computer security is a moving target. Researchers and hackers are constantly finding holes in software. And new revisions of software intended to add features can also inadvertently introduce new security bugs. Apple works hard to correct problems and periodically distributes corrections over the Internet. Out of the box, your Mac checks for available updates weekly. To check now, select ⌘⇨Software Update. You can change how often automatic checking occurs by selecting ⌘⇨System Preferences and clicking the Software Update icon. This is also the place to check which updates have already been installed, if you care.

Securing your e-mail

If you use programs such as Pretty Good Privacy (PGP, from `www.pgp.com`), Gnu Privacy Guard (GnuPG from `macgpg.sourceforge.net`), or Hushmail. com to encrypt and electronically sign e-mail, you'll be glad to know that Mac versions of these programs are available.

Remember to transfer your PGP keyrings with the rest of your files. Make sure that everything is working properly before disposing of your PC.

Watching out for phishing

As a PC user, you undoubtedly encounter *phishing,* or sending e-mail messages that look like legitimate requests from upstanding organizations. The message includes a link that opens what seems like the Web site of that organization, where you're asked to enter your account number, password, and any other personal info they think you can be conned into surrendering. If you have any doubt that the message is phony, do not click the link in the message. Go to the organization's Web site by typing its URL in your browser's address field and navigate to your account.

Locking it up

Computer security is almost meaningless without physical security. If a sophisticated attacker gets to spend quality time alone with your Mac, all the fancy technology may be of no avail. Laptops are easier to steal than desktop machines, but they're also easier to lock in a desk or safe. All Mac laptops and the Mac mini have a hole in the side, designed to accept a mechanical locking device, such as those made by Kensington.

Another cheap thing to do is to record your computer's serial number. Select About This Mac from the Apple menu. The serial number is listed in the hardware Overview section. Write down the number and keep it in your wallet, with a copy at home. You need the serial number in order to file a police report if your laptop is lost or stolen. You should also mark your computer with your name and address. You can place an address label inside your laptop's battery compartment. A colored sticker on the outside of your laptop makes it harder for a thief at the airport to hide in a crowd.

Securing empty trash and erasing free space

If you store sensitive data on your computer, particularly on a laptop, get in the habit of selecting Finder➪Secure Empty Trash whenever you want to empty the Trash. It's the Mac equivalent of the Windows *Recycle Bin,* the place where files are moved when you delete them. Otherwise, your data remains in unassigned areas of your hard drive until the operating system needs that space to store something else. With today's large hard drives, that may be never.

The Secure Empty Trash option can take a while if you're deleting large files, and even if you're careful to use it all the time, you should write over all the free space on your hard drive every so often. Apple supplies a tool for doing this, which works as follows:

1. **Open Disk Utility.**

   It's in the Utilities folder, inside the Applications folder.

2. **Select your hard drive and then click or select the Erase Free Space button.**

3. **Choose one of the three overwrite options.**

   The default option, which overwrites all free disk space with 0s just once, can take an hour or more — longer if your disk is big and relatively empty. The 7-pass method can take overnight, and the 35-pass method for the paranoid can take a couple of days.

I suggest using the default one-pass method, unless you're clearing an older hard drive — one with a capacity of 15GB or less. Current guidelines for the U.S. National Institute of Standards and Technology (NIST Special Publication 800-88) say that modern high-capacity drives "can be effectively cleared by one overwrite." I've also talked to someone at a major data recovery company, and it can't retrieve files that have been overwritten even once. For older drives, do the 7-pass erase — on a smaller, older drive, 7 passes won't take long. If the security provided by overwriting isn't enough, your best option is physical destruction. See the section in Chapter 6 on safely destroying your PC hard drive.

Checking checksums

Security-related programs are often distributed with a checksum or hash that lets you verify that the program you received hasn't been modified — a good practice. Two types of checksums are widely used: md5 and sha1. OS X can compute either type by using the Unix command line in the Terminal window. (See Chapter 19.) The command for md5 is just `md5`, followed by a space, followed by the file path. For sha1, type the command `openssl sha1`, followed by a space, followed by the file path.

Drag the file's icon to the Terminal window, and the file path is filled in automatically.

Virus protection?

Coming from the Windows world, you may feel naked without a virus-protection program. At the time this book was written, no reported OS X viruses were in circulation — the buzz phrase is *in the wild.* However, although Apple has done a good job with OS X security, no one claims that it's perfect, and Apple market share is increasing, making it an ever more tempting target for virus writers. Several PC antivirus companies offer programs for OS X and, of course, if you install Windows on your Mac and plan to connect it to the Internet, you should install a PC antivirus program for Windows in that partition. Based on the current situation, I think you can hold off buying a Mac antivirus program as long as you check Software Update regularly,

keep an eye on at least one independent Mac information Web site, and hang on to your PC-user caution about installing strange software.

One exception is if you regularly exchange files created in Microsoft Office. One class of virus uses the Office macro feature, and a few of those viruses can infect Macs if they're running versions of Office earlier than the 2008 version. More likely, you can spread a virus you got from one user to others in your office. The major antivirus vendors sell versions for the Mac. A free antivirus program for the Mac, ClamXav, is available from www.clamxav.com. It's based on the open source antivirus project ClamAV.

Part IV

More Software, More Choices

The 5th Wave   By Rich Tennant

TROUBLE ON THE SET

©RICHTENNANT

All the software in the world won't make this a great film. Only you can, Rusty. Only you and the guts and determination to be the finest Frisbee catching dog in this dirty little town. Now come on Rusty- it's magic time.

We're losing the light, Dad.

In this part . . .

Macs come with a ton of software. I introduce the Apple iLife digital lifestyle suite and discuss other software that comes with your Mac. These programs are simple, but powerful and fun to use. They let you buy and listen to music, manage your photo collection, edit your videos, make your own music, and put your creations on the World Wide Web. And, because they come from Apple, all the programs play well together. But if you're a long-time Windows user, there's likely to be an application in Windows that you miss. You have several options for running Windows on your Mac. I discuss them in the last chapter of this part.

Chapter 11

Easy Listening with iTunes

*I*f you have an iPod, you already know about iTunes. It's the lone program from the iLife collection that's available for Windows PCs, and it's absolutely necessary to use an iPod. Many Windows users who don't own iPods use iTunes as their music player. The short story is that iTunes on the Mac is pretty much the same as iTunes in Windows.

iTunes is a program for organizing and playing media — including music, video, and podcasts — on your Mac. If you have an iPod that you used with your PC, you're already familiar with iTunes because it's necessary for syncing your iPod. If not, you'll find iTunes a lot like Windows Media Player, only better — an easy way to find and enjoy

✔ Music

✔ Movies and TV shows

✔ Audible books and podcasts

✔ Other digital content

Digital rights management and iTunes Plus

In the past, music sold over the Internet has been protected by *digital rights management (DRM)* technology, which encrypts the music data and allows play only on authorized devices. The Apple iTunes Store now sells music without DRM restrictions. Such files aren't subject to the five-computer limit, and they can be played on any music player, not just on iPods. However, TV shows, movies, and software are still subject to DRM restrictions. Also, if you bought music from iTunes before 2009, it's likely to be protected by DRM. Apple allows you to remove the DRM encoding for 30 cents per song or 30 percent of an album's price. Remove the DRM by selecting Upgrade to iTunes Plus on the iTunes Store home page.

When you're ready to ditch the PC, I suggest you disassociate your PC from your iTunes library. Only authorized computers can play restricted media that you've purchased from the iTunes Store, and Apple limits the number of computers you can associate with your library. These restrictions don't affect the newer DRM-free music, but you might as well disassociate your old PC while it's still running. For the steps, see "Managing authorizations in iTunes," later in this chapter.

The Magical iPod

If you don't own an iPod or iPhone but you still love music, find something to use as a bookmark here while you go to the store and buy one. It's the greatest improvement in recorded music since the introduction of high fidelity in the 1950s. Owning an iPod welds music to your personal space. It becomes something you always have with you. William Congreve got it right in *The Mourning Bride,* back in 1697 (reportedly while attending an early Vista planning meeting):

> *Musick has Charms to sooth a savage Breast,*
> *To soften Rocks, or bend a knotted Oak.*
> *I've read, that things inanimate have mov'd,*
> *And, as with living Souls, have been inform'd,*
> *By Magick Numbers and persuasive Sound.*

The iPod isn't just a digital accessory — it informs our living souls.

Yes, an iPod can do other things. It can serve as a utilitarian portable hard drive, an older sibling to the flash drive. And, the spiffy video model can store (or play) movies, TV programs, music videos, games, and your photograph collection. An iPod is also helpful for listening to podcasts and recorded books. The iPhone and iPod touch can do pretty much anything a computer can do, and then some. But the ability to add one's favorite music to the unavoidable humdrum of the day — that's life changing.

Getting Started with iTunes

When you first open iTunes, you have a few setup tasks to complete. The first is completing the Setup Assistant, which lets you make iTunes your default music player. If you use iTunes on your PC, be sure to step through the section on importing your iTunes collection on your new Mac, later in this chapter. If you're new to iTunes, check out the tips on playing with iTunes, which explain a few basic tasks you need to know to work in the iTunes program.

Setting up iTunes

When you first get your Mac, you need to follow a fairly simple setup process to organize all your music. Follow these steps:

1. **Double-click iTunes, either on the Dock or in the Applications folder.**

2. **Work through the Setup Assistant, which offers to have iTunes handle audio content from the Internet, making it your audio-helper application.**

   Unless you downloaded other audio software, the alternative is to use Apple QuickTime.

iTunes then offers to search your home folder for MP3 and AAC music files. If you have transferred a bunch over from your PC, this is an opportunity to get them all organized by iTunes. Always double-check that you have backed up all the files. You can easily add them later, if you prefer. See the section "Importing your iTunes collection," later in this chapter, for details.

iTunes then offers to take you to the iTunes Store. The next section introduces you to the store.

Importing your iTunes collection

If you already have a collection of music and videos on your PC, copy the files from your PC to the Mac. (See Chapter 6.) Did that already? Then you may need to follow these steps:

1. **On your Mac, open iTunes and choose File⇨Add to Library.**

2. **Find the folder that contains all the music and video files you copied to your Mac.**

3. **Click the Choose button.**

iTunes on the Mac adds the PC files to its library, all neatly organized the way you had them. However if you had any `.wma` files you need additional software to play them. Inexpensive solutions that you can download are available from `Flip4mac.com` and `easywma.com`.

If your PC is so hosed that you can't recover your iTunes library and you don't have a backup, you still have hope. Apple allows you to transfer from your iPod to another computer the music you previously purchased from the iTunes Store. In iTunes, choose File⇨Transfer Purchases from iPod.

Two freeware programs, Ollie's iPod Extractor and Senuti, are also available to copy any songs from your iPod to your Mac, without duplicating the ones that are already there. Find them in a Google search or try your favorite download site.

Managing authorizations in iTunes

As I mention earlier in this chapter, the Apple digital rights management scheme lets you have DRM-protected media you purchased on iTunes playable on as many as five computers at any time. If you're planning to keep your PC for a while and you aren't close to the five-computer limit, you can leave the PC authorized.

To authorize your Mac, just try to play one of your purchased songs. iTunes asks for your Apple ID and password. Be sure to enter the ones you used to purchase the song. You have to do this task for one purchased song.

When you're ready to get rid of your Windows PC, be sure to deauthorize it first by following these steps:

1. **Open iTunes on your PC.**

2. **Choose Store⇨Deauthorize Computer.**

3. **Select Deauthorize Computer for Apple Account.**

4. **Enter your Apple ID and password and confirm your intentions.**

Apple determines a Windows computer's identity by looking at a number of factors, including the amount of RAM and the hard drive size, so don't mess with these before you deauthorize your PC. (Macs have a hardware serial number, so changing the hard drive or adding RAM, for example, doesn't affect things.)

If your PC is so messed up that you can't run iTunes to deauthorize, or if you just forgot to do it before you ditched the PC, it stays on the list of machines that count against your five-computer limit. However, you have an escape valve. When you reach the point where you have used up all five slots, you can blow them *all* away and reauthorize the computers you still want by playing a purchased song on each of them. However, Apple limits you to resetting the authorized computer list only once a year. To reset the list, follow these steps:

1. **Choose View My Account from the iTunes Store menu.**

2. **Enter your password.**

   If you've reached the five-computer limit and you haven't exercised this option in the past 12 months, you should see a Deauthorize All button on the Account Information screen.

3. **Click the Deauthorize All button.**

4. **Play a song on each computer that you want to authorize.**

Playing with iTunes

After you transfer your library to the Mac, it's time to enjoy your music and other media files in their new home. You won't find things much different from iTunes on your PC. If you're new to iTunes, here are a few popular tasks to help you get started:

✔ **To sync your iPod to your iTunes library:** Just plug its cable into a USB port on the Mac that has the library stored on it. You can sync to only one iTunes library.

✔ **To create a new play list:** Click the plus icon (+) at the bottom of the iTunes sidebar.

✔ **To add a tune to your playlist:** Simply drag it from the music list to the play list entry in the sidebar.

✔ **To create a mix disc:** Insert a blank writable CD and choose File➪Burn Playlist to Disc.

Filling iTunes with Music and More

You can fill your iTunes library in a few different ways. The iTunes Store is the hub for the many types of content iTunes can play, including music, movies, TV shows, and podcasts. Adding music on a CD to iTunes is easy, too. The following sections explain the more popular options.

Shopping the iTunes Store

When you first start iTunes, it opens the front window of the iTunes Store. If iPod has revolutionized the way we listen to music, the iTunes Store has revolutionized the way it is sold.

Notice that I said sold, not distributed. Only a small fraction of the songs in iTunes (or played on iPods) have been purchased through the iTunes Store. Much of it comes from compact discs that people already own and simply copy into iTunes. The rest comes from file-sharing programs such as BitTorrent and Lime Wire.

It seems that the recording industry didn't think through all the implications when it switched to CDs from the older vinyl LP records, the kind with a wiggly spiral groove that made a needle vibrate to reproduce sound. After computers and the Internet became fast enough, the digital data on CDs was too easily copied and shared.

Apple figured that many people would do the right thing and buy their music, instead of downloading it for free, if the price was right and the process was convenient enough. Users have downloaded more than 6 billion songs from the iTunes Store, and it ranks among the top three music retailers in the United States. Amazon.com now sells DRM-free MP3 music as well.

To get to the iTunes Store, open iTunes and click iTunes Store in the sidebar. You see a screen similar to that shown in Figure 11-1, with ads for various offerings and a list on the left of different types of content that are for sale. The following steps walk you through the store:

1. **Click the Sign In button in the upper-right corner.**

2. **If you already have an Apple account (for example, if you use iTunes on your PC), enter your account name and password.**

   Otherwise, click the Create New Account button and have your credit card handy. After you complete the signup process, you can move to Step 3.

3. **Browse by genre or use the search box in the upper-right corner of the iTunes window.**

   The iTunes Store has a huge selection of recorded music, but Apple makes it easy to find what you want. Search results appear in the lower half of the iTunes window, and you can sort by genre, title, artist, album, popularity, price, or running length. Just click the headings in the listing.

   If you double-click a song's entry in the list, you hear a 30-second selection from the song.

Figure 11-1:
The iTunes
Store front
window.

4. **To purchase a song or other item, click the Buy button, and you're asked for your password.**

    The song, album, or other item is automatically downloaded to your Mac and then to your iPod the next time you plug it in.

Apple has tried to make shopping simple at the iTunes Store by having an easy-to-understand price structure, but pressure from content owners has forced Apple to allow greater variation in pricing. In return, Apple is eliminating digital rights management (DRM) restrictions on downloaded music — though not on other content, such as movies and TV programs. At the time I write this book, songs cost 69 cents, 99 cents, or $1.29 apiece; TV shows are $1.99; and 30-day movie rentals are $3.99 for current hits and $2.99 for older flicks. Music albums, complete TV seasons and feature movies can range from $8 to $15 and up. High definition versions of TV programs and movies are often available for an additional charge.

Another big category on the iTunes store is applications for the iPhone and iPod Touch. Many are free; others range in price from 99 cents to $10 and more. The app store has been a runaway success with over 30,000 application titles and 1 billion downloads in the first nine months. You can even buy games for your older video iPod.

Copying CDs to iTunes

If you've never used iTunes, you'll want to add some music. If you own music CDs, you can add them to the iTunes library by simply sliding them into your Mac's CD/DVD slot. iTunes should open automatically, but if it doesn't, launch it in the usual way by double-clicking its icon. iTunes copies the files from the CD to its library while it plays the CD for you. The CD doesn't take as long to copy as it does to play, however, so you can stop the music when iTunes says the transfer is done.

The AAC compression scheme is used by default when iTunes imports CDs. You can change to another format, such as MP3, by following these steps:

1. **Select Preferences from the iTunes menu.**

2. **Click the General icon and then the Import Settings button.**

3. **Choose the import format you prefer.**

   Your choices are AAC, AIFF, Apple Lossless, MP3, and WAV.

   You can change many other options in the iTunes preferences, including playback options, such as subtitles and closed captioning, and setting parental controls for younger users.

Adding video to iTunes (and an iPod)

Transferring video is another matter. Of course, video you download from the store isn't a problem. But you can't simply put a movie DVD into your Mac and transfer the movie to view on your iPod. Movie DVDs have copy protection, whereas music CDs generally do not. You have to do two things to make such a transfer possible:

- Extract the movie from the DVD in an unencrypted format.
- Convert the file to one of the video formats that the iPod can understand.

Software is available that can perform each step. A Google search on *DVD to iPod* should find several resources. The first step involves getting past the copy protection on the DVD. The movie industry says that's illegal, though others say you should have the right to view DVDs you own any way you want.

Video that isn't copy protected, such as your home movies, must still be converted to an iPod-friendly format. One way to do this is to use iMovie, already installed on your Mac. Select iPod from the iMovie Share menu. I tell you more about iMovie in Chapter 13.

Subscribing to podcasts

Podcasts are talks, performances, or pretty much any kind of digital content that someone thinks someone else might be interested in. You can listen to podcasts on your computer, but what makes them special is that you can easily download them to your iPod or iPhone. Indeed, the introduction of the iPod made podcasts popular.

Podcasts can be just audio or they can be video. You find them in the iTunes Store by clicking Podcasts in the pane to the upper left of the main window. You find thousands of podcasts to choose from, on every imaginable topic, broken down into many categories. If you find one you like, you can automatically have others in the series downloaded to your iPod as they appear by clicking the Subscribe button. Podcasts awaiting your attention are marked with a blue dot in the Podcast section of your library. Podcasts you've listened to lose the blue dot and are automatically removed the next time you sync your iPod unless you mark them as unread by right-clicking their names.

iTunesU

Wouldn't it be nice if the top professors at the world's greatest colleges recorded their lectures as podcasts so that you can enjoy the best teaching the world has to offer as you commute to work or burn some calories on the treadmill? Well, they have, and you can. The Apple Store section iTunesU is chock-full of great talks and courses. Nothing but time and effort are required in order to benefit from the finest education the world's universities have to offer. Of course, iTunesU doesn't offer degrees and you miss the classroom camaraderie and beer parties in the dorms, but you don't go into lifelong debt paying tuition bills, either. Courses in iTunesU are absolutely free.

Chapter 12

Picturing iPhoto

· ·

· ·

*O*nce upon a time, taking photographs involved buying a roll of film, loading it in a camera, shooting 24 or 36 pictures, taking the film out of the camera (don't forget to rewind first!), taking the exposed film to a camera store or drugstore, waiting a day or so, picking up the pictures, selecting a few negatives to be copied or enlarged, sticking the rest in a shoebox until the day you have more free time to organize them (which birthday party was that, and who's the guy next to Aunt Harriet?), and then pasting them into a photo album. More serious photographers experienced a long interlude in a dark room with red lights and temperature-controlled trays of smelly chemicals.

Except for those who truly love the film process — and there's a lot to love — digital cameras have taken over photography. Good-quality digital cameras are inexpensive, and top-of-the-line models, which are becoming more affordable, rival the best film cameras for image quality. Try to buy a cellphone now that doesn't have a camera. The one in the iPhone is a respectable 2 megapixels. You have no more film to buy — just AA batteries and maybe a memory card or two. And, that shoebox is now a hard drive. But you're likely still waiting for the free time you need in order to organize your photos.

Wouldn't it be helpful to have a program that can suck down photos from any camera as soon as you plug it in, keep shots organized according to when you took them, let you see a large swath of your collection spread out on the screen like a light table, and let you annotate and organize photos into albums and slideshows? Shouldn't the program also display a slide show on your screen or television and maybe add music from your iTunes collection? And, why not allow you to ship those photos off for printing on your color printer or send them to a professional shop — and maybe even a place that will print a bound book of your photos so that you can have paste-free albums?

That's iPhoto in a nutshell. If you've used Google Picasa on your PC, you're familiar with the concept. But with iPhoto, you have nothing to download: It's waiting for you in the Applications folder. (If you love Picasa, you'll be glad to know that it has a version for the Mac. We discuss it later in this chapter.)

Getting Started with iPhoto

If you own a digital camera, you most likely can use it with iPhoto. iPhoto supports most brands and models. You can check to see whether your model is supported by visiting the iPhoto Web site, `www.apple.com/ilife/iphoto`, or just shoot a few pictures and plug your camera into the appropriate USB or FireWire port.

When iPhoto first starts, it asks whether you want it to take over every time you plug in your camera. iPhoto knows about almost every digital camera out there. You could go to your camera manufacturer's Web page to download its software, but why bother? Just say Yes.

You likely have many valuable images stored on your PC. You can move your collection from your PC to your Mac through iPhoto by importing photos. iPhoto adds your photos to its database and creates thumbnail versions for fast display. In the following sections, you find out what image files you can work with in iPhoto and the tips and how-tos you need to know before importing your image collection.

Checking out supported file types

iPhoto can read a wide variety of file types, including those listed in Table 12-1.

Table 12-1	Image File Types Supported by iPhoto	
BMP	FlashPix	GIF
JPEG/JFIF	MacPaint	Photoshop (with layers)
PICT	PNG	RAW
SGI	Targa	TIFF

RAW is the native format for high-end digital cameras. iPhoto supports dozens of models. Visit `support.apple.com/kb/HT1475` for the current list. A number of movie formats supported by still cameras are also handled nicely.

iPhoto lets you export files in their original form or converted to JPEG, TIFF, or PNG format.

Setting up a successful import

iPhoto can store up to 250,000 photos — about 250 shoe boxes' worth. But iPhoto has its own idea of how to store photos in its library. If you already have a large collection of digital photos, all organized in folders, you might want them kept that way. You can order iPhoto to do just that:

1. **Select iPhoto⇨Preferences.**

2. **Click the Advanced button.**

3. **Deselect the Copy Files to iPhoto Library Folder When Adding to Library check box.**

4. **Close the Preferences window.**

Now whenever you import photos, iPhoto leaves them organized the way you had them in the folders you set up, rather than use the normal method of filing the photos by date. However, if you edit one of those photos within iPhoto, it saves the edited version in its library, leaving the original where it was.

Importing your photos

To import your photos to iPhoto, follow these steps:

1. **Copy your PC photos to the Pictures folder.**

2. **Open iPhoto and choose File⇨Import to Library.**

3. **Find the folder or folders with the photos you want to import and select them.**

4. **Click the Import button.**

You can also just open iPhoto and drag the folder with your pictures to the iPhoto window.

You may want to experiment with bringing folders in one at a time to find the way of organizing the photos in iPhoto that works best for you. You might try the iPhoto folder import script at `http://scriptbuilders.net/files/iphotofolderimport1.0.html`. Drag a folder that contains photos to this script's icon and it imports all files in the folder and creates an appropriate folder and albums in iPhoto.

After you move all your photos from your PC into iPhoto, you should back up your OS X Pictures folder. If you enabled Time Machine, it does the backup for you. If not, or if you like the added security of having a backup in a separate place, copy your Pictures folder to a DVD-ROM or an external hard drive. For extra credit, find a safe place to store the backup that isn't in your home — maybe your office, a safe-deposit box, or even a friend's house. (A friend of mine's house burnt down recently, and he lost much of his photo collection.) I cover various ways to back up data in Chapter 6. Having all your photos organized and safely backed up offsite is a great feeling.

Organizing the iPhoto Way

iPhoto has its own way of storing and organizing photos. You can choose to look at them in several ways, listed on the left side of the iPhoto window:

- ✔ **Events:** iPhoto groups all photos you take in a single day as an *event* that you can name. As you slide your mouse pointer across an event's cover image (Apple calls it a *key photo*), you see all photos in the event, an effect that Apple calls *skimming*. You can move individual photos from one event to another by simply clicking and dragging. To merge two events, drag one event into the other. To split an event, open it by double-clicking, select the photo to begin the second half of the split, and click the Split button at the bottom of the screen.

- ✔ **Photos:** You see all your photos as though they were laid out on a light box. You can scroll through your entire library.

- ✔ **Faces and Places:** Apple has built face recognition into iPhoto and can organize your photos by who's in them and where they were taken. More on Faces and Places later in this chapter.

- ✔ **Albums:** An album is a named set of photos. A photo can be in more than one album. The photo is stored only once, however, so having photos in more than one album doesn't waste space. Albums work a lot like playlists in iTunes. To create a new album, choose File➪New Album or click the plus icon (+) in the lower-left corner. You add photos to an album by selecting and dragging them from the main display.

- ✔ **Smart albums:** A smart album contains photos based on search criteria you select. It works a lot like Spotlight. To make a smart album, choose File➪New Smart Album. Select your criteria, such as date in the range of 12/24/2008 to 12/26/2008, from the dialog that appears, and click OK.

- ✔ **Folders:** Folders in iPhoto are a way to add organization to your collection. You create a new folder from the File menu. Folders can contain albums and other folders. They can also contain slide shows, books, calendars, and other iPhoto projects. Again, you can drag things into and out of a folder and move them around as you want. Items can be in only one folder, however.

Viewing and sorting your photos

The main iPhoto display area, shown in Figure 12-1, shows small versions of your photos arranged on a dark background, much like a slide sorter from the film era. How small? The slider on the lower-right border of the iPhoto window lets you adjust the thumbnail size to suit your needs.

Figure 12-1:
The main
iPhoto
display in
Photo mode.

iPhoto offers a number of ways to see just what you want:

- ✔ Choose Photos in the sidebar, and all your photos are displayed.
- ✔ Click a folder or an album, and just those photos are shown.
- ✔ Choose View➪Sort Photos and then select one of the following options:
    - **By Event:** This is the default view.
    - **By Date:** The date is stored with the file when you import your photo.
    - **By Keyword:** Add these tags to a photo by clicking the key icon in the lower-right corner of the window or pressing ⌘+I. iPhoto comes with a simple set of keywords, but you can invent your own in iPhoto Preferences by clicking the Keyword tab.

- **By Title:** A photo's title is the name or number given to it by your camera, but you can change the name by clicking the small *I* icon in the lower-right area of the window.

- **By Rating:** The By Rating sort doesn't refer to how professional-looking iPhoto thinks your photos are. You assign your own rating to photos, from one to five stars. It's worth remembering the keyboard shortcuts. Select the photo or photos you want to rate and press ⌘+1 for one star, ⌘+2 for two stars — up to ⌘+5 for five stars. Pressing ⌘+0 means no rating. If you forget, choose Photos⇨My Rating. This menu choice has all the options and can remind you of the shortcuts.

- **Manual:** Move photos around by dragging them. This option is ideal for slide shows.

You can also select the Ascending or Descending sort order.

Finding faces

iPhoto can help you organize your photos by faces they contain and where you were when you took them. This section explains how it all works.

First, lower your expectations. Apple face recognition technology is far from perfect, but it's a big help if you have lots of photos of people. The technology has two parts: finding faces in images and assigning names to the individual faces. iPhoto is better at the first part than the second — you get a lot of wrong recognition matches, some weirdly inappropriate — but iPhoto makes it quite easy to correct wrong matches. And, yes, it can handle more than one face in an image.

To get started, follow these steps:

1. **Click on a photo in your iPhoto library that has a good face shot of a person you want iPhoto to keep track of.**

2. **Click the Name button at the bottom of the iPhoto window.**

   You see a white box around the face with a black label underneath.

3. **Type the name of the person in the label.**

   iPhoto tries to find a matching name in your Mac's address book.

4. **If iPhoto finds the right name, click it; otherwise, just finish typing the name you want to use for the person and then click that name when you're done.**

5. **Click the small arrow (>) next to the person's name.**

   iPhoto shows you other photos it thinks may contain the same person's face.

6. **Click Confirm Name at the bottom of the iPhoto window.**

   iPhoto shows you just the face in each photo that it thinks is the same person, with the words *click to confirm* underneath.

7. **Confirm or correct the names that iPhoto has matched with the faces.**

   To confirm, click each correct face once. The person's name appears under the face in green.

   To tell iPhoto it messed up, double-click a face and the name changes to red with the word *not* in front. If you're not sure of an image, just leave it unclicked.

8. **Review the photos you categorized. If you got one wrong, click the face to change from green to red or from red to green. When you have them all squared away, click Done.**

   iPhoto may show you another batch of faces. Later batches tend to include more erroneous matches, but also many good calls. In a few minutes, you'll have all photos of that individual tagged.

After you tag faces, you can click Faces in the sidebar to see a tile for each person you named. Double-click a tile to see all pictures in which you tagged someone.

Finding where in the world that picture was taken

Fancier digital cameras, including the one in the iPhone 3G, have a global positioning satellite (GPS) receiver and add location information to each image — a process known as *geotagging*. The geotag contains geographic coordinates, longitude, and latitude, but iPhoto knows how to read these geotags and translate the position into intelligible information, such as Boston or Paris. It even knows about popular spots where lots of pictures are taken, such as the *USS Constitution* or the Eiffel Tower.

To check out your photos' geotags, follow these steps:

1. **Click Places on the left side of the iPhoto window.**

   You see a Google map of the world with pins showing the locations where you took the geotagged photos in your library.

2. **Double-click near the pins to zoom in further — all the way down to street level.**

If your camera lacks GPS or you have old photos that aren't geotagged, you can add locations to individual photos or events because the shots made in a single day are often in the same locale. Follow these steps:

1. **Click a photo or an event to select it and then click the small *i* button in the lower-right area.**

   You see an information pane with space to type the location.

2. **Enter a city name. Or, type an address and ask Google to look it up.**

You can also name places that you use often, such as your home or a favorite campground. You can then use that name as a shortcut when geotagging your photos. In iPhoto, select Window⇨Manage My Places and then click Google Search and enter the address.

Editing Your iPhotos

Even the best photographers appreciate the ability to adjust digital photos after checking how they turned out. Although iPhoto isn't the most powerful photo editor, it comes with many tools for fine-tuning your photos.

When you select a photo in the main display and click Edit at the bottom of the window, iPhoto presents you with several editing icons, again at the bottom of its window, as shown in Figure 12-2. Unlike in higher-end editing programs, you aren't given a bewildering array of tools and options. iPhoto gets right to the point.

You have these options:

- **Rotate** turns photos in 90-degree increments. The default is clockwise. You can select counterclockwise in the iPhoto⇨Preferences dialog or press the Option key while clicking to see the opposite rotation.

- **Crop** selects the area of the photo you want to see using a gray overlay that you can move or adjust to size.

- **Straighten** lets you correct for a small tilt in your camera relative to the screen — up to plus or minus 10 degrees. A temporary grid overlays your photo to aid you in making the adjustment.

- **Enhance** applies filters that Apple thinks will generally do the right thing. They usually do.

- **Red eye** asks you to simply click the center of each eye in a portrait. iPhoto does the rest. This option doesn't work on photos of cats or dogs.

- **Retouch** gets rid of scratches and dust marks. Just rub over them with the cursor.

Figure 12-2:
Editing
options in
iPhoto.

✔ **Effects** displays a matrix of image treatments, such as Antique, Black & White, Boost Color, Edge Blur, Fade Color, Matte, Sepia, and Vignette, with your original in the center. Pick one you like.

✔ **Adjust** shows a pane with sliders to control individual attributes such as exposure, contrast, saturation, definition, highlights, shadows, sharpness, noise, temperature, and tint.

No matter what you do to your photo, you can always undo it all: Choose Photo⇨Revert to Original.

Sharing Photos in Slide Shows and Prints

What to do with all those photos? Why, show them to someone else, of course. iPhoto excels in having tools to share your images, including slide shows and easy ways to make prints.

The simplest way to share photos is online, on photo sharing sites or by e-mail:

- ✔ **Photo sharing sites and communities:** You can upload selected photos to your Facebook or Flickr account or to your Web Gallery on MobileMe, if you're a subscriber, letting the world see your photos or protecting them with a password.

- ✔ **E-mail:** To share your photos with friends by e-mail, just click the Email icon at the bottom of the window. iPhoto asks you to select which photo size to send.

If you want a fancier way to share your photos, try slide shows, prints, or photo books. The following sections explain these options in more detail.

Spicing up photos with a slide show

At its simplest level, creating a slide show involves selecting a bunch of pictures and putting them in order to tell a story. In iPhoto, that's just the beginning. Here's how to create a slide show:

1. **In iPhoto, select and arrange your photos in the main display.**

2. **Click the Slideshow icon at the bottom of the window.**

   An icon for your new slide show appears in the sidebar — you can rename it — and Slideshow view appears in the main display.

3. **Rearrange the thumbnails of the images that appear at the top, if you like.**

   At the bottom are icons that allow you to add excitement to your show. You can select from a variety of *transitions,* or ways to change from one slide to the next.

4. **If you like, select background music for your show from your iTunes library, GarageBand, or the sample selections supplied with iPhoto by clicking the Music icon in the lower-right corner of the window.**

When you're done, you can display your show onscreen, burn it to DVD, upload it to MobileMe, or use it in other ways such as podcasts or online presentations. See the Share menu for options.

Printing photos with iPhoto

Although slide shows and e-mail are handy, many people still appreciate photos they can hold in their hand. Until everyone carries a video iPod or iPhone, paper prints still have a role. To create prints, iPhoto offers the following options:

✔ You can print photos on your color printer by choosing File➪Print.

✔ You can order professional prints for a fee over the Internet. Click the Order Prints icon in the lower-right corner.

✔ You can use iPhoto tools to make custom greeting cards, calendars, and album books from your photos. You can drag photos one at a time or ask iPhoto to "flow" a bunch of them into the template you select. Click the appropriate icon at the bottom of the iPhoto window to get started (refer to Figure 12-2).

Moving Up to Aperture

Apple sells a more advanced photo-management software package, named Aperture, shown in Figure 12-3, that's aimed at professional photographers. It has more support for RAW images and can work with a much bigger photo library. It has more image-editing capabilities, but it can also integrate with Adobe Photoshop. You find tools to help you manage projects, including the ability to work with several versions of the same photo at a time. A handy image loupe magnifies a small area of the photo as you slide the loupe over the screen.

If you're serious about photography and have invested big bucks in camera iron and glass, the $200 Aperture price tag shouldn't be an obstacle to moving up.

Figure 12-3:
The Apple Aperture photo software with loupe tool.

The Picasa alternative

The Google Picasa photo management tool has long been popular on PCs. Perhaps you've been using it for your photos. The good news is that Google now has a version of Picasa for the Mac that you can download for free at http://picasa.google.com/mac. Like its PC cousin, Picasa for the Mac leaves your photos where it finds them — unlike iPhoto, which prefers to move all your images to its library. When you first launch Picasa on your Mac, it goes through all photos on your hard drive, even those in your iPhoto library. You can then look through all your images by date and folder. You can also make simple image edits, fix red-eye, make photo collages, and upload images to the online Google Picasa Web Albums. (A Google plugin lets you do this from iPhoto as well.) Google is extra careful with your iPhoto library, not making any changes but asking instead whether you want to store edited iPhoto images separately.

The only bad news, at least in the beta version that was available as I wrote this book, is that Google doesn't provide a way for moving your Picasa collection from the PC to the Mac. Sure, you can move all your photos and Picasa will preserve their folders, but other organizational changes you might have made on the PC side, such as making albums, aren't transferred.

Chapter 13

Producing Movies and Music on Your Mac

Some parts of what Apple calls the digital lifestyle appeal to most people who own a computer: surfing, sending and receiving e-mail, listening to music, organizing and viewing digital snapshots. But iLife also lets you do more exotic activities: edit and publish movies, create your own music and podcasts, and even learn to play an instrument. The Apple iMovie and GarageBand programs let anyone try their hand at these activities. What you do with these tools depends on you. I can only help you get started.

Producing Your Own Epic with iMovie

Great movies aren't created in a studio or on location. They're created in the editing room. The pioneering Russian filmmaker Lev Kuleshov proved the point by splicing a shot of a famous Russian actor between shots of a plate of soup, a girl at play, and an old woman in a coffin. It appeared that he was looking at each one. Audiences who were shown the short admired the different emotions that the actor displayed as he viewed each scene. But Kuleshov had used the same shot of the actor in each setting. The juxtaposition or montage created the strong emotion in the minds of the viewers.

For most of the 20th century, films were edited by cutting strips of film apart with a blade, arranging them artfully, and splicing them together to form the master image. Many specialized machines were invented to help in the cutting room. But no filmmaker in the first eight decades of motion pictures imagined the powerful editing capabilities that are supplied with your Macintosh for free, in the form of iMovie. Professional filmmakers now use still more capable software products. Apple makes one of the best, Final

Cut, which I talk about later. But if you've never edited film, the limitations of iMovie won't hold you back for some time. As Walter Murch, who won three Oscars for editing and sound mixing, put it:

Film editing is now something almost everyone can do at a simple level and enjoy it, but to take it to a higher level requires the same dedication and persistence that any art form does.

By the way, Murch was honored with a fourth Oscar nomination for *Cold Mountain,* which he edited using Apple's Final Cut Pro on a Macintosh G4, a wimpy machine compared to Macs now on sale.

Importing video from your camera

First things first: Make sure that you have enough hard drive space. Movies use lots of bits. Fifteen minutes of conventional video can occupy 3.2 to 10GB of space — the highest numbers apply if you're shooting in high definition (HD). Remember that you need space for all the raw footage you plan to edit, not just for the final product. I suggest buying an external hard drive with at least a terabyte of storage for any large film-editing project you undertake. If your Mac has a FireWire port, buy a drive that includes a FireWire interface. FireWire offers better video performance than USB 2.0.

If you have some digital camcorder footage you want to edit, follow these steps to import it into iMovie and begin editing:

1. **Connect your video camera to your Mac with the camera's cable and put the camera in the proper mode (typically, PC Connect).**

   You should see the iMovie Import window, and newer cameras present a list of clips. If not, select File➪Import from Camera.

2. **Select the clips you want to import in Manual mode, or select Automatic in the Import window to import them all.**

3. **When you're ready, click Import All or Import Checked.**

   FireWire camcorders show additional controls that let you rewind and fast-forward to the segments you want to download.

4. **Select the disk where you want the data stored and choose whether to add the video to an existing event or start a new one.**

   iMovie automatically divides your video into separate clips by looking at the time codes recorded on the tape. Stills from the beginning of each clip, and roughly every 5 seconds thereafter, appear in the Clips pane in the bottom of the iMovie window, shown in Figure 13-1. You adjust the interval between stills with the slider in the lower-right corner. As you move the mouse pointer over each clip, you see it play and iMovie stores video clips in a common library, by event, as iPhoto does. You see a list of events stored in your library in the lower-left corner.

Figure 13-1: The beginning stages of an iMovie project.

Importing video from your PC

If you have video you transferred from your PC, you can incorporate it into your iMovie project by using the File➪Import command. iMovie, which can accept any format that QuickTime understands, can work with high-definition video sources, including HDTV in 720p and 1080i formats.

One thing that vanilla QuickTime can't understand is Microsoft Windows Media (.wmv) files. Plug-ins from flip4mac.com can usually solve this problem.

Finding other sources for video

You can use the following other sources to insert video into your iMovie:

✔ **Built-in camera:** Want to try out iMovie but you don't own a digital camcorder? If you have a recent Apple laptop or iMac, you already have a built-in iSight camera, which you can use as an input source for iMovie. Just click the Camera icon on the central toolbar. iMovie shows you sitting in front of your keyboard, with a button that lets you start and stop recording from iSight. Lights, camera, *action!*

- **A Webcam:** Most FireWire Webcams and some newer USB Webcams work with iMovie. Many additional USB Webcams are supported using drivers available from the Macam project, (`webcam-osx.sourceforge.net`).

- **iPhoto:** Still photographs can be added to your iMovie project and animated by using the Ken Burns effect (see the nearby sidebar, "Ken Burns and his effect"). If your camera takes videos, you can grab those from iTunes as well.

- **Internet video:** A vast amount of video is available on the World Wide Web. Anything you download in a QuickTime-compatible format can be imported to iMovie. But be careful of copyright issues. (When I first typed the previous sentence, the fifth word read *copyfight*. That typo pretty much sums up what you want to avoid.)

Editing video in iMovie

Editing is where the fun begins. The following steps walk you through the basic process using iMovie:

1. **Edit each clip to show just what you want to include in your movie.**

   Click a clip, and an adjustable yellow box appears, showing the segment you selected.

2. **Drag the clip to the project pane in the upper-left corner, placing clips in the order you like.**

   You can use different segments from the same cut. If you just click a clip, iMovie selects a 4-second segment. To play a selected clip, press the spacebar.

3. **Add sound, photos, titles, scene transitions, and animated maps by using the icons to the right of the central toolbar.**

   Click an icon to see the options, and drag each one you want to your project window, placing them where you want them — even between clips.

   Sound sources include iTunes, two sets of prerecorded effects, and your Mac's microphone. To record narration, click the microphone icon.

4. **Continue editing your movie until the clips and effects are arranged the way you want.**

   You can rearrange elements of your movie by dragging. Click an element to edit it and press Delete to remove it from the movie.

5. **If you want to save your project, know that iMovie saves your project as you work on it.**

You can choose File⇨Versions to save a *checkpoint* (the current version of your movie) so you can go back to it if your later edits mangle what you've done up to this point.

6. **When your movie is ready, use the Share menu to transfer it to iTunes, an iPod, the Web, and more.**

One sharing option, DVDs, uses a separate iLife application that I talk about in "Burning Movies with iDVD" later in this chapter.

If your hand was a bit shaky when you took that once-in-a-lifetime shot, iMovie may be able to fix your precious video. Select one or more clips and choose File⇨Analyze for Stabilization. (You're also given this option when you import video from a camera, but the process can take quite a while, so you may be better off importing first and then stabilizing only the clips you want to use.)

Themes and precision editing

Like other iLife programs, iMovie comes with Apple-designed themes. Drag a bunch of clips to the project window. Rearrange them the way you like and pick a theme by choosing File⇨Project Properties⇨General and clicking the theme you want. iMovie then fills it in with your clips. You won't win any awards for editing, but after just a few minutes of work, you have a serviceable movie complete with title and credits to share a special vacation or birthday party with family members and friends.

At the other extreme, iMovie gives you fine-grain control of each clip transition. Select Window⇨Precision Editor (⌘-/) and iMovies replaces the bottom clip window with a screen that lets you get each transition just right — even carrying the audio from the first clip into the next one.

Moving up to Final Cut

You can accomplish a lot with iMovie, but it has its limits. When you're ready for the training wheels to come off, Apple has excellent industrial-strength solutions waiting for you, some at consumer-strength prices.

The top-of-the-line Apple video-editing suite is Final Cut Studio. It includes these features:

- **Final Cut Pro:** Not many computer programs win Emmys. It has also been used to edit more than two dozen feature-length films. It supports most high-definition formats.

✔ **Soundtrack Pro:** As Apple puts it, the soundtrack is half the picture. Soundtrack Pro includes more than 50 professional-effect plug-ins.

✔ **Motion:** This animation package creates motion graphics in real-time.

✔ **DVD Studio Pro:** Transfer HD content to optical disc formats.

✔ **Color:** Use this product for professional color grading.

✔ **Compressor:** This audio and video compression application automates encoding and format conversions.

Apple separately sells Shake, a video-compositing tool for professional special effects.

If you're still waiting to be green-lighted for that full-length epic, Apple has a scaled-down version of Final Cut, Final Cut Express, in the under-$200 class. It has the same interface as Final Cut Pro but not all tools and formats. It also comes with a scaled-back, but still powerful, version of Soundtrack. Figure 13-2 shows the rich interface of Final Cut Express.

For more on iMovie and the subject of the next section, iDVD, see *iMovie & iDVD '09 For Dummies* by Dennis R. Cohen and Michael E. Cohen (Wiley Publishing).

Figure 13-2:
Final Cut
Express.

Ken Burns and his effect

The documentary films of Ken Burns have brought to life, for millions of viewers, whole eras of American history — the building of the Brooklyn Bridge, the rise of jazz and baseball, and the development of radio. For his most acclaimed series, *The Civil War,* Burns faced an opportunity and a problem. The Civil War was fought after the invention of photography, and archives were filled with black-and-white images, some by excellent early photographers such as Mathew Brady. These archives presented an opportunity to visually tell the story of this horrific war. The problem was how to keep from boring an audience that was used to seeing movie footage of war. Burns solved the problem by panning the camera across the still images and slowly zooming in or out to create a sense of motion. *The Civil War* won numerous awards, including two Emmys, for its ability to not just convey the facts of history but also examine its emotional impact.

Apple has incorporated into its iLife suite the technique that Ken Burns made such masterful use of. It's even called "the Ken Burns effect." It operates by default in iPhoto slide shows and even in the OS X screen saver. But you can customize it by selecting starting and ending versions of the image. The same feature is available in iMovie (select a clip and press the C key), allowing you to incorporate iPhoto stills as dynamic images in your cinematic projects.

Burning Movies with iDVD

When your epic is ready, pull down the Share menu to find all the things you can do with it, from placing it in iTunes so that you can view it on your iPod or iPhone to uploading it to YouTube or your MobileMe Gallery to exporting it in QuickTime or another format that Apple FinalCut accepts. If you want to burn a DVD, you want to use iDVD. Read on.

Apple iDVD is something of a one-trick pony: It transfers content to DVD-R so that it can be shown on ordinary DVD players. The content includes stuff you created with other iLife applications (your iMovie films and iPhoto slide shows) and other video content you may have on your hard drive.

You need a Mac that can burn DVDs: the Apple SuperDrive. The MacBook Air doesn't have an optical drive, but Apple offers an optional external USB DVD burner.

If you want only to back up your media or other files to a DVD, you don't need to use iDVD. The OS X Finder lets you do that. Just don't try to play your backup DVD on your home entertainment center.

Most of what iDVD does is kind of boring: Convert stuff to the right video formats and put the bits in the place on the DVD where consumer players expect them. But Apple can add some pizzazz in one place: themes for the main DVD menu. Here's how it works:

1. **The main screen of iDVD shows a collection of Apple-created themes on the right side. Select one you like by clicking it.**

   In Figure 13-3, you can see the travel theme.

Figure 13-3:
The iDVD theme selection screen.

2. **Drag movies and photos from the Finder or any iLife application to designated image areas within the themes.**

   iDVD can even animate the images so that your menu is even more inviting.

   If you want a scene selection menu, iDVD can add one based on your iMovie chapter divisions.

3. **Choose File⇨Burn DVD.**

If you need to create a DVD quickly, use the OneStep DVD function that burns the entire contents of the tape in an attached DV camcorder. Just select OneStep DVD from the iDVD File menu.

Composing Using GarageBand

There's an old joke about someone asking a police officer in Manhattan how to get to Carnegie Hall. "Practice six hours every day" comes the reply. Making music has traditionally required both talent and manual skills that take years to master. People who don't start young and keep working at their instrument are consigned to taking guitar or piano lessons at adult education class, where they might progress to plunking out a few tunes at a party.

Computers have leveled the playing field somewhat. Programs such as Apple GarageBand, shown in Figure 13-4, come with prerecorded loops that you can transform and combine to create a sound you want. You can add your own tracks by connecting a keyboard or another instrument that has a MIDI or USB interface, or just use the onscreen keyboard. If your performance isn't quite up to snuff, you can try again or edit out the imperfections. You can also add tracks that were performed live and recorded with a microphone.

Figure 13-4: GarageBand lays down tracks.

Apple offers add-ins to GarageBand in the form of $99 Jam Packs, which include

- ✔ Remix Tools Jam Pack
- ✔ Rhythm Section Jam Pack
- ✔ Symphony Orchestra Jam Pack
- ✔ Voices
- ✔ World Music Jam Pack

You can export your composition to iTunes or use it as part of the soundtrack for your slide show or iMovie. The latter uses may be one of the most valuable aspects of GarageBand.

If you plan to distribute your iLife compositions beyond your circle of family and friends, you can't just dub in selections from your favorite group's album, even if you purchased it fair and square from the iTunes Store. What you bought entitles you to listen to, not incorporate into your own work, the copyrighted music. Original music and sound effects you create in GarageBand, even those that use prerecorded Apple loops, are yours to use as you see fit.

For an in-depth look at recording music with GarageBand, check out *GarageBand For Dummies,* by Bob LeVitus (Wiley Publishing).

Podcasting with GarageBand

If you want to try your hand at podcasting (creating audio or video essays that are distributed over the Net and often played on iPods), GarageBand has the tools you need.

You can use the built-in microphone in your Mac. GarageBand can enhance the sound and reduce background noise. If you use a musical soundtrack, GarageBand can automatically "duck" the soundtrack under your voice when you're speaking. Add sound effects, if you like — GarageBand comes with more than 200. You can also have a video track with a title screen and other photos you might want to add. If you have a MobileMe account, you can publish your podcast online with a single click.

Because programs such as GarageBand make podcasting easy, everyone can do it, and it seems like everyone *is* doing it. If you want your podcasts to stand out, follow these tips:

- ✔ Pick topics you know about.
- ✔ Take the time to develop an outline or a script.
- ✔ Pick one point and make it well.
- ✔ Keep it short.
- ✔ Lose the "umms" and "uhs" and "likes."

Learning to play an instrument with GarageBand

If you always wanted to play guitar or piano, or if you already play but want tips from some outstanding musicians, GarageBand can help. The program comes with two introductory lessons, one for each instrument. Click Learn to Play on the left side of the GarageBand window to try them out. You can download eight more free lessons for each instrument by clicking Lesson Store. But that's not all: The lesson store also has artist lessons you can buy, featuring popular performers — from Sara Bareilles to Sting. Each artist lesson teaches you to play a simple version of one of that artist's hits. All lessons are highly interactive, making clever use of the GarageBand power to help you practice. You can even record your practice sessions in GarageBand and save the tracks you like.

Moving up from GarageBand

Just as in iPhoto and iMovie, Apple has better music-creation tools ready whenever you are: Logic and Logic Pro. One classic rite of passage for a new musical group was coming up with the thousands of dollars needed to rent a sound studio for a few hours so that they could cut a demo tape. Modern groups have found that, for a lot less money, they can build sound studios in their basements to keep up with the pros. A Mac is often at the heart of this process. You need additional equipment, including good microphones, preamps, and a multi-input audio interface with a USB or, preferably, FireWire interface (if your Mac has a FireWire port). Sites such as www. tweakheadz.com have lots of resources to help you get started.

If you're serious about home recording and want a guide to help you learn professional techniques, check out *Home Recording for Musicians For Dummies,* 3rd Edition by Jeff Strong (Wiley Publishing).

Chapter 14

Building Your Space on the Web

*P*sychologist Abraham Maslow suggests that we have a hierarchy of needs. After our physical requirements for survival and safety are met and we have satisfactory personal relationships (friends, marriage, children), we seek to establish our presence in the larger world, a process that Maslow calls *self-actualization*. In the past, it might have meant running for political office, joining a performing group, or writing a self-help book. Now, more and more people seek recognition as individuals and find ways to make an impact on the world by creating a personal space on the Internet.

In this chapter, you find out a few popular ways to create your space on the Web:

- ✔ **Building a Web site:** Your Mac comes with excellent tools for expressing your thoughts, feelings, and ideas — iPhoto, iMovie, GarageBand — that I've talked about in the preceding three chapters. The final element of the iLife suite, iWeb (which I describe in this chapter) lets you pull together all that creative content and let others view it by way of the World Wide Web. You also discover how to get your own domain name and a few tips for building a successful site.

- ✔ **Having your Web storage and sharing space with MobileMe:** You can subscribe to MobileMe from Apple, and get not only a personal space for storing files and more, but also tools for hosting your site, simply sharing photos and synchronizing multiple computers.

- ✔ **Social networking:** If you haven't already, check out sites such as Facebook, MySpace, and LinkedIn.

Creating a Web Site

When you're setting up your own space on the Web, building your own site offers the most creative possibilities but is also the most technical. To make Web-page creation accessible to those without the technical knowledge, Apple iWeb brings the iLife predefined template concept to the process of building personal Web pages. The program comes supplied with 21 themes. Each theme has coordinated templates for the welcome page, narratives, photos, movies, blogs, and podcasts. See Figure 14-1. You can modify or customize the templates, if you want. iWeb relieves you from coding or other internal Web page tasks, and its automated tools simplify blogging.

If you have MobileMe, you can publish your page and update it with a single click, but iWeb supports other Web hosting services as well. I have more to say about MobileMe later in this chapter.

Figure 14-1:
An iWeb
template.

In the sections that follow, you find details about working with iWeb as well as tips for building a successful site and getting your own domain name.

Starting your first iWeb site

If iWeb isn't on your dock, you can find it in your Applications folder. Launch the program, and it first asks you whether you have a MobileMe account. If you already do, give it your username and password. If not, skip this step.

Next, you're asked to choose a theme for your Web site. Here's what you need to know about themes as you get started:

- ✔ **Your theme options enable you to set a look and feel for your site.** The Apple Web designers have supplied more than twenty themes, with looks that range from highly elegant and professional to frivolous and whimsical.

- ✔ **The themes help you coordinate pages for different types of site content.** Each theme includes matching page designs for a welcome screen, biographical information, photos, albums, movies, blogs, podcasts, and a blank theme page that you can easily customize for whatever inspires you.

- ✔ **You can switch themes easily.** Pick a theme to get started. Because all pages follow a similar organizational style, you aren't locked into your initial theme choice after you start building your page. For the most part, you can change themes at will.

Each theme page template, except the blank one, is filled with placeholder pictures and text so that you see what the result will look like. The body text consists of a Latin passage by the ancient Roman orator Cicero in which he explains that no one deliberately seeks out grief. (He wrote the passage centuries before Windows was created). You can customize the placeholders as follows:

- ✔ **Replacing text:** Double-click any bit of text to select it and then just type what you want or cut and paste it from another document.

- ✔ **Deleting placeholders:** To get rid of an element you don't want, select the element and press Delete.

- ✔ **Replacing placeholders with photos:** On the right side of your screen, you see the Media Browser, an area with headings labeled Audio, Photos, Movies, and Widgets. Click Photos and you see photos and albums from your iPhoto library. Select a photo and drag it to one of the placeholder images and your photo appears instead.

If you have lots of photos, you may find it more convenient to search in iPhoto itself and then drag the selected photo from iPhoto to the iWeb placeholder image. All iLife programs cooperate nicely.

Of course, you can continue to replace photos you selected with others until you find the one that best suits your purpose.

✔ **Moving and resizing images:** You can also click and drag images to move them, and you can resize them by clicking one and then dragging the control boxes that surround the image. If you move something by mistake, just choose Edit➪Undo or press ⌘-Z.

✔ **Adding new elements to a page:** You can add elements to any page, such as text boxes, shapes, images, and movies. For text boxes and shapes, click the appropriate icon at the bottom of the iWeb window. To add photos and other media, drag them from the Media Browser.

✔ **Putting a widget on a page:** Another type of element that you find in the Media Browser is a *widget,* which is a block of programming code in Hypertext Markup Language (HTML), the computer language that describes Web pages. Widgets perform specialized functions, such as displaying Google Maps or YouTube videos. You can even display paid advertising using the Google AdSense program. By *paid,* I mean that you're paid when people click the ads. See the later sidebar "Google AdSense" for more information.

The individual pages of your site have a navigation bar at the top that lets visitors move from one page to another. Clicking in that bar while you're in iWeb to select a different page to edit is tempting, but it doesn't work. You have to use the navigation pane on the right side of the iWeb window to access different pages in the site you're editing.

Saving your pages is no different from any Mac or Windows app: File➪Save. If you forget, like all apps, iWeb asks if you want to save your changes when you quit the program.

Publishing your site

Just because you build a site in iWeb doesn't mean it's online for all to see. When you're ready to share your creation, you have to publish it to the Web.

Before you share your site with others, take a look to make sure that all placeholders have been replaced with your content. Also be sure to give your site a name. To get ready to publish your site, follow these steps:

1. **Click the top icon in the navigation bar on the left side of the iWeb windows.**

2. **In the Site Publishing Settings pane that appears, you name your site, provide a contact e-mail address, and (optionally) make your site private by requiring guests to enter a password you select.**

3. **(Optional) Tell iWeb to automatically notify your Facebook profile whenever you change your site. Just select the Facebook check box at the bottom of the pane.**

4. **In the Publishing settings pane, you also select where you want to publish your site, either your MobileMe account or another Web hosting service using File Transfer Protocol (FTP).**

   Your hosting service should provide you with the necessary server address, username, password, directory path, and protocol you must use with FTP.

5. **To close this pane, click some other element on the navigation bar.**

6. **After you enter all the information, click Publish at the bottom of the iWeb screen.**

   Apple nags you to ensure that you have rights to all content you're putting online. Publishing can take a few minutes, so don't close iWeb until you receive confirmation that your site has been published. The confirmation box tells you the Web address of your site, which is information you should write down somewhere, and gives you the option of announcing your site by either sending e-mail or visiting the site immediately.

If you find mistakes (everyone does) or information you want to change or add, don't worry. Open the site again in iWeb, make your changes, and click Publish again.

The Internet can be a dangerous place for young people. Before you let your kids set up their own Web pages or join social networking sites, take a close look at the section in Chapter 17 that talks about Macs for kids.

Moving up from iWeb

iWeb is narrowly focused on personal Web pages. You might be able to adapt its templates to a simple business, but that's about it. Apple lacks a high-end program for Web page design. If you're looking for a program that's more robust that iWeb, I suggest looking into the following options:

✔ Adobe Dreamweaver is probably the tool that's most often used by professionals using Macs and Windows. For help creating a site with Dreamweaver, check out *Dreamweaver CS4 For Dummies* or *Web Sites Do-It-Yourself For Dummies,* both by Janine Warner (Wiley Publishing).

✓ You can find a good free, visual Web page editor at `www.kompozer.net`, though you may need to load Rosetta in order to use it. Rosetta is in the Optional Installs folder on the restore DVD supplied with your Mac. See the section on installing software in Chapter 5. The SeaMonkey Web application suite. `www.seamonkey-project.org`, also includes a Web editor.

Making Web sites that work

With tools such as iWeb, creating a Web page is easy. Making one that accomplishes your goals is another matter. Here are some tips for making your Web site effective:

✓ **Make sure that you're providing information that someone else cares about.** You don't need a large audience, but you must address the needs of your niche. Content counts.

✓ **Say what you most need to say on the first page a visitor sees.** Keep it simple. You have, at most, ten seconds to convince visitors to delve deeper into your site. Be sure to include any keywords that you want Google to index in the initial paragraphs.

✓ **Pick an easy-to-remember Web address.** Pick one that's in the `.com` top-level domain, if you can. No, they aren't all taken. If a name you like isn't taken, register it immediately. One-year registrations are cheap. Mark the renewal date a month ahead on your iCal calendar so that you don't forget to renew. Some domain name registrars, such as GoDaddy.com, automatically renew you, but you must keep your credit card information up to date. After you settle on a name, don't change it. Links to your site are priceless.

✓ **On the garish World Wide Web, restraint stands out.** Use color and graphics to enhance your messages. Avoid clichés such as animated `.gif` files and Under Construction signs. If one of your pages isn't ready, don't link to it.

✓ **Put up what you have now and improve it later.** The visitors you missed today won't be back tomorrow.

✓ **Test your site by using different browsers.** Include Internet Explorer in Windows (a good use for your old PC) and Firefox on Mac and Windows. Test your site on a dialup connection, too.

✓ **Ask someone who doesn't know your site to find it and check it out while you watch.** Keep your mouth shut during the evaluation — it isn't easy — and take notes or, better, videotape the session. You want to understand how a new visitor experiences and navigates your site so that you can make any changes needed to improve the user experience and make sure your visitors do whatever you're hoping they'll do on your site.

✔ **Keep your site current.** Inspect it at least one a month. Out-of-date information destroys the credibility of your entire site. Regularly purge references to "upcoming" events that have already happened and to dead external links. Don't include high-maintenance items such as *events* if you aren't prepared to keep them updated. Less is more.

✔ **Give visitors a compelling reason to return to your site.** That reason depends on the goals of your site, but it must have a clear benefit for visitors, not just for you.

Getting your own domain name

Having your own domain name makes you a first-class citizen on the Internet. Web addresses have several parts strung together by periods, like this:

```
www.dummies.com
```

You decode a Web address from right to left:

✔ **Top-level domain, or TLD:** The rightmost part of a name (`com`, in the preceding example).

✔ **Organization or Web site name:** Located to the left of the TLD (`dummies`). Two-letter TLDs are reserved for different countries, such as `us`, `fr`, or `uk`. Three-letter TLDs denote a type of use. The most widely known is `.com`, typically used for commercial sites. Many browsers, including Safari, insert `.com` in the Web address if no TLD is specified, so this TLD is particularly desirable.

✔ **Particular service within the organization:** The part to the left of the organization name (`www`).

Google AdSense

If you sign up for the Google AdSense program and place the AdSense widget on your site, Google automatically puts ads on your page. You can select from a number of ad formats, from the discrete to the garish. Google selects ads to show to your visitors based on the content of the site and on information that Google and its partners have accumulated about your visitor. Yes, all your Web activity is being tracked, and, if you use AdSense, you're helping with the tracking. You won't get rich with AdSense, unless you have a spectacularly popular site. Google pays you each month, but only after your earnings exceed $100. The folk singer Linda Lavin once complained, "You can make hundreds of dollars as a folk singer." That limit on expectations applies to Web sites using AdSense, even ones that receive hundreds of hits a day.

The www, which stands for World Wide Web, is common in Web addresses, but large organizations often further subdivide their Web addresses by site or department.

The last two hunks of a hostname are known as the *domain*. For example, dummies.com is a *domain name*. (In some countries, an extra hunk identifies broad categories, such as in bbc.co.uk, in which co has a meaning similar to .com.)

Domain names are assigned by various registrars. Their price varies from $8 to $35 per year, and you usually have to pay the first year up front. I've had good experiences with GoDaddy.com. For a list of organizations that can register a domain name for you, see

```
www.icann.org/registrars/accredited-list.html
```

Internet service providers often charge substantial additional fees for setting up and supporting new domains. But registrars such as GoDaddy often offer a free service that sends people who enter your domain name in their browser to the more clunky address that your Internet provider chooses. For example, visitors to ditchmypc.com are automatically redirected to http://web.me.com/agr/Site/Welcome.html.

MobileMe for You

MobileMe is the Apple collection of online services that are available by subscription. (It used to be named .Mac — or "dot-mac" — and iTools before that) MobileMe costs $99 a year or $149 for a family pack that supports as many as five users. MobileMe works for PCs and Macs, but Apple offers a 60-day free trial to new Mac buyers. For the $99 fee, you receive these services:

- ✓ **Web hosting:** You can have one or more Web sites, all managed by iWeb, as described earlier in this chapter. Note that the Apple terms of service for MobileMe say that it's "designed for personal use and not intended to be used for commercial business purposes, including, but not limited to, transacting online sales or software distribution via an e-commerce site." But you can show Google AdSense advertisements.

- ✓ **A me.com electronic mail account for each user:** For example, SteveJobs@me.com. Mail addressed to your MobileMe account is automatically sent to your Mac, your iPhone or iPod touch, and even to Microsoft Outlook. You can even access your mail on someone else's computer by using a Web interface.

✔ **iDisk online storage:** Access it from your Mac just as you would access an external hard drive. You can use iDisk for backing up or to share files with others — under password protection, if you want. You can access your iDisk from a PC as well. The basic plan offers 20GB of total storage space, including your e-mail, photos, and Web sites. Additional users on the family plan have 5GB each, and, of course, Apple will happily rent you more space, if you need it.

✔ **Contacts and calendars:** MobileMe can synchronize all address books and calendars that live on your desktop or laptop or your iPhone or iPod and in Microsoft Outlook, the Windows address book, Google, and Yahoo! Plus, you can access your information from a Web application.

✔ **Photo gallery:** Upload and store your photos from your computer or iPhone. The gallery is integrated with iPhoto and Aperture for effortless uploads. Friends can view pictures and even add their own to your gallery. MobileMe even works with AppleTV, letting your viewers see your photos on their big-screen TVs.

Many services that MobileMe provides are available for free or less expensively from other Internet services. For example, Google and Yahoo! offer free e-mail with address books and online storage. And, sites such as Flickr.com host your photos for free. MobileMe ties up everything in a single package that's reliable and easy to use. The time you spend in figuring out how to use a bunch of free services is worth something, too.

Social Networking from your Mac

You don't need your own Web site to establish a personal presence on the Internet. Several sites designed to give individuals a place to do their thing have become wildly popular:

✔ LinkedIn (www.linkedin.com) focuses on your work life and helps you find and network with people who can help your career.

✔ Facebook (www.facebook.com) was originally intended for college students, but it's increasingly used by people in older and younger age brackets.

✔ MySpace (www.myspace.com) is a bit more freeform, with everything from dating to business sites to music distribution and the promotion of TV shows and movies.

✔ Twitter (www.twitter.com) lets you send short text messages, or *tweets,* from your computer or cellphone so that your friends and others can read them.

If you already have an account on one of these social networking sites, you don't have to do anything when you switch to a Mac — just log in to the site with your Safari browser and do what you usually do there. You need your site passwords, however. If you forget them, the sites will generally mail you a new password to the e-mail address they have on file for you. So test your passwords to make sure they work (and write them down) before you abandon your old e-mail account. See Chapter 10 for tips on password management.

This list describes some social networking resources specifically for your Mac:

- **Facebook Widget**: A dashboard widget that's designed to show notifications such as messages, pokes, friend requests, and group and event invites. You can download it from `facebookdesktopwidget.com`.

- **FMenu**: Adds an icon to your menu bar that lets you quickly access your Facebook pages. This product (at `http://sourceforge.net/projects/fmenu`) tells you about various Facebook events, such as new wall posts, new inbox messages, status changes, and the release of the Facebook Growl feature. In addition, it lets you quickly access almost all your Facebook pages. See `www.applesource.com.au/os-x/soa/Mac-plugins-for-Facebook` for more examples.

- **Spyder**: A fast, versatile MySpace browser (`www.spyderx.com`) aimed at OS X.

- **Twitterrific**: A free, ad-supported application from IconFactory that lets you send and receive tweets from your Mac in a little side window that floats in front of your other windows so you'll never miss the latest hot tweet. (Give them $15, and they'll drop the ads.) You can find it at

  ```
  www.apple.com/downloads/macosx/email_chat/
          twitterrific.html
  ```

- **OS X support groups for Mac users:** Often accessible on social networking sites. Try searching for *macintosh computers* on Facebook.

Should you friend your teenager?

Facebook and other social networking sites allow only a member's full content to be viewed solely by other members who have mutually agreed to be friends on the site. That arrangement raises the question of whether parents should insist that their kids make them friends (or "friend them," in the argot) on these sites. Parents need to supervise younger kids' Internet activities, but the case can be made to allow older teens some privacy online. They'll be on their own in a few years anyway, and having the opportunity to experiment and even make mistakes online while you're still active in their lives can be a good learning experience. It's a tough judgment call that you have to make. Still, a review of the online guidelines for young people that I present in Chapter 17 is always in order.

Chapter 15

Enjoying Other OS X Goodies

● ●

In This Chapter

▶ Filling the Dashboard with widgets

▶ Finding the window you need with Exposé

▶ Organizing the screen with Spaces

▶ Searching your Mac with Spotlight

● ●

Mac OS X is filled with programs and features that make time spent in front of your computer more productive, more interesting, and more fun. In this chapter, I introduce some of my favorites.

Adding Handy Widgets to the Dashboard

Dashboard provides an easy way to see and use *widgets,* which are mini-applications that grab specific information from the Internet or help with narrow but useful tasks. Figure 15-1 shows a typical Dashboard arrangement, including a calendar, clock, translator, flight tracker, weather program, and more. Of course, you can move widgets around, add new ones, and drop stale ones. You're in charge. Some widgets are silly, some are fun, and some seem indispensable after you're used to having them around.

To work with widgets, you just need to know a few tips:

- ✔ **To make your widgets appear:** Press F4, the key with a meter icon on it. The desktop you've been working on "grays" into the background, and a layer with colorful widgets appears.

- ✔ **To add more widgets:** Click the plus sign (+)in the lower-left corner. A scrolling list appears at the bottom of your screen. Click the icons for the widgets you want to add.

- ✔ **To delete widgets:** Click the plus sign to do this task, too. When you do, all current widgets show up with an *X* in their upper-left corner. Click the *X,* and they're gone.

✔ **To adjust settings:** Many widgets have a lowercase *i* in their lower-right corners. Click the *i,* and the widget flips over to show you which settings you can adjust to customize it.

Apple includes a collection of widgets with OS X, but many more are available from www.apple.com/downloads/dashboard. Many are freeware, and some ask for a fee. Many work only when your computer is connected to the Internet.

Figure 15-1:
The
Dashboard.

You can have multiple instances of a widget running simultaneously with different customizations, such as a clock with different time zones or weather reports from different locales. Some of the widgets supplied with OS X are described in this list:

✔ **Address book:** Gain easy access to your contact list.

✔ **Calendar:** What day is the 23rd of next month?

✔ **Dictionary and thesaurus:** Don't guess — look it up.

✔ **Flight tracker:** Where's that flight now? When will it arrive?

✔ **Language translator:** Translate a sentence or two between Chinese, Dutch, English, French, German, Greek, Italian, Korean, Russian, and Spanish.

✔ **Movies:** Find what's playing where, see previews, and buy tickets from Fandango.

✔ **Phone book:** Let your mouse do the walking.

✔ **Ski report:** Packed ice or fresh powder?

✔ **Stickies:** These items don't fall off your monitor.

✔ **Stocks:** Watch your favorite securities and funds fluctuate.

✔ **Tile game:** Check out this classic.

✔ **Unit converter:** Sure, it can convert from metric to English, but it also knows currency exchange rates.

✔ **Weather:** Look up the temperature highs and lows and a six-day forecast.

✔ **World time:** Is it too early to call Tokyo?

You even have a Widget widget to help you manage all your widgets. To see the widgets available and add some to your Dashboard, press F4 to open Dashboard and then click the plus sign (+) in the lower left of your screen.

Download more

You can find many more widgets to play with. Here are some examples — all are freeware:

✔ **Countdown Dashboard:** Make a countdown timer to any event you choose: graduation, vacation, dental appointment, or book deadline, for example.

✔ **Corporate Ipsum:** Generate nonsense text whenever you need it, such as "interactively orchestrate superior portals without team-driven platforms, collaboratively actualize plug-and-play outsourcing and maintainable applications, distinctively simplify front-end platforms before backward-compatible relationships."

✔ **Fans:** Your Mac has cooling fans inside that spin at different rates depending on how hard your CPU is working. Seriously. The first time my normally quiet MacBook started to sound like an airplane taking off was a tad alarming. The Fans widget shows animated fans spinning to match the current speed of your real fans.

   ✔ **I Love Lamp:** You've seen or heard of the infamous lava lamp from the 1960s?

   ✔ **iStat Pro:** Display the status of the CPU, memory, hard drives, internal and external IP address, bandwidth, battery, uptime, and fans.

   ✔ **Kennedy Space Center Video:** Watch what's happening at everyone's favorite spaceport. You have more than a dozen Webcams to choose from.

   ✔ **Mirror:** See yourself onscreen and touch up your hair (uses your iSight camera).

   ✔ **Starry Night:** See the planets and constellations as they appear right now at any location on Earth.

   ✔ **Sudoku:** Get your rivals at work hooked on this wildly popular number game. Sudoku and career success are ensured.

Thousands more widgets are available, and more keep popping up.

Roll your own

You can select a portion of a Web page and create a widget that shows the latest version of just that piece, a feature Apple calls *WebClips*. Follow these steps:

   1. **Open Safari and go to the Web site you want to "widgetize."**

   2. **Choose File⇨Open in Dashboard or click the Dashboard icon.**

   3. **Select the section of the page you want to capture.**

      In the upper-right corner of Figure 15-1, you see two Web clips I made. One is from the U.S. Department of Homeland Security (www.dhs.gov), showing the current terrorist threat level; the other, from Dummies.com, shows a search box for finding the latest *For Dummies* titles.

Apple even provides the Dashcode program to help you build your own widget. Make a widget to track your favorite blog. The possibilities are endless. Dashcode is in the Xcode folder on your OS X installation DVD.

Controlling Windows Fast with Exposé

The more useful computers become, the more cluttered the screen gets. At any given time, you may be working with half a dozen applications at one time, each with multiple windows open. Exposé provides the following shortcuts to help you find the window you're looking for:

✔ **Press F3.** All open windows shrink and arrange themselves on your screen so that none of them overlaps. (The icon on the key suggests the separated windows.). You see an overview of everything. Click the window you want and it moves to the front, or press F3 again and your screen returns to its previous mess.

✔ **Press Control+F3.** It works like pressing F3, but rearranges only the windows from the application you're working on. Or click and hold any application's icon in the Dock to get the same effect for that application.

✔ **Press ⌘-F3.** Make all windows disappear so that you can see your desktop. (The windows don't completely go away — you can see the edges of the windows along the border of your screen. Clicking one of those window edges moves you out of Exposé with that window in front.)

✔ **Press F4.** Open the Dashboard.

Apple sometimes moves these keys around depending on the keyboard you have. Also, you can pick different keys to perform these functions and also make the corner of your screen a hot spot for the same actions. Follow these steps to check on your key assignments and to make changes:

1. **Choose ⌘➪System Preferences.**

2. **Select Exposé & Spaces.**

   You see a pane similar to the one shown in Figure 15-2.

3. **Select the keys or onscreen corners for which you want to perform an action.**

Figure 15-2:
The Exposé preferences pane.

Organizing Work Areas with Spaces

I'm one of those people who always has several projects going on at a time. My fantasy is to have a studio where I can have a table or workbench for each project so that I can walk up to it whenever I want and pick up where I left off. Apple hasn't offered me a studio, but OS X provides the next best thing — a bunch of virtual work tables named Spaces. You can have as many as 16 of them. Specific applications can be assigned to specific spaces, or an application can be available to all spaces. You set up Spaces this way:

1. **Choose ⇨System Preferences.**

2. **Select Exposé & Spaces, and then click the Spaces tab.**

   You see a window like the one shown in Figure 15-3.

3. **Add the applications you want and assign them a space or set them to be available to all spaces.**

   Figure 15-3 shows Spaces with three spaces populated. (See the Application Bindings area of the dialog.)

   When you're done with the setup, activate Spaces by pressing Fn+F8 and selecting the space you want. (Again, choose System Preferences⇨Exposé and Spaces for the key on your Mac.) Or, switch spaces by holding down Ctrl and pressing either the arrow key or the number key that corresponds to the space you want.

Figure 15-3: Preferences for Spaces.

Searching for Files with Spotlight

After you use computers for a while, sooner or later you encounter difficulty in finding a file, even though you *know* that it's in there somewhere. The Spotlight search tool helps you find that file by typing words that the file likely contains and other characteristics, such as its name, the date you created it, and which kind of file it is. Searching through gigabytes of hard drive space can take some time, even on a fast computer, so Spotlight keeps an index of every word you use in documents, e-mail messages, and other areas. It does this in the background, so you hardly notice. But these indexes make searching very fast.

A Spotlight icon is located on the menu bar in the upper-right corner of your screen. Click it to open a search box. You also see search boxes in each Finder window. You can also press ⌘+F when the Finder is open.

Customizing searches

You can tell Spotlight your search preferences and how you want to see results by clicking the Spotlight icon in System Preferences. You see a pane similar to the one shown in Figure 15-4. Deselect the items you don't want to search. You can drag individual lines up and down to reorder the way items appear in a search.

Figure 15-4:
Customizing
the Spotlight
search
order.

Of course, you may have information that you'd prefer not be found in a search. Click the Privacy tab in the Spotlight preferences pane and drag into the window those files and folders you don't want to be searched. Spotlight doesn't return matches from those files and folders.

Spotlight normally tries to match all the words you type in its search box. If you want to search for dogs *or* cats, type **dogs | cats**. If you want to search for pets but no dogs, type **pets -dogs**.

You find downloadable plug-ins that let Spotlight search other file types at `www.apple.com/downloads/macosx/spotlight`.

Searching with Smart Folders

Wouldn't it be convenient to find all files associated with the Zorchcastle Project without having to do a search every time? Spotlight offers a tool to do this: Smart Folders. Here's how it works:

1. **In the Finder, create a folder by choosing Finder⇨New Smart Folder.**

   Of course, if your project isn't named Zorchcastle, you're out of luck. Smart Folders works only with "Zorchcastle." Just kidding.

2. **In the Smart Folder's search area, enter the words or other criteria you want.**

   You add more criteria by clicking the little plus-sign button (+).

3. **To keep your handy new Smart Folder around, click the Save button and give it a name.**

   Keep the Smart Folder around, and it will always show the files that match the criteria you set, including new files you saved after you set up the Smart Folder. The Smart Folder stays wherever you put it, such as on the desktop or in your Documents folder. You can find it the same way you find any other folder.

   Figure 15-5 shows a Smart Folder looking for files created in the past month whose name starts with the letters *Ch*.

Figure 15-5:
A Smart
Folder.

Saving Time with Automator and AppleScript

Every now and then, you face a task that's highly repetitious. A bunch of photos have to be sized to fit a catalog, or some illustrations have to be numbered a certain way to work with a publishing system, for example. Apple provides a couple of techniques for completing the task.

If you're comfortable with computer programming, OS X comes with a scripting language named AppleScript. Most OS X applications can be invoked from AppleScript programs, so you can use the applications as tools in your program, say to extract an address from Address Book or rotate an image using Preview. You can find all the details in *AppleScript For Dummies,* 2nd Edition by Tom Trinko (Wiley Publishing).

Most of us aren't eager to write programs every time a tedious chore presents itself, so Apple has a simple way to automate your life, named, interestingly, Automator. OS X includes a library with hundreds of Automator actions you can choose from. See Figure 15-6. You can even ask Automator to watch what you're doing as you work through the routine once and record your actions. You can then play back or edit your actions.

Apple has a nice tutorial on using Automator at `www.macosxautomation.com/automator/`.

Figure 15-6:
An Automator workflow to send birthday greetings.

Chapter 16

Oops, It's a PC: Running Windows on Your Mac

● ●

In This Chapter

▶ Understanding the different ways to run Windows

▶ Getting Started with BootCamp

▶ Using virtualization to run OS X and Windows

▶ Running Windows using API translation

● ●

*T*he Earth moved on June 6, 2005. Pigs flew. All flights to Hades were canceled because the runway had frozen over. On that day, Apple CEO Steve Jobs announced that Apple would begin using microprocessors from Intel in all its new products.

Since the beginning of the rivalry between Apple and Microsoft, one constant point of contention was the underlying hardware. Microsoft designed its products to run on the Intel *x*86 microprocessor series. Apple used Motorola 680x0 "micros," later switching to the PowerPC, jointly developed by Motorola and IBM. Apple ran ads showing Army tanks guarding a G3 Mac, briefly subject to U.S. arms export regulation, while stating that Windows PCs were harmless.

Jobs concluded that Intel had a better plan for developing the kind of microprocessors Apple needed and did the unthinkable. The transition went surprisingly smoothly. All Macs sold now not only have Intel microprocessors inside but also closely adhere to industry standards for PC design. They are truly PCs. If you take a fancy to the elegant Apple hardware but have eyes for only Windows 7, you can get the Mac you like and just run Windows 7 on it. You do have to buy a Windows 7 license separately — an added expense — but otherwise you have just another Windows machine.

The real win for Mac owners is having the ability to run, quite easily, both Mac OS X and Windows applications on the same Mac. The tricky part is choosing which of several methods exist for doing this. You have three main candidates. Here's a quick rundown (I explain each one in more detail in this chapter):

  ✔ **Dual-booting:** You pick your poison when you boot up your computer: OS X or Windows. Dual-booting capability is built into OS X, but, again, you need to obtain a Windows license. Apple named this technology *Boot Camp.*

  ✔ **Virtualization:** Run both operating systems at the same time and switch between them effortlessly. OS X and Windows play nicely together. Two vendors now offer this solution: Parallels.com and VMware.com.

  ✔ **API translation:** Run Windows applications on your Mac without installing Windows. This method doesn't yet work for all applications, but if you need to run only a few applications or games that are on the "okay" list, you save money and aggravation by not buying and installing Windows. See "CodeWeavers — Wine on a Mac," later in this chapter.

Pulling the Rabbit Out of the Hat

Magic starts with understanding the obvious. How can you run both OS X and Windows? Well, if you bought a Mac and still have your old PC, it's easy — just turn them both on. You have the situation shown in Figure 16-1. I labeled one computer a Mac and one a Dell, but the second one can be any Windows PC. Indeed, as I just mentioned, because your new Mac is a PC, the computer on the right can be another Mac.

Figure 16-1:
Two computers, two operating systems.

Mac

Dell

If you don't care about spending money, you can buy two Macs, leave OS X on one, and replace OS X with Windows on the other. You'd be in the same situation as shown in Figure 16-2, which isn't much different from Figure 16-1.

When you install an operating system on a computer, it's stored on your hard drive. Well, you can have two (or more) hard drives and install a different operating system on each one. You can then tell your Mac (and your PC) from which hard drive you want to *boot* (start up).

Figure 16-2: Two Macs, two operating systems.

Mac 1   Mac 2

You don't even need two physical drives. You can use Disk Utility to split or *partition* your hard drive into two (or more) sections, called *volumes*. From then on, the computer considers each volume a separate hard drive, and you can install different operating systems on each volume, with only one physical hard drive. This situation is depicted in Figure 16-3.

Why can't I run OS X on a Dell?

You may be wondering, "If Macs are just like any other PC, why can't I run OS X on a Dell or an HP or any other Windows box that doesn't come from Apple?" It's a good question. And, it has two answers. First, some components in the Windows PC probably require drivers that aren't available for OS X. Windows drivers don't work in OS X. Apple makes drivers only for the components it uses in making Macs. This reason prevents cross-use only to a point. You find overlap in components, and some people are skilled enough to make the necessary drivers, at least for the more popular configurations of Windows PCs, and make them available. If you want an unsupported, possibly unreliable, possibly illegal installation, I won't say which Google search to try.

The other reason is that Apple doesn't want you to run OS X on a Windows box — at least for now. Apple makes money selling the complete package: hardware and software. At the moment, it isn't ready to license OS X for other computers — it may never be — and it certainly doesn't want people to pirate OS X. So Apple has built tests into OS X that can detect a non-Apple PC. Exactly how closely guarded a secret is it? The company has even applied for patents on certain techniques for concealing the methods they use.

One benefit of having OS X run only on Apple hardware is that Apple doesn't require registration for each new OS X installation. Microsoft, by contrast, requires such registration in its Windows Genuine Advantage program, and changes to a PC's configuration can trigger a request to reregister.

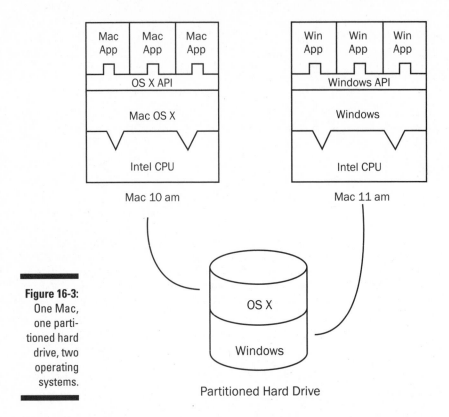

Figure 16-3:
One Mac, one partitioned hard drive, two operating systems.

At 10:00 a.m., you boot your Mac in OS X to check your mail and search the Web for information you need for a presentation you're working on. At 11 a.m., you reboot into Windows to run some corporate applications that require Internet Explorer. At 11:30, you reboot into OS X to finish that presentation in Keynote. It's a tad tedious, but it all works.

Getting Started with Boot Camp

Boot Camp is included with Mac OS X 10.6 (Snow Leopard) and the earlier 10.5 (Leopard). To use it, you need these two items:

- ✔ An Intel Mac with at least 10GB of free hard drive space
- ✔ A bona fide installation disc for Microsoft Windows XP (Service Pack 2 or later, Home or Professional), Windows Vista, or Windows 7

After you install Windows by using Boot Camp, you select which operating system you want, Windows or OS X, by holding down the Option key (the Alt key if you're using a Windows keyboard) while starting up. If you don't hold down the option key, you get OS X, unless you change the default, by selecting ⌘➪System preferences➪Startup Disk. I would include a screen shot of Boot Camp in action, but you already know what Windows looks like.

Virtualize Me

Dual-booting is helpful if you need to use Windows only every so often. Dual-booting can grow old fast if you need to switch several times a day. Wouldn't it be wonderful if you could run both operating systems at the same time and switch between them as easily as you switch between applications in OS X? The technology that makes such a switch possible has been around since the 1960s, but it has taken off in the past few years and has become one of the hottest topics in computing: *virtualization.*

With virtualization, an extra layer, a *hypervisor,* is inserted between the operating system and the computer. Operating systems include *supervisor* software, so the term *hypervisor* was invented to connote something with even more authority than a supervisor. The hypervisor's role is to divide the CPU's attention between two or more virtual machines, each with its own operating system. This concept is shown schematically in Figure 16-4. Each virtual machine looks to its operating system as though it had a complete, unvarnished CPU all to itself. The hypervisor ensures that each virtual machine gets a fair share of the real CPU's resources and decides which operating system gets to appear on the real computer's display and where to direct mouse and keyboard actions.

Figure 16-4: In virtualized computing, each OS thinks it owns the lone CPU.

In the following sections, you find out about the pros and cons of virtualization as well as about programs you can use to add this hypervisor to your system. The two virtualization solutions for OS X are Parallels from Parallels.com and VMware Fusion from VMware.com, which is owned by EMC Corporation. I explain both products in more detail later in this section.

The pros and cons of virtualization

Virtualization is the most convenient solution to running Windows on a Mac. Both operating systems run at the same time, and you can quickly switch back and forth, with no rebooting. Virtualization also supports a wide variety of operating systems. You want MS-DOS or OS/2 on your Mac? No problem.

Virtualization has these disadvantages:

- It's the most expensive solution to running Windows on a Mac because you must buy the virtualization package and obtain a Windows license.

- The hypervisor layer causes a small performance penalty, though special hardware, known as Intel Virtualization Technology (VT-x), in the Intel Core processors used in Macs is designed to speed virtualization.

- You have to deal with two different operating systems.

- It discourages you from making the leap to OS X, because the more familiar Windows programs are always easily available.

- Peripheral support may be less than ideal.

Parallels

Parallels is the first company to sell virtualization for OS X. Its product, Parallels Desktop, runs on any Intel Mac, though Parallels recommends having 1GB of RAM or more and 15GB of free hard drive space. It supports a wide range of guest operating systems, 32- and 64-bit, including the ones in this list:

- Most versions of Microsoft Windows, starting with 3.1, 98, Me, NT Server, Server 2000, Server 2003, Server 2008, XP, Vista, and Windows 7

- Many popular Linux distributions, including CentOS, Debian, Fedora Core, Mandriva, Red Hat, SUSE, Ubuntu, and Xandrox

- FreeBSD 4 and 5

- The legendary IBM OS/2 Warp 4.5

- Sun Solaris 9 and 10

- MS-DOS 6.22

Parallels has a Parallels Transporter feature that migrates your existing PC to the Mac, which greatly simplifies the process of getting on the Mac. It can also use a Boot Camp partition if you have previously created one.

Perhaps the sweetest feature of Parallels Desktop is Coherence, which lets you run Windows applications from the Mac desktop as though they were Mac applications. You don't even have to look at Windows. You can even drag and drop files between the two operating systems. Windows apps show up on the OS X Dock with a *W* symbol, indicating their Windows origin.

Parallels offers a separate tool, Compressor, that the company claims reduces the size of a virtual machine stored on your hard drive by 50 percent or more, saving disk space and improving performance.

Parallels has support for USB 2.0, Windows 3D and DirectX 9. You can even use the built-in camera on your Mac. See `http://kb.parallels.com/en/5028`.

VMware Fusion

VMware largely started the *x*86 virtualization business in 1998. The company is a leading supplier of virtualization products, such as its VMware Workstation, in the Windows and Linux enterprise markets. Its virtualization product for the Mac, VMware Fusion, is based on the same proven technology. So, even though VMware entered the OS X market a little later than Parallels, it brings along considerable depth of experience, supporting over 60 guest operating systems. Virtual machines created with other VMware products can run on the Mac, and similarly, virtual machines created with VMware Fusion on the Mac can run on other systems. VMware has a Virtual Appliance Marketplace, where you can try one of hundreds of preconfigured virtual solutions on your Mac.

One neat feature allows you to take a snapshot of your VMware virtual machine when you have it set up the way you like it. You can then roll back to that configuration with a single click whenever you want. You can copy and paste text between Windows and Mac applications and drag and drop files from one to the other. VMware also offers full USB 2.0 support and can run some games that depend on DirectX 9.0. VMware has similar installation requirements as Parallels Desktop.

Choosing between Parallels and VMware is tough. They're both good products, and both offer free trial versions, so check out both products. If you work in an organization that uses other VMware products, that might tip the decision in favor of VMware.

Imitation, the Sincerest Form of Flattery

One problem exists with both the dual-boot and the virtualization approaches: You need a copy of Windows. That's an added expense, and it means that you have one more operating system to maintain, update, and defrag, for example. You probably just want to run some Windows-only applications. Suppose that you could sneak them onto your Mac without having to install the whole Windows boat? You can do that, too — sort of. I say "sort of" because it works with only certain Windows applications, though the list is growing.

Why running Windows applications will (or won't) work

To understand how this approach works, it helps to first consider why it's a problem. Windows programs run on the same Intel microprocessors as newer Macs. So why can't you just insert a Windows program disc in your Mac and start it up? The reason is that all applications have to talk to the operating system to receive basic services, such as opening files or being notified whenever the user clicks a mouse button or presses a key. For programmers who create applications, an operating system is nothing more than a giant catalog of services they can call. Hundreds of services exist. The geek phrase for the collection of services an operating system provides is *application program interfaces,* or APIs. Unfortunately, the APIs that Mac OS X provides are set up quite differently from the ones Windows provides. They speak different languages, in effect.

Although the languages are different, the underlying concepts are the same. Some people came up with the idea of building a layer of software that would sit on top of one operating system and provide the APIs that a program for a second operating system would expect. This approach is illustrated in Figure 16-5, showing a compatibility layer known as Wine. On a case-by-case basis, translating each operating system service isn't hard. Intercept a request address to the second operating system to open a file, and convert it to the open-file request in the host system. What's hard is getting it all exactly right for the hundreds of services involved.

The Wine project, www.winehq.org, was originally aimed at running Windows programs, particularly Microsoft Office, on Intel-based Linux computers. Microsoft doesn't offer Office for Linux. The Wine project started in 1993, and people have been working on it ever since. One problem is that every time Microsoft releases a new version of Windows, dozens of new APIs must be added and others may have changed in subtle ways. And, Microsoft doesn't always document its APIs as thoroughly as Wine developers might want, so a certain amount of trial and error exists in the Wine development process.

Figure 16-5:
API
translation:
translating
calls to one
API into
calls to
another.

CodeWeavers — Wine on a Mac

Mac OS X shares a common Unix heritage with Linux. So when Apple announced it was switching to Intel microprocessors, it created the possibility of running Wine on Macs. It was such an attractive idea that a company, CodeWeavers.com, decided to make a business of creating the OS X version of Wine. The company offers three products:

✔ CrossOver Mac, for Windows applications, except games

✔ CrossOver Games, for selected Windows games, including most of the Steam repertoire

✔ CrossOver Pro, includes both of the above plus additional support

The good news is that these solutions cost a lot less than a Windows license. The bad news, which CodeWeavers freely admits, is that they work fully with only a few Windows programs, though the list is expanding.

At the time I wrote this book, CrossOverMac officially supported the following applications:

✔ Microsoft Office 2007, 2003, XP, 2000, and 97 in Word, Excel, PowerPoint, and Outlook. Access is supported only in Office 2000.

✔ In addition to Office, CrossOverMac supports Microsoft Internet Explorer 6, Microsoft Project, Microsoft Visio, and Quicken.

CrossOverGames officially supports these games:

✔ *EVE Online*

✔ *Guild Wars*

> ✔ *Prey*
>
> ✔ Steam games, including *Call of Duty 2*, *Civilization IV*, *Counterstrike, Counterstrike: Source*, *Half-Life 2*, *Max Payne 2*, *Peggle Extreme*, *Team Fortress 2*, *World of Warcraft*

Many other programs work to a usable degree, and improvements are continually being made. You can check the status of the program or programs you're interested in by visiting the CodeWeavers compatibility center. The company even has a process by which you can influence its priorities in getting applications to work. See `www.codeweavers.com/compatibility`.

As a Windows user, you probably already have several of the supported programs and games. Because CodeWeavers offers a free trial period, you have little to lose — except some time — and a lot to gain by downloading the trial versions and checking out your favorite apps and games. You may even find that old games that no longer run on the Windows software you use come back to life on your new Mac.

One other important use for CrossOver exists. If your organization has Windows applications and you want them to work on Macs, CodeWeavers can test the application to see whether it works on CrossOver, and if not, attempt to make it work by fixing problems the way developers fix any bug. CodeWeavers even has tools to help you. Because a free trial period is available, you have little to lose in giving it a try.

Security issues

It's neat to have Windows at your disposal on your Mac, but remember that it's still Windows. You should follow all security and antivirus guidelines recommended for Windows on a PC, including enabling Windows Update and having up-to-date antivirus software installed. As a former Windows user, you know the drill.

Be wise and retrieve your mail and do your Web surfing in OS X, and restrict Internet access on the Windows side to situations where it's needed, such as accessing sites that you already know about and trust and that require Internet Explorer or ActiveX. You should also pick a password for Windows that's different from the one you use on the Mac. See Chapter 10 for password suggestions.

One advantage of running Windows on a Mac is that you can keep important files on the Mac side, using shared folders. Then, if your Windows machine becomes infected by nasty malware, you can simply delete the Windows virtual disk and restore a copy that you saved when you were sure it was in a clean state, or simply reinstall Windows from the original disc. Virus hunters use virtualization for this very reason.

Part V
Specialty Switching Scenarios

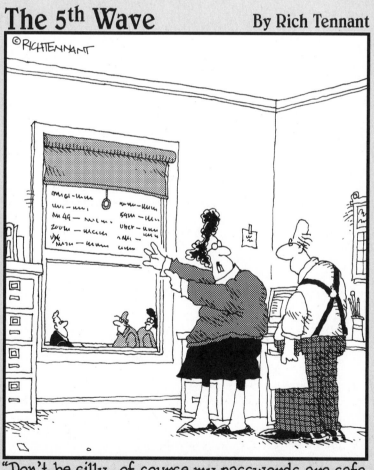

"Don't be silly - of course my passwords are safe.
I keep them written on my window, but then I
pull the shade if anyone walks in the room."

In this part . . .

We're all different and the problems and opportunities we encounter when we switch computer systems depends on our situation and needs. In this part, I deal with topics that may not interest everyone who switches. The first chapter of this part covers kids, seniors, and people with disabilities. Then I discuss using Macs in business settings, the heartland of Windows dominance. The last chapter in this part dives a bit deeper into OS X and introduces the Unix layer underneath all the graphical glitz. (Folks who are switching from computer operating systems other than Windows XP might want to check out the Bonus Chapter on this book's Web site at www. dummies.com/go/switchingtoamacfd2e. In particular, users of older Mac operating systems can find upgrading to OS X challenging.)

Chapter 17

Switching with the Whole Family in Mind

*B*uying a computer for home use involves a special set of challenges. In a work environment, personal computing may just mean that each employee has his own machine. But in a family setting, *personal* means much more. Computers become part of us, woven into our daily routine and even into our psyches. The choices we make in which computers we give our children and how we set them up can affect their development. For an elderly person or someone with a disability, having the right computer can improve their quality of life.

In this chapter, you find out about features and software on your Mac that help kids, parents, and the whole family enjoy their home computer that much more.

Macs for Kids

Kids take to computers like raccoons to suburbia. It may not be the environment that nature intended, but kids quickly become comfortable — perhaps too comfortable — in front of a screen.

Check out these positive factors about computers for kids. Computers do the following:

✔ Provide an outlet for artistic expression and creativity

✔ Offer information about every topic imaginable (much of it true)

✔ Let kids chat with friends and be at home at the same time, without running up minutes on their cellphone accounts

✔ Offer opportunities for personal contact with new people and cultures

✔ Help develop and improve reading, writing, and language skills

✔ Support kids with special needs and their parents

You find some big negative aspects as well:

✔ Video games can be unbelievably addictive, especially for boys.

✔ Time spent in front of a computer is time not spent doing chores or homework or engaging in ordinary play.

✔ Our kids are getting fat from a lack of physical activity. TV is the main culprit, but computers are catching up.

✔ Kids generally can't resist the temptation to download music and videos without paying for them.

✔ It's also too tempting to copy material from the Web and pass it off as their own schoolwork.

✔ Like suburbia must seem to raccoons, the Internet is littered with "garbage cans."

Establishing parental control

If you're switching your kids to a Mac, you have a unique opportunity to regain some control over their computer use. You have to act fast, though. Your kids probably know more about computers than you do, so you should set things up correctly from the beginning. I go over the steps in more detail here than for other topics because establishing control over your kids' computer use is vital and because I know how harried and time constrained most parents are.

The first thing you must do is make yourself the administrator for your kids' Mac. *You* should be the one to work through the start-up sequence described in Chapter 4 and become the first user of the computer. If you're adding your kids' accounts to the Mac you use, you have in effect already done this.

Next, set up a separate account for each child who will use the computer. If you have more than one child and are giving each one her own Mac (what good parents you are!), you should still give each kid an account on each machine. That way, if one child borrows an older sibling's Mac, she still has the restrictions you impose.

Computers and young children

I'm not convinced that young kids (the fourth grade or younger) need to have computer access. Young kids need to relate to the real world and, especially, to other people. They do that by playing with toys, kids, and adults. Computers are mostly a distraction from the task of being children. Perhaps you can make an argument that computers are less passive babysitters than television. But neither is particularly desirable, and kid computer use should be supervised anyway.

Think long and hard before introducing your kids to computers, and make careful choices about what kind of programs and Web sites they're exposed to.

Setting up accounts is easy. Follow these steps:

1. Select ➪System Preferences and click the Accounts icon.

It's the one with a silhouette of two heads. You see the pane shown in Figure 17-1.

Figure 17-1:
The Accounts system preferences pane.

2. Click the plus sign in the lower-left corner to add a new account.

You may have to click the Lock icon first and enter your password.

3. When you see a pane that asks for the name and password of the new account, as shown in Figure 17-2, fill in the name and password you want your child to have.

New Account: Managed with Parental Controls

Name: Billy

Short Name: billy

Password: ••••••••

Verify: ••••••••

Password Hint: 3rd grade teacher
(Recommended)

☐ Turn on FileVault protection

(Cancel) (Create Account)

Figure 17-2:
The New
Account
pane.

Here are some tips for choosing names and passwords specifically for kids:

- Because the account name and short name are used in OS X for many purposes and may show up during Internet use, *do not include your kids' last name on the account.* Billy or Billy R should do fine.

- In Chapter 10, I emphasize the security value of using random passwords. If anything, security is more important for kids on the Internet. You can ask OS X to suggest a short, 8- to 10-character, random password of letters and numbers by clicking the Key icon next to the password field.

- An alternative for kids who are very young is to combine a name and number from two different parts of their lives, such as a character from a favorite story and their room number in school.

- Tape your child's password to his bed until the child memorizes it. It doesn't take long.

- While you're at it, help your child make up a separate password for all the junk Internet sites that require registration. Some sites reportedly collect passwords and offer them for sale for nefarious purposes.

4. **Because this account is for a child, select New Account⇨Managed with Parental Controls.**

Other account options include Standard and Administrator. Don't give your kids administrative privileges. They will pester you from time to time, though, to enter your password so that they can do something that requires these privileges, such as installing downloaded software. Trust me: You want to know about these events. Ask questions about how the software will be used, and ask to visit the Web site from which it came. Don't be afraid to veto the installation.

5. **Click the Create Account button.**

   When you're done, you see the Accounts system preferences pane again, shown in Figure 17-3, this time with the new account highlighted.

Figure 17-3:
Billy's account is ready for parental controls.

6. **Select the account you just created, if it's not already selected, and select the Enable Parental Controls check box.**

7. **Click the Open Parental Controls button.**

   The Parental Controls System pane appears, as shown in Figure 17-4. You see tabs for several other panes:

   • System

   • Content

   • Mail & iChat

   • Time Limits

   • Logs

8. **Each pane has settings that let you sculpt your child's computer and Internet usage. Using the information in the sections that follow, set up the controls for the account.**

   By logging on as the administrator under your own account, you can return to the Parental Controls settings to adjust them, if needed. Just open System Preferences from the Apple menu.

Figure 17-4:
The
Parental
Controls
System
pane.

The System pane

The first item in the Parental Controls System pane (refer to Figure 17-4) lets you require Simple Finder for this account. Simple Finder replaces the usual OS X desktop with a screen that contains big, square buttons. Each button launches an application from the list of those you permit. Many applications provide reduced menus when Simple Finder is in use. Simple Finder removes much of the complexity of the OS X interface and makes the computer more of an appliance.

Below that choice is an area where you can limit the applications this user can launch to only those you specify. Simply deselect those you don't want to allow access to. At the bottom of the pane is a series of check boxes that lets you give this user specific privileges:

- **Can Administer Printers:** This option might be a good idea for kids who are a little older. They might learn enough to help you with printer problems.

- **Can Burn CDs and DVDs:** Wait on this one until you set clear guidelines on what your kids can and cannot share with friends.

- **Can Change Password:** Knowing your kid's password makes it easier to check what's on the computer, but you have other ways to do this.

- **Can Modify the Dock:** Let young kids mess with the Dock, and they pester you to find the stuff they dragged off it (just to watch it go poof). Don't select this check box.

The Content pane

OS X offers a number of options to limit what content your kids can see, using the Content pane depicted in Figure 17-5. One example is the Hide Profanity in Dictionary check box. However, at some stage in your child's development, it might be better for her to find out what words mean from a dictionary rather than on the street. You can also ask OS X to try to limit access to adult sites automatically. If you then click the Customize button, you can list sites you want added or specifically banned. The third option restricts your kids to only those sites you specifically choose.

Figure 17-5:
The Parental Controls Content pane.

The rest of the Content pane offers you some choices about what kind of content your kids get to see online:

- ✔ **Allow Unrestricted Access to Websites:** Select this check box only for older kids. You can still check the logs to see where they're going.

- ✔ **Try to Limit Access to Adult Websites Automatically:** This option uses filters that attempt to determine what is and isn't kid appropriate. The filters aren't foolproof, occasionally letting bad stuff in and, at the same time, limiting access to sites that are harmless. And, you find a third class of sites to consider: those that provide sound information on health, sex, and what's happening to kids' bodies as they mature. If you select this check box, a Customize button appears. Click it and you see a pane with two text areas. In the top one, you specify sites that are always allowed, perhaps a site you reviewed with health information for kids. The bottom one lists sites that are never allowed, a trickier proposition because so many exist.

✔ **Allow Access to Only These Websites:** This option may be the sanest one for the younger set. You can surf sites first and add ones that you deem appropriate. You can even add Safari bookmarks and folders to this list.

The Mail & iChat pane

As I mention in Chapter 8, your Mac is an excellent communication tool. Your kids will figure out that much faster than you do. The Mail & iChat pane, shown in Figure 17-6, lets you decide to whom they can talk to by way of e-mail or instant messaging (IM). Note that the controls in this pane apply to only Apple Mail and iChat. If your kids can download another mail or IM program, such as AOL AIM, all bets are off. Some mail programs, such as Yahoo! Mail and Gmail, require only a Web browser. So, if you want your white list restrictions enforced, you must limit the programs your children can download and also block access to e-mail sites.

Figure 17-6:
The
Parental
Controls
Mail & iChat
pane.

This pane also lets you specify an e-mail address — yours, presumably — where notifications are sent when someone not on the white list attempts to contact your kid in Mail or iChat.

The Time Limits pane

I love this feature. Other programs for limiting kids' use are often too complex for mere parents to understand, much less set up and explain to their kids. This one is easy. You have two types of control, as shown in Figure 17-7. One limits the amount of time a child can use the computer each day. The other blocks any usage after bedtime. And, you find two sets of controls for each limit: one for weekdays and the other for the weekends. It's simple, and it works.

Figure 17-7:
The easy-to-use Time Limits pane.

The Logs pane

OS X keeps track of what your kids are up to online. You can see the logs by periodically visiting this pane, as shown in Figure 17-8.

You can choose to see logged activity for Web sites your child visited, Web sites he attempted to visit but access was blocked, applications he used, and iChat conversations he engaged in.

Setting limits

Having all these tools at a parent's disposal is great, but setting limits can be hard. It's always easier to start with more restricted access and add time and privileges as the child matures and demonstrates responsibility. For very young children, not having computer access may be the easiest starting point.

Discuss reasonable computer limits with other parents in your circle. A group consensus can be easier to enforce. And, pay attention to your own computer usage. Kids learn by example.

Figure 17-8:
The
Parental
Controls
Logs pane.

Keeping kids safe online

Incidents in which kids get hurt and that have any connection to the Internet always get great play in the press. Incidents in which kids get hurt on the street or at the playground often don't. Still, your kids need to develop some online smarts about online conduct. Here are some tips you can share with them. Avoid heavy-handed lectures with threats of draconian punishment, though. You want your child to feel safe coming to you if she encounters anything that feels creepy.

Here are some basic guidelines that you should review periodically with your kids:

- ✔ **Keep your personal information private.** Consider your last name, address, and phone number private information that's not to be shared with people you meet online. Be careful if the online person asks a lot of questions about you, such as where you go to school or what your parents do for a living.

- ✔ **Protect your password by keeping it to yourself.** No one should ever need it.

- ✔ **Be aware that people often aren't who they say they are.** Sometimes, people on the Internet pretend to be quite different from who they truly are. A child may pretend to be an adult, or an adult might pretend to be a kid. Someone may pretend to be a teacher or doctor or police officer when they aren't. A boy can even pretend to be a girl, or vice versa.

- ✔ **Ask your parents or guardian before meeting someone in person.** Never agree to see someone in person whom you first met online without asking your parents first.

- ✔ **Remember that people can find out a lot about your family on the Internet.** If someone you don't know says that he's a friend of your family and asks you to go with him, don't go just because he seems to know a lot about you and your parents.

- ✔ **Let your parents or a trusted adult be your confidant.** If someone is making you feel uncomfortable or scaring you, tell your parents. Especially be sure to tell your parents if the person asks you not to. Don't close the chat window or turn off the computer.

Social networking sites

Social networking Web sites, such as MySpace.com, Facebook.com, and Twitter.com, have integrated themselves into the social lives of teenagers. Facebook, originally aimed at high school and college students, has more than 200 million active users. (It had 16 million when I wrote the first edition of this book.) MySpace has more than 100 million users. Facebook and MySpace encourage their members to build profiles with personal information, including accounts and photographs of recent activities. Members designate other members as "friends" who then gain additional access to their page. Both sites have privacy options that members can select that can limit which information nonfriends can see and which information will be revealed about them in a search. Members use the site to send messages to other users.

MySpace requires members to be at least 14 years old and sets privacy restrictions on members 16 and under. Restrictions are also in place for members over 18 connecting with the youngest members. However, kids and adults can always lie about their age. Potential employers and colleges might also look at candidate profiles on these sites.

Young people start using these social networking sites about the same time as they stop listening to what their parents say. Still, it's worth having a conversation with your teen about the short-term and long-term privacy concerns and the dangers of meeting, in person, people you know only online. At some point, they won't bring you along, but you can still implore them to at least bring along a friend for the first meeting.

Also see Chapter 14 for more on whether parents should "friend" their kids.

Downloading music

Another aspect of kid culture on the Internet, downloading music without paying for it, continues to generate controversy. The recording industry blames the practice for a slowdown in sales. Others question this and point to high prices for CDs and a lack of compelling product as the cause.

The Recording Industry Association of America (RIAA) has managed to shut down free file-sharing sites such as Napster and Grokster early, through legal action, but other peer-to-peer systems, such as BitTorrent.com, which have no central indexing service — and which are used for other purposes — have proven more difficult to stop. So the RIAA has started taking legal action against individual downloaders and their parents. Although some people have fought these suits, most are forced to accept expensive settlement terms.

If I give my kids a Mac, won't they be unprepared for a Windows world?

I've heard this objection more than once. For now and the foreseeable future, the working world is dominated by Windows. Many colleges require entering students to have a Windows laptop — though some prefer Macs. One answer, of course, is that Macs can run Windows (see Chapter 16). So, if your child takes his MacBook to school, he can use whatever software is required. But you have a better response. For years, Microsoft has followed Apple's lead in introducing new interfaces and features. Several reviewers have remarked on the similarities between Windows 7 and OS X. So, giving your kids a Mac may be the *best* way to prepare them for the Windows of the future.

Whatever you think of the RIAA tactics and their justification, much can be said for staying out of their gun sights. Most people agree that performers deserve to be compensated for their work. Giving your kid an iPod and a computer without giving him the means to pay for songs is asking for trouble. You might give a monthly allowance at the iTunes Store, perhaps based on chores or schoolwork. Go to the iTunes Store and click the iTunes Gifts link in the Quick Links section.

Finding software for kids

Kids have lots to do with just the iLife suite supplied with all Macs. You can buy or download many other titles for free. However, adult supervision is required whenever software is downloaded from the Internet. One source for children's software that runs on Macs is the Apple Macintosh Products Guide, at `http://guide.apple.com/uscategories/kids.lasso`. You can also check out the education page at `http://guide.apple.com/uscategories/education.lasso`. Many major Web sites have special sections for kids. And, a Google search for *kid-safe Web sites* turns up several guides to this type of site. But no substitute exists for checking out new sites yourself before letting your kids visit.

Macs for Seniors

The extraterrestrials who monitor our television signals must be certain that no one over 40 buys Apple products because no one older ever shows up in its TV commercials. The truth is that people over 40 are *more* likely to buy Macs. One reason may be that older consumers seek quality over price. They remember how difficult it was to use computers, and they know who made it easy.

A still-older generation, composed of the parents of the 40s and 50s set, in many cases has never used computers. Personal computers offer many ways to improve the lives of these seniors, and Macs are the ideal choice for them. Although some seniors start riding motorcycles and take up scuba diving, most have a harder time picking up new skills.

If you're buying a Mac for your parents, consider that you may end up as their main source of technical support. Buying them a computer that's easier to set up, easier to show them how to use, and less likely to require help with problems such as viruses and malware will save you time and money in the long run.

More importantly, giving your folks a computer that's easy to use and less trouble-prone makes them more likely to use it and derive benefit from it. Seniors can benefit by using a Mac in these areas:

- ✔ **E-mail and instant messaging:** These are great ways to stay in touch with friends and family, particularly grandchildren who are away at school.

- ✔ **Video iChat:** This feature can enable seniors to be part of family events, even if they can no longer travel easily. During a recent visit to my cousins in California, their new granddaughter ate her first solid food as the other grandparents, in New Jersey, watched by way of iChat on my cousins' iMac.

- ✔ **Voice over IP (VoIP) services:** These can help keep phone bills down, especially for relatives in the "old country."

- ✔ **Social networking:** Sites such as Facebook aren't just for college students any more. Seniors are finding them a helpful place to connect with old friends and make new ones, by posting photos of grandchildren, vacation trips, and other mementos.

- ✔ **Health maintenance and medical condition sites:** Online support groups exist for almost every medical condition imaginable.

- ✔ **Internet shopping:** Seniors who have limited mobility can be empowered by shopping on their own.

- ✔ **Disability sites:** The Mac's clean interface can make it easier for seniors with disabilities to use. I talk more about Macs and people with disabilities in the next section of this chapter.

A useful way to preserve family history is to digitize old family photos by using a scanner or commercial service and asking your parents to annotate them in iPhoto. If typing is a problem, you can put the photos in a slide show and have your parents record their comments in GarageBand as they step through the photos.

Simple Finder, which I mention earlier in this chapter as a way to make Macs easier for young children to operate, can perform the same function for seniors who may be unfamiliar with computers. To give your elder family member a complete guide to using a Mac and its software, written with the needs of a computing beginner in mind, check out *Macs For Seniors For Dummies,* by Mark Chambers (Wiley Publishing).

Determining which model to buy

For seniors who travel regularly, a basic MacBook is an inexpensive, do-everything companion. By seeking hotel accommodations that include Internet access, seniors can stay in touch anywhere in the world. Using their digital camera and iSight, iPhoto, and iWeb, they can share their travel experiences with family and friends almost as these events happen.

For those who mostly stay at home, the iMac is hard to beat. It's a single unit, so no wires will become accidentally disconnected, resulting in panicked service calls to you. The low-end model has everything seniors need.

If seniors enjoy sharing photos of their grandkids, an iPhone or iPod touch is another useful gift, allowing them to always carry a whole library of photos with them.

Speeding photos to the grandparents

Perhaps the best application for grandparents is the iPhoto photocasting capability. You put the latest photos of your kids into an iPhoto album and click the Photocast This Album button. The album is uploaded to your MobileMe account, where it's "published" for authorized subscribers.

Assuming that the grandparents' computer subscribes to your family photo feed, a simple one-time setup, the photos are automatically downloaded to their iPhoto library, where they can be watched immediately. The photos can even be displayed as their screen saver. As you add new photos to the photocast album, they're automatically uploaded and then downloaded.

To subscribe to a photocast, in iPhoto, choose File⇨Subscribe to Photocast. Fill in the address of the photocast when you're prompted. Alternatively, you can click a link to the photocast on your Web page or in an e-mail message.

You make a photocast display as the screen saver by following these steps:

1. **Select ⌘⇨System Preferences.**
2. **Click the Desktop & Screen Saver icon in System Preferences.**
3. **Click the Screen Saver tab.**

4. **In the list that appears on the left side of the Screen Saver pane, shown in Figure 17-9, scroll down to Pictures and then click MobileMe and RSS.**

5. **Click the Options button.**

6. **In the pane that appears, select the feeds you want to display in the screen saver.**

   You can reorder the feeds shown by dragging them to the new order.

   Your latest photos of the kids now appear on the grandparents' Mac as soon as you add them to your photocast album in iPhoto.

Figure 17-9:
The Screen
Saver pane.

Macs for Specific Needs

OS X provides an array of accessibility features that enable people to use the Mac in ways that are different from — or more comfortable than — the standard setup of reading onscreen at the default sizes and using the keyboard and mouse to give computer commands. You control most of these features from the Universal Access pane in System Preferences. (The lone exception is VoiceOver, the Apple screen reader, which has its own setup utility in the Utilities folder, but that utility can also be easily accessed from the Universal Access Seeing pane. See Figure 17-10.) The following sections introduce the available options and describe how they work.

Figure 17-10:
The
Universal
Access
Seeing
pane.

Setting up the screen when you have limited vision

When you click the Universal Access icon, you see the Seeing pane (refer to Figure 17-10), where you can control features that aid people with vision difficulties. Note that the pane appears in large type to avoid the Catch-22 problem where someone with limited vision can't use the tool to increase the type size because the tool's type size is too small.

Here's a quick introduction to the available features:

- **VoiceOver:** This pane turns VoiceOver on or off and can send you to the VoiceOver setup utility. I explain VoiceOver in more detail in the next section.

- **Zoom:** When you enable the handy Zoom feature, you can magnify the screen by pressing ⌘+Option+=. Pressing ⌘+Option+- (⌘+Option+hyphen) reverses the magnification.

- **Display:** In this section, you can change the screen from black on white to white on black, if it helps. Move the slider to adjust the contrast, if you like.

- **Enable Access for Assistive Devices check box:** Selecting this check box enables your Mac to work with a variety of assistive technologies and software packages designed to help users with special computer-use needs. For more information, see the Macintosh Product Guide at `http://guide.apple.com/uscategories/assisttech.lasso`.

Listening rather than reading

The Apple VoiceOver screen reader was designed to make using a Mac easier by speaking the contents of the screen. Although that may seem to be a simple and obvious idea, for someone trying to use a computer in this way, a poorly designed screen reader is almost useless. A user wants the screen reader to speak the text of interest at the moment and as little else as possible. The user also wants to be able to speed up the reading as much as possible without losing intelligibility. Otherwise, work becomes painfully slow.

Therefore, it isn't surprising that VoiceOver comes with a plethora of customizable options. It also offers several different voices, including Alex, a voice that's engineered to work well when it's sped up. Figure 17-11 shows the VoiceOver Utility Verbosity screen.

Figure 17-11:
The
VoiceOver
Utility
Verbosity
screen.

You find eight options in the sidebar, each with many more options:

✔ **General** lets you control portable preferences.

✔ **Verbosity** controls how much VoiceOver says in various situations, such as when it encounters a misspelled word. For example, a user might want a different behavior when reading a memo she received versus proofreading her own writing.

✔ **Speech** lets you choose among some two dozen virtual speakers and adjust their settings. Most are more fun than productive. Voices with real names, such as Alex or Kathy, tend to be more suited for serious use than nicknames such as Bubbles. But you can find exceptions. Princess isn't bad, but Albert is. The Pronunciation tab lets you customize how special characters, initialisms, abbreviations, and other elements are spoken.

✔ **Navigation** determines what VoiceOver does as you move around the screen and change focus.

✔ **Web** controls how you hear the content of Web pages — from beginning to end (DOM) or with common elements grouped together for faster scanning.

✔ **Sound** controls sound output.

✔ **Visuals** controls how VoiceOver elements, such as its cursor, are shown onscreen.

✔ **NumPad** lets you assign special functions to the numeric keypad keys.

✔ **Braille** has settings for Braille input and output for people with visual disabilities.

Adjusting settings in the Hearing pane

Compared to the Seeing pane, there's not much to the Hearing pane. A personal computer is controlled primarily by visual cues, anyway. In this pane, you can tell OS X to flash the screen when it issues an alert, a handy feature for those of us with full hearing. You also find a button that opens the Sound System Preferences pane, where you can adjust the volume of your Mac's audio. You can generally do that also by using your keyboard.

Changing how the keyboard works

The Keyboard pane, shown in Figure 17-12, offers settings that can make using a keyboard easier:

Figure 17-12:
The
Universal
Access
Keyboard
pane.

✔ If you have difficulty completing complex key presses, such as the ⌘+Option+= combination for Zoom, mentioned earlier in this chapter, try turning on Sticky Keys. The Sticky Keys option, which is controlled from this pane, lets you press the keys one at a time to effect the combination you want. For example, you first press ⌘, and then Option, and then the equal sign (=). You can also control what feedback OS X gives you when you do this.

✔ Another problem that some people have is unsteady hands; they may accidentally press a needed key more than once. Another option in this pane lets you set a time delay between key presses to reduce this problem.

✔ Note that you can find additional settings related to the keyboard in the Keyboard & Mouse pane of System Preferences.

Speaking of keyboards, a number of specialized keyboards are available to assist with various problems, ranging from repetitive stress injuries to users who can use only one hand. As long as a specialized keyboard uses a USB interface, the keyboard should work on a Mac.

Mousing the way you like

Some people have a hard time using a computer mouse or trackpad. If the default mouse or trackpad setup doesn't work well for you or someone in your household, give the following options in the Mouse & Trackpad pane a try:

✔ **Turn on Mouse Keys:** For people who have trouble using a mouse, Apple provides an alternative, where you move the cursor around the screen by using the numeric keypad. After Mouse Keys is turned on, pressing any digit other than 5 or 0 moves the cursor a short distance in the direction of that key (relative to 5). The 5 key acts like a mouse click. The 0 key acts like press and hold — say, if you want to drag a file to a folder. When you have the file where you want to drop it, press 5 to release the hold.

Mouse Keys work best with a keyboard that has a separate numeric keypad. If you have a laptop or standard sized keyboard and want to make extensive use of this feature, consider adding the Apple Keyboard with Numeric Keypad or an external USB numeric keypad.

Mouse Keys is a feature worth knowing about if your mouse or touchpad is ever unusable and you're in a rush to finish something.

✔ **Increase the mouse cursor size:** Another feature that's located in the Universal Access Mouse & Trackpad pane and that's valuable for all users is the ability to make the mouse cursor arrow bigger. Particularly when it's at high-resolution display settings, you can easily lose that sucker in the desktop clutter.

✔ **Tab to access menus:** You can also eliminate the need for mouse use to access menus. Instead, you press Tab to move between control items and press the arrow keys to select within menus. This option is turned on by using the Keyboard & Mouse window in System Preferences, on the Keyboard Shortcuts tab. The Full Keyboard Access option is at the bottom.

If mice don't work for you, options other than Mouse Keys are available for Macs:

✔ **Trackballs:** Have a smooth, round ball on top that you roll in various directions to control the cursor.

✔ **Touchpads:** Allow you to control the cursor by sliding your finger on a sensitive surface. Apple laptops have touchpads built-in, but you can buy third-party units to use with your desktop setup.

✔ **Graphics tablets:** Have a flat surface with a position-sensing pen. If you use one, you can take advantage of the Apple Inkwell technology, which can turn handwriting into text that you can use in any application.

Again, you should buy one of these with a USB interface. More than one pointing device can be attached and active at the same time. Even if you like using a mouse, having an alternative way to enter text can reduce problems with repetitive stress.

If you use your mouse a lot and feel pain from repetitive stress, one suggestion I've found useful is to move the mouse and mouse pad to the other side of the keyboard so that you use it with your nondominant hand — the left hand, in my case. It takes a little getting used to, but if you're starting to feel fatigued in your dominant hand, it's worth a try.

Chapter 18

Switching Your Business to Macs

Microsoft owns the enterprise desktop. Owns it. Most of Apple's small market share comes from home and educational users. Many large companies have strict Windows-only policies. Lots of business software is available only for Windows. So why even think about using Macs? Why did we kill a bunch of trees to bring you a chapter pushing Macs for businesses?

In this chapter, you find out how Macs can produce a good return on investment for a business, as well as services and products that help small and midsize businesses stay nimble and competitive, with Macs working for them behind the scenes.

Why Use Macs in Your Business?

The cop-out answer is that Macs now run Windows too, as I explain in Chapter 16. That does at least answer the concern about Windows-only software you might need for your business. But by itself, it's not much of a reason. It doesn't make business sense to buy a Mac that may cost a few hundred dollars more and then pay Microsoft for a Vista license, just to get a pretty computer that runs Windows. Sure, iMacs look spiffy in front offices and MacBook Airs turn heads at meetings, but that won't convince the bean counters.

Total cost of ownership

Another common justification given for businesses switching to Macs is *total cost of ownership*. Macs may cost a bit more up front, but savings can be achieved down the road. Here's why:

- ✔ There's no need for antivirus software.
- ✔ Training costs are lower because Macs are easier to use.
- ✔ Support costs are lower because Macs have fewer software problems and users can often fix their own problems.
- ✔ Macs seem to have a longer service life than Windows machines, so they don't need to be replaced as often.

The total cost of ownership argument has some merit. One organization I work with pays over $1,000 per year in support for each Windows PC it owns. Cutting that down would go right to the bottom line.

But the counterargument usually given is that the organization has already made large investments in a Windows-oriented support organization. Firewalls and antivirus and intrusion detectors are already in place. In the short run, adding Macs may increase the cost because any additional support costs are a new expense. Who has time to worry about the long run?

Increased productivity

You can easily count the initial purchase price of computers you buy. Support costs are more difficult to calculate, but a well-run organization has a handle on those as well. The impact of your choice of computer platform on individual worker productivity is much harder to measure. Most organizations don't have expense-tracking codes for "I'm purging viruses," "The network is down," "I can't get the printer to work," or "I'm waiting for tech support to call back." Pesky problems like that don't just eat up time — they sap energy, enthusiasm, and morale.

You get what you pay for

To succeed in the intense competition of a global economy, everything a business does has to stand out from the crowd. Mediocre tools ultimately lead to mediocre work. Your salesperson's PowerPoint presentation will look like every other salesperson's PowerPoint presentation. The huckster with a Mac and a Keynote show will stand out.

Although it's hard to gauge productivity, it's not so hard to measure the effect of improvements. Suppose that working with a Mac increases productivity just 5 percent. (I think it's more.) Sum up the annual pay of each worker who uses a computer. Add in fringe benefits and direct overhead — stuff like the cost of office space and administrative support. Now multiply that number by 0.05. That's how much using Windows costs you each year.

Plays well with Linux

In most organizations, some workers have little or no creative component in their computer work. Surely they don't need a Mac. They may not need Windows, either. A number of Linux distributions can support workers whose main job is data entry or telephone support. Mac OS X and Linux share a Unix heritage and generally work well together. A great deal of Linux software has been ported to Macs, so tools can be used on both platforms. Best of all, you don't need to buy new computers to run Linux. It should run fine on the older PCs you're replacing with Macs.

The only constant in business is change

The best reason to switch to Macs is because computer technology is changing, and it's changing the world along with it. And Apple, not Microsoft, is leading the charge. Microsoft is too busy making money off the way things were. Stay hitched to Microsoft and you'll always be safely in the middle of the pack — except that the middle of the pack is where businesses wither and die.

What are some of these changes? Here's a partial list:

- **Mobile computing:** Our electronic lives are migrating from our desks to our laps and now to our pockets and purses. Some of us feel naked without a live Internet connection at hand. We carry our most important files in our pockets or purses on flash drives. The Apple iPhone and iPod touch have created an integrated mobile computing future where we have all the tools we rely on with us wherever we go.

- **Electronic commerce:** The Internet now drives economic growth and levels the playing field between large and small companies. People who buy online shop online, and word-of-Web drives sales. First impressions of early customers are aggregated by blogs and RSS feeds and spread worldwide. Lapses in quality are magnified. You have to get it right the first time.

✔ **Web 2.0:** The World Wide Web is now a two-way medium. Consumers are spending more of their time viewing content produced by other consumers. A clever YouTube spoof can undo a multimillion-dollar marketing campaign. Speed is of the essence. It can't wait 'til the Monday morning staff meeting.

✔ **Globalization:** Your next competitor could emerge from a country you never heard of. And so could your next technology supplier. And so could your next market.

✔ **Open source business software:** The open source model — which has been quite successful in the development of BSD UNIX, Linux, and Gnu — is being taken up by groups trying to create nonproprietary software systems. These groups are using open standards and open source code to create software that meets basic business needs. The wide adoption of XML as a standard for data interchange has spawned many efforts to create nonproprietary data exchange formats for specific business needs, such as `hr-xml.org` in human resources. As these efforts mature, they provide viable, platform-independent alternatives to expensive software packages.

✔ **Software as a Service (SaaS):** The other new approach to business software is for vendors to host the software on their own servers and sell the services over the Internet on a subscription basis, typically a per-user, per-month fee. This solution reduces the need for in-house hardware and support personnel and allows employees to access the service from remote locations. SaaS systems are accessed by way of standard Web browsers, reducing the importance of being on one operating system versus another.

✔ **Virtualization:** The relationship between computers and operating systems is no longer monogamous. One operating system can span several processor cores, and one processor can support several operating systems at one time. The impetus for standardizing on the operating system you've always used makes less business sense. Pick the best tool for the job. You can find an introduction to virtualization in Chapter 16.

✔ **Computer crime:** In the good old days, malware, such as computer viruses and worms, was created by hobbyist hackers interested in the intellectual challenge. Now such activities are a big, if illicit, business and a significant distraction for legitimate businesses. Direct costs occur in terms of data theft and denial of service and the indirect costs of cleanup, damage remediation, and reporting. Finally, there's the hard-to-measure loss of customer trust and its impact on sales. The malware-free Apple track record has saved its users expense and can instill confidence in customers.

✔ **High-definition TV:** Some of us remember the transition from black-and-white to color television. At first, color sets were bulky and expensive. Programming was limited to a few shows that proclaimed "in living color" during their introductions. It took more than a decade, but eventually *everything* was in color. The same sort of transition is under way with high-definition TV (HDTV). Apple is following a strategy of "skating to where the puck is going to be" and incorporating HD throughout the Macintosh line. If your business needs to be HD ready, get Macs.

✔ **Internet content delivery:** Widespread high-speed Internet access has led to the Internet becoming a primary means of information content delivery. Traditional media is feeling the heat. College students with the right concept, like the students who created YouTube and Facebook, can become billionaires almost overnight.

✔ **Lean and mean organizations:** To stay competitive in a tight economy, businesses are streamlining, outsourcing grunt work, flattening organization charts, and increasing the span of control and the number of workers per manager. The emphasis is on lean-and-mean organizations where each employee has the ability to recognize opportunities and to respond to challenges, and is held accountable for performance. These workers need the best tools available.

If some of the changes described here are felt in your business, stop thinking of computers as a cost center, like lights and lavatories, and realize that, used properly, they are competitive weapons. Realize that many of the most creative employees prefer Macs, and respecting their choice attracts them to and retains them for your firm. Realize that the quality of the tools you give your workers affects your products and services in ways that are hard to measure but are inescapable.

Macs in Small Businesses

The case for Macs is easiest to make in a small business. You're unlikely to have legacy software written in Cobol or a staff of information technology professionals wedded to doing things "the Microsoft way." To run a small business and grow it into a bigger business, you must have a can-do attitude. Two of the most important software tools for small businesses, Microsoft Office and QuickBooks (from Quicken.com), already run on Macs. FileMaker Pro, from Apple, is highly regarded as a database that can be easily customized by nonprogrammers. It's a cross-platform solution between Mac and Windows, with shared access using your in-house network. You can also find many specialized programs for Macs, such as computer-aided design and cash register operation. Although the selection is smaller than what is available for Windows, the vendors are dedicated to the Mac market and generally enjoy the support of a strong user community.

Software as a Service (SaaS) applications, such as ConstantContact.com, Salesforce.com, and SugarCRM.com, are a natural fit for small businesses because they allow you to have world-class applications at affordable prices without the need to hire IT support staff. And, choosing Macs makes a statement to prospective staff and customers that you are forward thinking and open to new ideas.

Macs in Midsize Businesses

Midsize businesses need an edge to survive against increasingly large corporate giants. Small businesses find niches too insignificant to attract the giants' attention. But when a midsize firm finds a good market, a large company is soon sniffing around. The midsize firm had better be more nimble and creative and in closer touch with its customers' needs.

The World Wide Web makes reaching customers easier for midsize firms. Internet advertising, such as Google AdWords, targets customers who have already shown interest in your product categories. The networks of self-published writers known as the blogosphere can make or break your product. Having selected employees write blogs about your industry can be more effective than advertising in traditional ways, such as in trade magazines. OS X has tools that make blogging easy. Video iChat simplifies and speeds the coordinating of responses from different groups in different locales without expensive travel.

Macs for the Enterprise

I'm under no illusion that this book will convince any large company to toss all its Windows boxes and switch everyone to Macs. I'd be happy if the book lowered the barriers to using Macs in a few organizations. The IT staff in many companies promulgate strict Windows-only rules. The common exception is the graphics department, which produces print and other media for outside consumption. My only suggestion is to give Macs a try in other places. Equipping a small department or field office with Macs is a low-risk experiment. The computers can be converted to Windows, if need be. What do you have to lose?

For more on Mac applications in businesses, visit the Apple business site, www.apple.com/business. Also try www.macenterprise.org, a community of IT professionals sharing information and solutions to support Macs in an enterprise.

Chapter 19

Desktop to Dashcode: OS X Advanced

· ·

· ·

Apple OS X is a complex piece of software. It draws on rich heritages, including earlier versions of Mac OS; Unix, particularly the Berkley System Distribution; NeXTstep, developed by a company Steve Jobs founded when he left Apple; and the Mach kernel project at Carnegie Mellon University. In this chapter, I dive into some of the OS X inner workings. Feel free to skip this chapter if you aren't interested in these details.

Peeking at the File System Structure

One of the most visible influences of Unix on OS X is the way the file system is organized. A top-level directory or folder contains these folders:

✔ **Applications:** Holds the entire iLife suite and applications that come with OS X. Applications you install, such as Microsoft Office, normally go here. It also contains the Utilities folder, where programs such as Disk Utility are found.

✔ **Library:** Contains other "under the hood" files that are needed system-wide. A Library folder also exists within the System folder, and one Library folder is available for each user.

✔ **System:** Contains OS X itself. Nothing you would want to work with directly dwells in this folder.

✔ **Users:** Holds each user's home folder. You can see other users' folders, but you can't look at files within them without permission, unless you're an administrative user.

You can add files and folders at the top level, but it generally isn't a good idea unless you have a good reason. This situation is more difficult for OS 9 users to get used to. Normally, you only add files to the Applications folder, as part of installing software, or to your user folder.

Exploring the User folder

Each User folder also has a standard set of subfolders. Some longtime computer users become quite irritated by all this structure when they first encounter it, but later versions of Windows have a similar structure. Swallow hard; it's worth getting used to.

The standard folders in a new User directory are described in this list:

✔ **Desktop:** This folder holds all files on your desktop. Having them in a folder like any other is handy. If your desktop gets too cluttered to find things easily, you can see its contents in a Finder window instead and use the folder-sorting tools to arrange the files and folders on the desktop by name, date, size, and other criteria. The Desktop folder is also handy when making manual backups, because you can simply copy all desktop content to an external hard drive, thumb drive, or optical disc.

✔ **Documents:** Apple intends for you to put all your documents in this folder. You don't have to, of course, but doing it the Apple way avoids hassles. You can, and should, add subfolders to whatever depth you want within the Documents folder. This is the place to go wild and make yourself at home.

If you have all your files neatly organized on your old computer, copy them all to the Documents folder. Then move pictures, movies, and music to the appropriate folders listed in the following bullets.

✔ **Library:** Programs store data that's unique for each user, such as preferences and caches. You normally don't add files here yourself, with the possible exception of Fonts or some plug-ins. (It's not the place to store your e-books.)

✔ **Movies:** Store your iMovie projects.

✔ **Music:** Stash the iTunes library.

✔ **Pictures:** Store your iPhoto shoebox.

✔ **Public:** Each user has this special folder with permissions set so that any user on the Mac can access the folder. Within this folder is a folder named Drop Box, in which other users can place files and folders but can't look inside. Only the user (and a computer administrator, of course) can see what's in the Drop Box folder.

✔ **Sites:** This folder contains Web page files you created for OS X Web Sharing to publish on the Internet — or on your organization's intranet.

Understanding file permission basics

Permissions determine who can do what with a file. Traditionally, you find three levels of permission in a Unix system:

✔ **Owner:** Each file in OS X is owned by someone, such as a user with an account, or something, such as the system.

✔ **Group:** A file is also assigned to one group. Groups consist of one or more users. You can belong to more than one group, and groups can include other groups.

✔ **Other (sometimes called World):** Other refers to anyone with authorized access to the computer.

Also in the Unix tradition, you can do these three things with a file:

✔ Read it (r).

✔ Write to it (w).

✔ Execute it (x).

The execute permission takes a bit of explaining. For program files, including scripts, it means that you can run the program. For directories, it means that you can see which files are inside the directory. It doesn't mean that you can open those files; you just see their names. The letters next to each action are abbreviations that are sometimes shown in directory listings.

With this structure, you have nine possibilities: Each level of ownership can have any combination of read, write, and execute access to a file, so long as owner has privileges at least as high as group, and group at least as high as world.

This approach to organizing permissions may seem complex, but it isn't complex enough for some situations. A file can be assigned to only one group. What if you want different groups to have different permissions? I hope that your personal life isn't convoluted, but in large organizations, it easily can be.

A more complex set of permissions in OS X is named Access Control List, or ACL. Each file and directory can have an *ACL*. It's an ordered list of rules. Each rule says so-and-so can do such-and-such. OS X ships with ACLs turned off, fortunately. The tools to administer them are included in OS X Server.

If you right-click a file and select Get Info from the shortcut menu (or just press ⌘+I), you see the Info window shown in Figure 19-1. It's somewhat analogous to the Properties window in Windows.

Figure 19-1:
The Info window for a file. I clicked the disclosure triangles to show details.

Permission information is toward the bottom. You may have to click the tiny disclosure triangles to view all the details.

Because permissions are so important to the underlying system software, OS X keeps track of what permissions are supposed to be for system files and applications installed with the Apple installer. Disk Utility, in the Utilities folder, has a Repair Permissions option, for setting the permissions back to their pristine values. You should run Repair Permissions every month or so.

Commanding Unix

When I say that OS X is built on top of Unix, you might imagine that I mean the way a house is built on top of a foundation: A door or hatch is at the ground level, and if you open it, you walk down a creaky set of stairs to a place that's damp and kind of dark, with pipes and wires going every which way. It's good to know about if you blow a fuse or if the heat isn't working, but it's no place to hang out.

Uh-uh. That's not what I'm talking about. What I mean is more like a city built on top of another city. Tap on a magic mirror, and you're transported to an underground metropolis. The people dress funny and speak a different dialect, but the place has lots of interesting places to visit and things to do.

You find a brief introduction to Unix in the sections that follow. You can find more online at www.freebsd.org, or pick up a copy of *UNIX For Dummies*, 5th Edition, by John R. Levine and Margaret Levine Young (published by Wiley).

The magic mirror is Terminal

The magic application that takes you from the outer world of OS X to the inner world of Unix is appropriately hidden and unpretentious. It's Terminal, and it's in the Utilities folder inside the Applications folder. Double-click the Terminal icon, and you see a window such as the one shown in Figure 19-2. The window is labeled Terminal – bash – 80x24.

```
Terminal — bash — 80×24
Last login: Wed Mar 28 15:46:23 on console
arnold-reinholds-macbook21:~ agr$
```

Figure 19-2:
The
Terminal
window.

Here's a rundown of what you see in the Terminal window:

- ✔ The last number indicates that the window holds 24 lines, each one 80 monospaced characters long.

- ✔ Drag the lower-right corner of the window and you can make it bigger or smaller, but the 80-character initial width has a long history. It's the number of characters in an IBM punch card. (Remember those?)

- ✔ The word *bash* in the window label isn't requesting an aggressive act. It's the name of the Unix program attending you, something that the Unix world calls a *shell*. It's much like the Windows XP command interpreter, cmd.exe.

- ✔ The $ character in the Terminal window is the bash prompt — Windows uses a right-facing arrow (>) for its prompt. Type anything at the prompt. Press Return and the shell program — bash by default in OS X — tries to carry out your wishes.

- ✔ The letters bash stand for Bourne-again shell. It's an open source remake by the Gnu project of an earlier shell (sh) written by Stephen Bourne when he was at Bell Labs. sh and other popular Unix shells (csh, zsh, ksh, tcsh, for example) are available as well, in case you grew up with one of them and prefer it.

Bash is more powerful than the Windows cmd.exe, but Microsoft is offering a new Windows PowerShell that's comparable. (My technical editor says "Yeah, comparable in the way that a Geo compares to a Maserati.")

Bash ain't Windows

You find a number of differences as well as similarities between the Windows command line and Unix. Many of these differences go back to the early days of DOS and were deliberately introduced to avoid legal problems from AT&T, the original developer of Unix:

- ✔ **Pathnames:** A pathname specifies where a file is located, starting at the top-level or root directory. Windows separates names with a backslash (\), and Unix, like the Internet, uses a forward slash (/). Versions of Mac OS 9 and earlier used a colon (:).

- ✔ **Hidden files:** Filenames that start with a period (.) are normally hidden and are often used to store the settings for various programs. Type **ls –a** to see them.

- ✔ **Home directory:** Unix uses the tilde character (~) as an abbreviation for the home directory. You sometimes see this on the Internet as well. One URL for my home page is http://theworld.com/~reinhold. (www.arnoldreinhold.com redirects you there.)

✔ **Switches:** Like Windows commands, Unix commands have switches that follow the command name to modify its action. In Windows, switches are indicated by a forward slash. In Unix, switches are usually indicated by a hyphen (-).

✔ **More about commands:** Windows uses `help`. Unix uses `man`, which stands for manual. In Unix, type this line:

```
man command-name
```

OS X comes with thousands of man pages mostly copied from BSD UNIX. Unix aficionados love man pages because they don't waste verbiage on cute analogies and historical asides, and they tend to be authoritative. Beginners often find them maddeningly terse. Use the `apropos` command to search through man pages.

Working in the Terminal window

As in Windows, you can use an asterisk (*) as a wildcard in a filename in most commands. Also like Windows, `bash` can complete a partially typed command or filename, if it can figure it out, when you press Tab.

You can copy text from the Terminal window, but you can't cut or insert text. If you can paste text into the terminal window, it's appended to whatever you already typed after the prompt.

If you drag an OS X file or folder icon to the Terminal window, the pathname of the file or folder is inserted where you're typing.

Introducing Unix commands

Unix has many commands, but I discuss just a few important ones: some that work with directories, some that work with files, and a few miscellaneous but commonly used commands.

Folders are called *directories* in Unix. Commands that refer to filenames, as most do, assume that you're talking about files in the working directory. When you open the Terminal window, the working directory is set to your home directory, abbreviated ~. You see the current working directory and your username to the left of its prompt. Table 19-1 lists common directory-related commands.

Table 19-1	Unix Directory Commands
Command	**What You Do with It**
ls	List the names of the files in the working directory. For more complete information, use ls -alF (see Figure 19-3).
cd *directoryname*	Change the working directory to the one you named.
cd ..	Move up one directory level.
cd	Return to your home directory.
pwd	Display the pathname of the current directory.
mkdir *newdirectoryname*	Make a new directory.
rmdir *directoryname*	Remove (delete) an empty directory.

Figure 19-3: Listing files with the Unix ls -alF command. Characters on the left are file permissions.

```
● ○ ○                   Terminal — bash — 80×24
Last login: Wed Mar 28 15:46:23 on console
arnold-reinholds-macbook21:~ agr$ ls -alF
total 24
drwxr-xr-x  11 agr    agr      442 Mar 23 08:58 ./
drwxr-xr-x   5 root   admin    238 Mar 21 13:18 ../
-rw-r--r--   1 agr    agr        3 Feb  2 12:50 .CFUserTextEncoding
-rw-r--r--@  1 agr    agr     6148 Mar 23 08:58 .DS_Store
drwx------   3 agr    agr      204 Mar  8 17:06 .Trash/
drwx------   7 agr    agr      238 Mar 28 15:56 Desktop/
drwx------   4 agr    agr      238 Mar 23 07:44 Documents/
drwx------  33 agr    agr     1190 Mar 20 16:18 Library/
drwx------   2 agr    agr      102 Feb  2 12:50 Movies/
drwx------   3 agr    agr      136 Feb 13 14:20 Music/
drwx------   2 agr    agr      136 Feb  2 12:50 Pictures/
drwxr-xr-x   3 agr    agr      136 Feb  2 12:50 Public/
drwxr-xr-x   3 agr    agr      170 Feb  2 12:50 Sites/
arnold-reinholds-macbook21:~ agr$ []
```

As in Windows, you can redirect the output of a command to a text file. So, if you want a record of the files in a folder, follow these steps:

1. **Type** cd **followed by a space.**

2. **Drag the folder's icon to the Terminal window.**

   Its pathname should appear after the cd command.

3. **Press Return.**

4. **Type** ls > mydirectorylist.txt **and press Return.**

   A file named mydirectorylist.txt appears in the folder you chose.

   You can open the file in TextEdit to see a list of the files in that directory.

Table 19-2 lists commands commonly used when working with files in the Terminal window; Table 19-3 explains other handy commands that anyone getting started in Terminal will likely want to know.

Table 19-2	Working with Files
Command	*What You Do with It*
cp *filename1 filename2*	Copy a file.
chmod	Change permissions for access to a file. Study the man page before using this one.
diff	Compare two files line by line (assumes text).
more *filename*	Display a text file one page at a time. Press the spacebar to see the next page; press Q to quit. The man command works through more.
mv *filename1 filename2*	Move a file or change its name.
rm *filename*	Remove (delete) a file.

When you're working in Terminal, you don't have a trash can to which deleted files are moved pending their ultimate disposal. Delete it and it's gone. In general, Unix has no Undo function.

Table 19-3	Miscellaneous Commands
Command	*What You Do with It*
Control+C	Terminate most operations.
date	Display the current date and time.
echo	Repeat whatever appears after the command (after expansion).
help	Display a partial list of bash commands.
history	Display the last commands you typed. You can redo a command by typing an exclamation point (!) followed immediately (no space) by the number of that command in the history list. To repeat the last command, type !!. To repeat the last filename, type !*.
pico	Use a simple Unix text editor.
ps	Display a list of running processes.
sudo	Carry out commands for which the account you're using lacks authority. You're asked for an administrator's password.

Text files

Plain-text files seem like the simplest, least complicated form of computer data. But differences exist in the ways Windows, Unix, and Macs format these files. For the most part, if you use standard word processing applications, you needn't worry about these differences, but if you're mucking around with the innards of OS X or moving text files back and forth between different operating system, it helps to be aware of the issues.

Unix text files terminate lines with an ASCII LF (line feed) character (decimal value 10). Windows uses the pair of characters CR (carriage return) and LF (decimal values 13 and 10, respectively). Mac OS 9 and earlier used just CR (decimal value 13). Carriage return and line feed go back to the days of mechanical teletype machines, which had a printing element that went back and forth on a carriage across a roll of paper. Moving the paper up one line was a separate operation from returning the carriage to the left edge of the page.

OS X would rather forget about text files altogether. By default, TextEdit can read any of them, but doesn't save in text format, preferring the RTF format. (You can tell TextEdit to use text format in its Preferences.) Many third-party Mac text editors use the OS 9 convention, ending lines in CR, though they often give you a choice. The Unix commands in OS X speak Unix, however, and expect LF unless you specify otherwise with a switch.

Developing Software on a Mac

Many years ago, my parents asked what I wanted for my 16th birthday. "A computer," I replied. They asked what that was — few people had heard of them back then. Then they asked what one cost. "Five hundred thousand dollars," I replied. It was a bad joke on my part (the first of many, you might be thinking). The smallest computer IBM made would occupy most of our apartment, and back then, half a million dollars was a lot of money. We all had a good laugh and I ended up with a shortwave radio receiver.

The reason I wanted a computer was to run programs I would write. That's what one did with a computer for the first couple of decades. It was lots of fun. The iMac I'm writing this book on is a million times faster than the computer I lusted after as a 15-year-old. That's not hyperbole — it's probably closer to ten million times faster.

But the iMac is harder to program. Sure, much better programming languages (too many of them) are available, and compilers do their thing in seconds for all except the biggest programs. But everything is so-o-o much more complicated.

Introducing Xcode

Apple hasn't figured out how to make programming a Mac anywhere near as easy as using one. No one has. But Apple is trying its best, and a complete programming environment comes with your Mac. You only have to pop in the discs that come with it and install *Xcode.* That's what Apple named its integrated development environment. Xcode supports a variety of compiled programming languages: Objective-C, C, C++, Java, and AppleScript. Objective-C is the native language for OS X, but the others can be used as well. Apple also supports scripting languages, including Perl, Python, and the hot Ruby on Rails. Xcode is built on top of many standard Gnu-Unix tools, including the GCC compiler and GDB debugger. All the standard Unix tools are there in their native form as well.

Xcode also has many Apple-specific tools, such as Interface Builder. The Xcode package includes most Apple developer documentation. You even find a Research Assistant to help you find application program interface (API) details and other arcane stuff you need in order to write programs these days.

Xcode supports both Intel and PowerPC Macintosh environments and produces universal binaries that run on both. It can produce programs that support either 32- or 64-bit addressing.

Dashing to the Dashboard with Dashcode

Apple provides a much simpler environment than Xcode for creating Dashboard widgets. It's *Dashcode,* and it includes templates that let you quickly create an RSS feed, a podcast or photocast viewer, a countdown timer, or a gauge. A blank widget template is also available if you want to be more creative. You can find out more at `developer.apple.com/tools/dashcode`.

When you're ready to release your spiffy widget, Dashcode collects all the little bits of stuff that must be present and packages them for distribution as a professional-looking widget. Apple distributes selected widgets on its Web site: `www.apple.com`.

Programming the iPhone

Over 30,000 applications have been developed for the Apple iPhone and iPod touch. The Apple iTunes app store distributes these applications on a 70–30 basis — the developer keeps 70 percent of the sale price, and Apple keeps 30 percent. Many people have made a nice side income from iPhone applications they develop. Maybe you have some programming skills and a novel idea for an app. First make sure that your app doesn't already exist, by searching the app store and Google. Then you need to register as an Apple developer at `http://developer.apple.com/iphone`. (It's free, but you agree to the Apple terms and conditions, which include a nondisclosure agreement.) Then download the iPhone Software Developer's Kit (SDK) — it's available only for OS X. You can test your application on an iPhone simulator included in the SDK, but to test it on a live phone and to release it to the store, you have to pay a fee that covers issuing you a digital signature that you use to sign your code. Apple doesn't want anonymous software in the iPhone.

For help getting started with the actual programming, check out *iPhone Application Development For Dummies* by Neal Goldstein (Wiley Publishing).

The Sun ZFS file system

Mac OS X Snow Leopard Server supports ZFS, a new file system developed by Sun Microsystems. A file system is the internal plumbing of an operating system that organizes and stores computer data files on mass storage devices. OS X supports several file systems, including HFS+, Apple's own file system; the Unix file system, UFS; and a couple of Microsoft variants.

Why add another file system to the OS X repertoire? Because ZFS is an amazing technological achievement. After decades of problems with file system design, Sun synthesized a new approach that offers nearly unlimited capacity and built-in reliability. The Apple HFS+ file system achieves its high reliability by keeping side notes on what it's doing so that it can recover in case its operations are interrupted by a power failure or software crash — a process called *journaling*. ZFS eliminates the need for journaling by protecting the old version of data until the creation of a new version is complete. So, you have no need for disk recovery utilities and the like. ZFS has lots of other neat features, such as integrity checks on every file, the ability to add disk drives without creating separate volumes, and better techniques for using multiple disks to create a redundant array (RAID) that protects data even if a single disk drive dies. Some people think that ZFS may become the Apple standard file system.

Part VI
The Part of Tens

The 5th Wave   By Rich Tennant

HELP DESK

TECHNICAL   ETHICAL

In this part . . .

The tense tenor of tens extends tenacious tendrils, testing our tentative tenets. This tract's top text tackles ten terrific OS X troubleshooting tricks . . . and then ten techniques to tame Terra's terrifying trials. Text three portends thy PC's termination, tendering ten tenuous but tenable extensions to its tenure.

Chapter 20

Ten Terrific Troubleshooting Tips

*M*acs have a deserved reputation for reliability. But they're not perfect. Computer software is extremely complex, and stuff happens. In this chapter, I present some suggestions for dealing with problems that can arise and tips for preventing problems in the first place.

Take Care of First Things First

Take two aspirins and call me in the morning. Every field has its basic nostrums. Here are the basic remedies every Mac user should know:

- ✔ **Back it up:** It's the first rule of computing. The Apple Time Machine automates the process if you attach a second hard drive and turn on Time Machine (see Chapter 5). In addition, I recommend a periodic manual backup of your most important files to DVD-R or to an additional external hard drive.

- ✔ **Reboot:** Select Restart from the Apple menu. See the section "Reboot a Hung Mac," later in this chapter, for more details. You should reboot every week or so, whether or not you need to.

- ✔ **Check the hard drive:** Run Disk Utility in the Utilities folder. Select your hard drive. Click the Repair Permissions button. Then click the Verify Disk button. If Verify Disk reports a problem, you can boot from the installation disc that came with your computer by inserting it and holding down the C key when you reboot. Running Disk Utility from that system gives you the option to repair your disk. Do it.

  If you can't find your installation disc, do a safe boot: Shut down your Mac. Press the power button. Right after the startup "boing," hold down Shift. After the safe boot is complete, restart your Mac. Safe booting repairs your file system as it starts up.

✔ **Fix the preference file:** If an application is acting up, the file where it keeps your preference settings (the *plist* file) might be messed up. One way to deal with this problem is to change some preference settings and close the application. For Finder problems, also change the System Preferences Appearance settings.

Another approach is to close the troublesome application, open the Library folder in your home directory, and then open the Preferences folder. Find the `.plist` file for the troublesome application and change its name by tacking `.old` or something similar to the end of the filename. Then restart the application with its default preferences.

✔ **Zap PRAM:** Every Mac stores some basic info it needs in a small, separate memory area known as *parameter RAM, or PRAM.* To reset it, hold down the P and R keys while you reboot.

✔ **Replace the system battery:** If you have a new Mac, you won't run into system battery problems for years. Its small battery keeps the clock and PRAM working when power is off; it's not the one that powers your laptop. But if you have an older Mac that's behaving weirdly (a common symptom is the wrong date at startup), the small battery on the motherboard that keeps the clock and PRAM working might have run down. These batteries are easy to replace on the Mac Pro and older Mac desktop machines; it's a service call on all-in-one units and laptops.

Replacing the battery is also a common solution to problems with wireless devices. If you use a wireless keyboard and mouse and they don't seem to be working, replace their batteries.

✔ **Figure out whether it's the hardware:** If your Mac is crashing frequently, it might have a hardware problem. For starters, disconnect all peripherals and see whether you still have problems. If they go away, reconnect devices one at a time to try to isolate the evildoer. If the problems don't go away, run the diagnostic disc that came with your Mac. It typically offers you a fast and more thorough mode. Try fast mode first. Then do the slow test overnight. If the diagnostic program reports an error, write down exactly what it says, with all the error numbers, and bring that info along with the sick computer to your service tech or have it ready when you call AppleCare.

Watch the Spinning Beach Ball

Macs rarely crash, but applications sometimes hang. That means the application is no longer responding to input from the keyboard or mouse. A common indication is a spinning beach ball cursor that doesn't go away. The spinning beach ball is normal from time to time when an application is busy. It's the equivalent of the hourglass cursor in Windows. You can tell that a specific application is responsible if the spinning beach ball shows up only when the cursor is over one of that application's windows.

Show a little patience. The application might be waiting on an Internet resource or reorganizing its sock drawer. Go have a cup of coffee. Safari, in particular, sometimes takes awhile. If the beach ball is still spinning when you get back, I recommend handling the problem as follows:

1. **Try pressing ⌘+Tab to cycle to other applications you might have open, and save your work.**

2. **Close these applications using the Quit command. (Press ⌘+Q.)**

   If the Quit command doesn't work, you can try a more drastic measure: Force Quit. Follow these steps:

   a. *Select Force Quit from the Apple menu or press ⌘+Option+Esc.*

      This step opens a small window showing all applications that are active. If one of yours is hung, OS X probably notices and marks it as not responding in the Force Quit window.

   b. *Select the hung application in the window and click the Force Quit button.*

      If the Finder is hung, pressing ⌘+Option+Esc may offer you the option to relaunch it. Otherwise, you must reboot.

Reboot a Hung Mac

Hold down the power button while you slowly count to ten. That's not to calm you down. A little power management processor in your Mac looks for the extended push and shuts down the main computer.

If that doesn't work, unplug the computer from its power source and, if it's a laptop with a removable battery, remove it. To do the latter, follow these steps:

1. **Close the screen and gently turn the machine over. (It has been bad but doesn't need to be spanked.)**

   You see a metal circle with a slot in it.

2. **Insert a coin in the slot and turn it to the unlocked position.**

3. **Remove the battery.**

4. **Count to ten again and put the battery back in.**

5. **Press the power button briefly (count to one), and your computer should reboot.**

   This restart may take a little longer than usual because your Mac knows it wasn't shut down normally and is checking things out.

If your Mac keeps hanging while it's booting up and you've tried everything else, lift it about half an inch and drop it right after you reboot it. The resulting jar is often enough to get a stuck hard drive spinning again. If this works, take the hint: You're hard drive is dying. Back up your files *now* and bring your Mac in for service.

Reconnect to the Internet

Your browser whines that you aren't connected to the Internet. Mail complains that it can't find the server. Debugging Internet connectivity problems can be frustrating. Many steps are involved in getting you online, and any of them can be the problem.

Safari offers you a Network Diagnostics button in the dialog that appears when Safari can't connect. Click it. You see a list of the steps needed to connect, with colored lights that show green if that step has passed successfully and red if it hasn't.

If the Network Diagnostics feature doesn't help you resolve your problem, the following list offers other testing advice:

- ✔ **Test for service:** Before you spend too much time tracking down possible problems, try these simple tests. If you're connected by a telephone line (dialup or DSL), ensure that you have a dial tone on your landline telephone. If you use a cable modem, ensure that you have TV reception. If not, the problem isn't in your computer equipment. Call your phone company or cable company.

- ✔ **Check the blinking lights:** If you have a modem and router or a WiFi/AirPort access point, check that their lights are on and appear normal.

- ✔ **Can you hear me now?** If you're using WiFi/AirPort, determine whether you have a strong enough signal — at least two solid arcs on the Signal Strength icon on the menu bar. If not, click the icon to turn it off and back on. Move your laptop. Moving closer to the router or access point is usually better, but any move can help. See Chapter 9 for more tips on getting a signal and solving interference problems.

- ✔ **Follow the wires:** If you're using a wired Ethernet connection, check that all cables are connected properly. Disconnect and reconnect them at each end. You have to press a little tab to remove the cable, just like on a telephone cable. You should hear a little click when it snaps into place as you reconnect. Follow the wire to make sure that the one entering your computer is the same one entering the router or modem and that it hasn't been damaged.

- ✔ **Cycle the power:** Shut down your computer and turn off power to every device. Count to 30. Then, one at a time, power up each unit, starting with the modem, and then the router and access point, and then the computer.

- ✔ **Check network settings:** Select System Preferences from the Apple menu and click the Networks icon. Make sure that its settings match the instructions your ISP gave you. Also, check your router's settings. See Chapters 8 and 9.

Handle Printing Problems

Most long-term Mac users have gotten calls from friends that go something like this: "I know you suggested I buy a Mac, but the salesman said the ZorchPC is just as good and he saved me $300 on a package. I got it set up all by myself, but the printer doesn't work. Could you come over and help me?" The Apple Bonjour technology has made connecting a printer much simpler, even in the Windows world. But sometimes you click the Print button and nothing happens. The following steps can help you resolve your problem:

1. **Click the Print & Fax icon in System Preferences.**

2. **Make sure your printer is listed in the window that appears.**

   Your printer manufacturer and model number should be listed in the window. If not, make sure the printer has power and check the connection cables.

3. **Look at the printer's lights and display for any error messages, such as one saying that it's out of paper or ink. Press its Resume or OK button.**

4. **Turn off the printer, wait until it shuts down completely, and then turn it back on.**

5. **Ensure that all cables are connected.**

   Refer to the "Follow the wires" bullet in the preceding section.

6. **Download the latest drivers from your printer manufacturer's Web site.**

   Avoid using drivers on the disc that came with the printer. They're often out-of-date.

If you've done all these things and still don't have a solution to your printing problem, check the printer manual for other suggestions and the service number to call.

Reset Passwords

Okay, everybody forgets a password sooner or later. That's why I advise most users to write down passwords and keep them in a safe place. See Chapter 10. Here's how to handle forgotten passwords:

- ✔ **If a user on your Mac forgot his password:** Reset it to a new password by clicking the Accounts icon in System Preferences. You must click the Lock icon and then enter your administrator password. If the person forgot the user's keychain password, use Keychain Access, located in the Utilities folder.

- ✔ **If you forgot your administrator password:** Reset it by inserting the installation disc that came with your computer and holding down the C key while you reboot. Select Reset Password from the menu that appears.

Eject CDs, DVDs, and Flash Drives

Most Macs come with *slot-loading* optical drives: You insert a CD or DVD into the wide, thin slot on your Mac where it just fits. Never insert a miniature-size CD or DVD into the slot. If you're having trouble ejecting a CD or DVD, here are some tips:

- ✔ The Eject button is on the keyboard, in the upper-right corner, and is marked ▲.

- ✔ You can also right-click the disc's icon in the Finder and select Eject from the menu that appears, or click the eject icon next to the disc's name in a Finder window sidebar.

- ✔ OS X won't eject a disc if a program thinks it's using it. If your disc doesn't eject when you press the button, close the application that was last using it (or close all applications, if you're not sure which one is using it).

- ✔ If all else fails, restart the computer while holding down the mouse or trackpad button. That should eject the disc.

Flash drives and other removable hard drives have to be "ejected" as well. There's no mechanical response; you still have to unplug them yourself. But ejecting tells OS X to finish what it was doing and leave the file system on the removable device in a proper state. Right-click the drive icon and select Eject from the shortcut menu. Wait for the icon to disappear from the desktop and then a few seconds more before unplugging.

If you removed a flash drive prematurely, the file system may be damaged. Even if the drive isn't readable on your Mac (try a reboot first), it might be readable on another computer, including your old PC. If you're able to read it, back it up by copying its contents to the hard drive of the machine that could read it. You can reformat a flash drive on your Mac by using Disk Utility. Select the FAT file system format. You lose all data on the drive.

Track Down Weird Noises

If your normally quiet new Mac starts making loud noises that sound a bit like a jetliner revving for take off, don't be alarmed. The Intel processors in your Mac use more power when they're thinking hard, as when rendering movies or 3D images. They can sense their own temperature and call for the fans in your Mac to blast some air to cool things down. Sometimes an application crashes in a way that keeps the processors and the fans at full tilt. A reboot usually quiets things. The Dashboard widget iStat Pro from www.islayer. com reports on system temperatures and fan speeds. CoreDuoTemp from macbricol.free.fr puts temperature information on your menu bar.

Prevent Running Out of Disk Space

If you find that your Mac's hard drive is filling up for no reason, you can try several fixes. For starters, empty the Trash. The command is on the Finder menu.

Next, check for extraordinarily large files to delete or back up to a removable drive or disc:

1. **In the Finder, open a new Finder window (press ⌘+N).**

2. **Open your home directory — it's normally the House icon in the sidebar.**

3. **Choose Finder⇨View⇨As List.**

4. **Choose Finder⇨View⇨Show View Options, and select the Calculate All Sizes check box.**

   When this check box is selected, OS X makes the added effort to show you how big each folder is, not just each file. The calculation takes a few minutes, typically.

5. **Look to see whether any of your folders seems unreasonably large. If so, look for unnecessary stuff to delete or move elsewhere.**

   Do the same procedure on subfolders as needed.

Another possible cause of disappearing disk space is overgrown log files. UNIX can generate lots of logs as applications do their thing. Mac OS X runs special maintenance programs periodically to clean them out. They run in the wee hours of the morning, so be sure to leave your Mac on overnight sometimes. A reboot can often help. You can also use shareware programs that clean out the logs. Yasu and Onyx are two popular programs.

A final possibility is to defragment the hard drive. OS X tries to keep individual files from fragmenting, but the disk structure as a whole can suffer from having too many small, unused patches. Apple recommends against defragmentation for most users, as long as they aren't doing disk-intensive work, such as video editing, and their hard drive isn't close to being full.

Of course, your hard drive might be filling up because you have lots of files you want to keep. In that case, consider getting a large external hard drive and moving less frequently used files and folders to it. You generally should keep free at least 20 percent of the space on your main drive.

Keep Your Mac Safe and in Tiptop Shape

Taking care of a Mac is mostly common sense. For the most part, no special tricks are required. You just need to pay attention to the software, hardware, and your habits every so often.

To maintain the software, keep these points in mind:

- ✔ OS X checks Software Update once a week, unless you change its settings. I suggest leaving them as is.

- ✔ Dig out Disk Utility from the Utilities folder every few weeks and run Repair Permissions. If security is a concern, run Erase Free Space as well. Do this overnight because it can take awhile.

- ✔ Be judicious in the software you download and install. Although malware hasn't been a big problem on Macs, there's always a first time.

  The biggest risk in installing every software gizmo that catches your eye is that some are poorly written and can make OS X less stable.

- ✔ When your Internet connection is working properly, take a look at your router and modem — the box that connects your network to the telephone line, TV cable, or satellite dish. Note what the blinking lights look like when everything is okay so that you can recognize the difference when it isn't.

Following these tips can help you keep the hardware in good working order:

✔ The MagSafe connector is designed to keep an Apple laptop from falling if someone trips on its power cord. But avoid balancing yours precariously on top of books, papers, and other work-surface litter. Remember that MagSafe protects only the power cord. Someone tripping on an Ethernet, USB, FireWire, or audio cable can still send your laptop flying. And avoid sharp bends in the power cord, particularly where it meets the MagSafe connector, to prevent eventual failure.

✔ Don't use cleaners that contain alcohol or ammonia or other strong solvents on your computer. And, don't spray any liquids directly on your computer. Apple suggests a soft cloth dipped in a little plain water for cleaning display screens. If that's not sufficient, Klear Screen from klearscreen.com is recommended.

✔ Your Mac is designed to run in an ordinary home or office environment. Avoid running it in excessively hot locales or exposed to direct sunlight. If you put your laptop on a soft or cluttered surface, make sure that the fan exhaust, which is at the hinge, isn't blocked.

✔ Keep an eagle eye on your laptop in public places. Be especially vigilant while walking through airport security.

Last but not least, the following tips can keep you computing comfortably day in and day out:

✔ If you spend much time at your computer, you owe it to yourself to take ergonomic precautions. Repetitive motion injuries are best avoided altogether. Comfortable seating that puts your keyboard and mouse or trackpad at a level where your forearms are at right angles to your body tops the list. Apple has extensive suggestions at apple.com/about/ergonomics.

✔ Finally, you weren't put on this planet to be a computer peripheral. Practice the push-away exercise several times a day. Place both hands at the edge of your desk and slowly push your body away from the keyboard. Then get up and walk outside for a while.

Find Help

I mention some common problems here and suggest how to fix them. But I can't foresee everything that can happen. You have a number of places to turn when problems arise that these tips don't fix.

Google

I always check the Internet first. Usually someone else has come up with an answer to the same problem, and Google (www.google.com) can find it if you come up with the right search request.

Be sure to include the term *OS X* or *Mac* in your search; otherwise, the answer gets lost in PC replies. Google seems to know that *OS X* is a single search term, even though a space is in it. But don't be too specific at first. You may have a MacBook, but the person who solved your problem may have seen the same problem on an iMac. Try searching different ways, such as once with the word *printer* and once with your printer's make and model.

Also try your search at Google Groups. Click the More link at the top of the Google home page.

The online Mac community

The fabled loyalty of Mac users is reflected in a strong online community of Mac Web sites. Some are dedicated to rumors of new products; others strive to keep up with the latest problems and their fixes:

- **MacInTouch.com:** One of the most comprehensive sites, with a strong focus on reviews and issues with new products and freshly released software
- **VersionTracker.com:** Lets you know if you have the latest software
- **MacOSXHints.com:** Filled with tips on solving problems and improving performance
- **Macnn.com and MacRumors.com:** Lets you read the latest Mac stories, along with user discussions
- **LowEndMac.com:** Has resources you can use with an older Mac

Apple

It may seem surprising that I don't list Apple first when searching for help. But Google and the online communities can be checked in seconds and often pop up relevant links to the Apple Web site. So many problems are quickly resolved this way that it's worth a try before calling AppleCare or visiting your local Apple store's Genius Bar.

But Apple is the ultimate resource. New Macs typically come with 90-day free telephone support. You can extend this period by purchasing AppleCare, which is generally a good idea if this is your first Mac. See Chapter 3 for more on the Apple service options.

User groups and consultants

Numerous Apple user groups are scattered about the planet. Apple tries to find one near you if you visit `www.apple.com/usergroups`. Getting to know the folks at your local user group can be valuable when you're stuck and in a hurry. Having a Mac-knowledgeable friend you can call can make all the difference. Your local user group can also recommend good Mac consultants in your area and give you some idea about what fees to expect. You meet some nice people too.

Chapter 21

Ten Ways Your Mac Can Help the Planet

. . . .

In This Chapter

▶ Saving energy

▶ Running on alternative power

▶ Putting your idle Mac to good use

. . . .

*Y*ou can use your Mac to get your work done, stay in touch, and just have fun, but you can also employ it in ways that help the environment and humanity. In this chapter, I describe just a few.

Saving Energy with Energy Saver

The Energy Saver control panel, shown in Figure 21-1, lets you adjust settings that can reduce your Mac's energy consumption. To see it, choose ●⇨System Preferences⇨Energy Saver.

Figure 21-1:
The Energy
Saver
System
Preferences
pane.

If you have an Apple laptop, you have a choice of settings: one for operating on battery power and one for when you're connected to the power adapter. The default settings are based on the assumption that you want to use less power when you're operating on battery power in order to extend battery life. But there's no reason to waste energy when you're on the power adapter. To select the energy-saving setting while you're using your power adapter, follow these steps:

1. **Choose Settings For⇨Power Adapter.**

2. **Choose Optimization⇨Better Energy Savings.**

   While you're at it, make sure that Better Energy Savings is selected under the Battery option.

If you find the Better Energy Savings setting a bit annoying — for example, if the system is going to sleep too often — you can select Custom from the Optimization menu and pick a longer sleep time.

Organizing Your Accessories for Power Savings

Ever notice any of those tiny power adapters you have plugged in around your home or office? They power or charge the increasing number of electronic gadgets you have: computers, printers, modems, routers, cellphones, and video games, for example.

Whenever an adapter is connected to an electrical outlet, it consumes a little power even when the device it powers is turned off or disconnected. If all your adapters are plugged in all the time, that power adds up to significant energy use. Unplugging the adapters when they aren't in use is one way to save energy, but it can be a bit tedious. An alternative is to plug into their own power strip all the chargers that can be turned off at night so that you can turn them all off together.

If you want to make this process a bit more automatic, consider getting a Colman Cable Smart Strip. This unit looks like an ordinary power strip, with color-coded outlets. One is a control outlet where you plug in a device (such as your computer) that you turn on and off. The strip senses when this happens and turns six other outlets on and off automatically, in sync with the control device. If you plug accessories (such as displays and USB hubs) into the smart strip and they're off when your computer is off, you save standby power. The strip also has three outlets that are always on for devices that need to stay on, such as a router that others use.

Running on Alternative Power

Generating your own power — running off the electrical grid — by means of renewable power is the ultimate form of energy saving. Taking your entire home or business off grid is one way to do this, but it's beyond the scope of this book (Check out *Solar Power Your Home For Dummies,* by Rik DeGunther, if this topic appeals to you).

If you want an off-grid Mac, a laptop is your best bet, because it consumes less power and it come with a battery so that you can work when the sun is behind a cloud or at night. All you need is a solar battery charger. A number of chargers of this type are on the market, but many don't fit the MagSafe power connector on your Mac laptop. Two products that offer this vital link are

- ✔ **The Solar Cell Apple Juicz:** From `quickertek.com`
- ✔ **The Voltaic Generator Solar Laptop Charger:** From `voltaicsystems.com`

Neither is cheap, but if you need to be online from someplace sunny with no commercial electric power or you just want to make a green statement, they may be for you.

A final option is to see whether your electric utility lets you choose your energy supplier and sign up for one that generates electricity from an alternative source, such as wind, hydro, or solar.

Monitoring Power Use

Your computing setup consists of more than just your Mac. You might have a printer, a display, an external hard drive, a scanner, a camcorder, a router, an HDTV, and other devices. If you're keeping your PC, it and its peripherals will be plugged in as well. But how much energy does each one use?

Measuring the power and energy consumption of peripherals and other electronic gadgets that run off wall outlets is easy with the Kill A Watt EZ electricity usage monitor from P3 International (`www.p3international.com`). This compact meter, which costs about $50, plugs into a standard outlet or a power strip. You plug the unit to be tested into the outlet on the front of the Kill A Watt. An LED display shows you the power and energy usage since the last time you reset the meter. The Kill A Watt can also display instantaneous power, voltage, current, and power-factor levels. (The *power factor* measures how close a load comes to an ideal resistor; low power factors mean energy is being wasted.) You can check other appliances in your home that plug into a 120-volt outlet, such as refrigerators and lamps. After you know how much energy your equipment uses, you can identify the best ways to reduce energy consumption, whether it's turning off peripherals or installing compact fluorescent bulbs in your desk lamp.

iChat AV: The Green Way to Visit

Transportation fuel use — for automobiles and airplanes — is a major source of carbon dioxide, a gas that traps heat in the atmosphere and contributes to global warming. Cutting down on travel can reduce your carbon *footprint* — the amount of carbon dioxide you produce as a result of your activities. It can also save you money.

Short-notice airfares have long been the bane of small business. If you live in Boston and want to visit Aunt Ellie in L.A. and can plan your trip two weeks in advance, you can often easily find a nonstop round-trip flight online for less than $300. But if you need to go tomorrow to solve a customer's problem or make that last-minute presentation to win a sale, you spend close to $1,000.

Using the Apple iChat AV to hold a videoconference, rather than catch that last-minute flight, can save you enough to cover the cost of your Mac with just one trip avoided. The iSight camera built into your iMac or laptop is all you need. Plug-in cameras are available for Mac minis and Pros. You can even video-conference with Windows users by using AOL Instant Messenger for Windows.

You always see yourself as well as the other people on the call. If you have visual materials to make your case, iChat Theater lets you share an iPhoto slide show or a Keynote presentation while letting your audience see you as you talk them through it.

If you're working on a proposal or report with a remote colleague who also has a Mac, you can both edit the same document or search the Web together with iChat screen sharing, which lets one chatter control the other's desktop. If security is a concern, connecting through MobileMe allows you to automatically encrypt your chat. Look for the Lock icon in the upper-left corner.

For more on iChat AV, see Chapter 8.

Automating Your Home

Years ago, home automation meant buying X10 lamp modules from Radio Shack and putting a controller on the night table so that you could dim the lights from your bed. Home automation now means that you control every electrical device in your home, fine-tune your heating and air conditioning, and even patch in alternative forms of energy. You can also add video surveillance and intrusion detection systems, with security images shipped off-site where an intruder can't get at them. And, you can control all these tasks remotely and securely over the Internet.

The Indigo software package from `Perceptiveautomation.com` lets your Mac control both X10 and the newer Insteon family of home automation controls.

 If you're using your Mac as a home controller, be sure to select Energy Saver in System Preferences, click Options, and check the Restart Automatically after a Power Failure box.

Living the Paperless Portable Life

Okay, this is a pet fantasy of mine, but did you ever think about how much of our living situation is devoted to storing and managing papers? Imagine scanning every piece of paper that matters to you and storing it all on an external hard drive (such as Time Capsule, covered in Chapter 5). Legal documents you need in original form can be stored in a rented safe-deposit box, along with jewelry and small mementos. If you have books and bigger tchotchkes you can't part with, rent a small storage room or a corner of a friend's basement. Imagine getting everything you need down to a laptop and portable hard drive. You're free! You can go anywhere, at any time.

Even if you aren't ready to go this far, you can still cut your use of paper. You're probably already using texting and e-mail to stay in touch with friends. Here are a few other suggestions:

- ✔ **Use online bill-paying systems.** Your bank or broker probably offers such a service.

- ✔ **Ask to get bills and statements via e-mail rather than on paper.** Many banks, utilities and other vendors offer this service.

- ✔ **If you're in school, ask your instructors whether they accept essays and other submissions in electronic form.** It never hurts to ask.

- ✔ **Turn off your printer and see how long you can get by without it.** You save on ink and toner cartridges as well. (Don't forget to recycle your old ones — many stationary stores take them back for credit.)

Curing Cancer

Your Mac is one powerful computer. How powerful? One Mac sent back in time to the 1940s or '50s could alter the balance of power in the world. Yet yours spends most of its time patiently waiting for commands. Can I find you a Web page? Can I? Can I maybe read you your e-mail? Pretty please?

Rather than consign your Mac to total boredom, you can give it interesting work to do — work that helps cure cancer and other diseases. Living cells assemble proteins by linking different amino acids in a sequence specified by the cell's DNA. As the protein is completed, it folds itself up into a 3D shape that determines how it functions in the cell. These days, biologists can determine a protein's sequence from the DNA, but figuring out how it folds up takes extremely demanding calculations. The Stanford University Folding@home project uses the idle cycles on your Mac to help carry out these computations. Visit `folding.stanford.edu` and download the OS X client. You have lots of options to choose from, but start with the Screensaver version, which makes only moderate demands on your computer and quickly gets out of the way when you want to get your work done. After the Folding@home screen saver has run long enough to produce some results, it displays the molecules it's working on so that you can see what's being accomplished.

Retiring Old Electronics Responsibly

Computers wear out. Mac last longer than PCs on average, but even they die or become obsolete eventually. Disposing of them improperly can add to landfill pollution. Worse, in many cases, old computers are shipped to Third World countries, where they're stripped of valuable parts in unsafe conditions, often by children. The section in Chapter 22 on recycling equipment safely explains better ways to get rid of old equipment.

Switching a Friend to a Mac

The Mac model's environmentally friendly design and long service life make them ideal for environmentally conscious users. Apple competes against computer companies battling to see who can produce the cheapest Windows computer. These perpetual price wars lead to corner cutting and products that need frequent replacement.

The one thing that has kept Apple alive through difficult years is the loyalty of its customers. If you like having a commercial alternative to Microsoft and Windows, consider helping a friend make the switch. If you found this book helpful, the friend might too.

Chapter 22

Ten Creative Uses for Your Old PC

A s you wean yourself from Windows, you may wonder what to do with your old PC. Here are ten suggestions, some more creative than others.

Before you send away your computer, be sure to clear its hard drive of all sensitive files. Dragging items to the Recycle Bin and then emptying it doesn't erase your data. See Chapter 6 for instructions for better ways to delete data.

Sell It on Craigslist

If your PC is of fairly recent vintage, it may have some resale value. I suggest listing it on your local craigslist (www.craigslist.org). It's free to use and less complicated than eBay.com. Because Craigslist enables you to create a local listing, you can ask the buyer to pick up the PC, avoiding shipping hassles. You can get an idea of what your computer is worth by checking what's now on sale — but don't assume that the listed asking price is what people are getting.

Load Ubuntu Linux on It

I love OS X, but Linux — the free, open source operating system — is also becoming an important alternative to Windows. You can download and burn a CD to load your PC with the friendly version of Linux, Ubuntu (www.ubuntu.com).

By the way, this is the only way I recommend giving your old PC box to your kids. I'd rather see them have a Mac, but setting up and using Linux has real educational value — and fewer games are available. Get the kids a copy of *Ubuntu Linux For Dummies*, by Paul G. Sery (Wiley Publishing), and let them figure it out.

Give It to Charity

Donating your computer to a worthwhile organization is an admirable thing to do, and you may even get a tax deduction. However, most charitable organizations aren't interested in computer donations from individuals — they're inundated with them. Your best bet is to contact organizations you know. An offer to help set up the PC may be appreciated. Don't take offense if they say no.

A posting in the free section of craigslist.org often works — you can specify a preference for charities, but often a donation to an individual can be a good deed. In any case, be sure to include all software discs and documentation that came with the PC, if you still have them.

Use It as a Pedestal

Years ago, my employer sold all its computers to a leasing company and leased them back on a seven-year note. The equipment was obsolete after three years, so we kept the racks they were mounted in, which is where the leasing company's inventory tags were affixed, and used them for printer stands. The bean counters from the leasing company dutifully came around every six months and were satisfied to see that the stuff that secured their loans (and our printers) was still there. A PC makes a great plant stand, but be sure to install the antitipping hardware that probably came with it. Two PCs of the same height with a wide board across them creates a nice work surface for young kids.

Have Your Kids Take It Apart

These days, kids don't get much opportunity to see how things are put together. Place the computer on an old bed sheet, give the kids a screwdriver set, and see how far they can go in taking apart the computer. Hard drives are a bit tricky to open — you usually find one or two screws under the "you'll void the warranty" labels — but they're full of fascinating parts, including some powerful magnets.

Adult supervision is required. Some parts have sharp edges. Those magnets are strong enough to pinch if two snap together. This activity isn't one that kids younger than five should be anywhere near, because small parts are a choking hazard. And *never* try to take apart a video monitor or any computer that includes a CRT display — it has high voltages inside, and its CRT tubes can implode violently. See "Recycle It Safely," at the end of this chapter, for disposal tips.

Enjoy It As Art

If you've never looked closely at a computer's circuit board, you're missing a cultural experience. Those *objets d'art* are marvels of design, filled with colorful electronic components, including numerous integrated circuits in mysterious black slabs and covered with thousands of tiny copper traces that carry all the signals. I think they're worthy of hanging on the wall. Some craftspeople even use them as raw material for jewelry.

Use It for Target Practice

I'm not seriously suggesting this one. It can be dangerous and may be contrary to laws in some locations, but years ago, when I had a gig at a local company that made spreadsheet software, someone brought in a 386 PC filled with .30 caliber bullet holes. Everyone appreciated the gesture.

Disconnect from the Internet

One way to continue to use a Windows machine safely is to disconnect it from the Internet. Unplug its Ethernet cable and remove any wireless networking card. If the machine has built-in wireless capability, such as Intel Centrino, change the password on your wireless network hub and don't give the PC the new password. For extra credit, turn off wireless networking in the Network Connections section of the Control Panel or remove the wireless card, because the PC can still connect through a neighbor's open hub. When you need to move files between the PC and your Mac, use a USB flash drive.

Keep It for Old Media

If you have a PC old enough to have 5¼-inch floppy drives , wrap it in one of those big plastic bags you get from the dry cleaner and store it in the basement. Sooner or later, the world will no longer be able to read those old disks, and you'll be a hero for saving your machine. Or not. (And if some of the dire predictions for cyberwar come true, old machines may be the only computers that still work.)

Recycle It Safely

Keep computers and displays out of the town dump. Did you know that an old CRT monitor can contain four pounds of lead? Also, many computer recycling operations send computers and displays to developing countries, where they're dismantled under hazardous conditions — often by child labor — and worthless parts are simply dumped somewhere. Here are a few tips to help you find a good way to safely recycle an old and unwanted computer:

- In the United States, the Apple take-back program accepts your old computer and monitor — regardless of manufacturer — when you buy a new Mac. It also takes back old cellphones and iPods, even if you don't buy anything.

- Several other brand-name PC manufacturers, including HP and Dell, have recycling programs that use safe and responsible methods. Check the home page of the folks who made your PC.

- Also check with your municipal trash collection department to see what programs it offers for old PCs and monitors.

- Finally, you can find out about organizations that take PCs and recycle them responsibly at the U.S. Environmental Protection Agency's Web site, `www.epa.gov/plugin`.

Mac Speak versus Windows Speak: A Translation Glossary

~ : The tilde character, used in Mac OS X and other Unix operating systems; an abbreviation for "the home directory of." Sometimes called *twiddle*.

.Net: Also known as "dot net," the Microsoft software framework for Web services. See also ***Mono***, a compatible system that runs on other platforms, including Mac OS X.

.ps: A PostScript file.

.sit file: A StuffIt compressed Mac file. (A version for Windows exists, too.)

10BaseT, 100BaseT, 1000BaseT: Ethernet signaling standards at 10, 100, and 1,000 megabits per second. The last is also called Gigabit Ethernet.

16-bit, 32-bit, 64-bit: When referring to a program or operating system, the maximum size of program addresses used. More bits allow more memory to be addressed; the amount doubles for each added bit.

68K: Motorola 68000 series microprocessors, used in the original Macintosh. Superseded by the PowerPC and then the Intel Core line.

accessibility: The ability of software and hardware to be used by people with disabilities.

ACID: A set of criteria for database systems intended to ensure that all transactions are handled properly — completed either completely or not at all — even if a system failure occurs during processing. The letters stand for atomicity, consistency, isolation, and durability.

Acid2 test: A series of documents used to test browser compliance with industry standards. The Apple Safari browser passes.

Acrobat reader: A free program from Adobe.com used to read PDF files. The OS X Preview feature performs many of the same functions.

ADA: The Americans with Disability Act, a U.S. law requiring reasonable accommodations for workers and customers with disabilities. Also, Ada, a computer programming language developed under the auspices of the U.S. Department of Defense.

ADB: Apple Desktop Bus, a technology used in older, pre-USB Macs to connect keyboards and mice.

adware: Software that's provided for free but displays advertising.

AES: Advanced Encryption Standard, a strong encryption cipher developed in Belgium and adopted by the U.S. government. See Chapter 10.

AFP: Apple File Protocol, used in AppleShare.

AIFF: Audio Interchange File Format, an Apple-developed format for sound files. It's lossless, but tends to be large compared to compressed formats such as MP3. It's the same idea as Microsoft WAV format.

AIM: AOL Instant Messenger, an instant messaging (IM) system supported by AOL and iChat.

AirPort: The Apple brand name for Wi-Fi wireless networking; also called IEEE 802.11.

alias: A small file that points to another file.

Android: An open source operating system for smartphones, sponsored by Google.

Apache: A popular program, supplied with OS X, for serving Web pages over the Internet. Visit `www.apache.org`.

Aperture: The high-end Apple program for still photographers. Not included in OS X.

API: Application program interface, a set of services that one program, such as an operating system, provides to another.

Apple I and II: The original Apple computers, based on an 8-bit microprocessor, the 6502.

Apple key: A key with the Apple logo (🍎) and the command symbol (⌘). Also called the Command key or fan key. Newer keyboards have only ⌘ on the key, but the name persists.

Apple lossless: An audio file format that features lossless compression. Can be played on most iPods.

Apple remote control: A small, infrared remote that can command Macs and Apple TV and most iPod models.

Apple store: Apple retail outlets, including a Web site, `store.apple.com`, and brick-and-mortar (more often glass-and-silicone) stores that you can walk into. They're located in many major cities and shopping centers.

AppleScript: A programming language that allows repetitive tasks on a Mac to be automated. Many Mac apps can respond to AppleScript commands and are said to be Apple scriptable.

AppleShare: The Apple file-sharing technology for local networks.

applet: A small program in the Java language that can be automatically downloaded and executed by your browser.

AppleTalk: An older Apple networking technology that has been largely replaced by industry standard technologies such as AirPort, Ethernet, and TCP/IP.

AppleWorks: A suite of office applications, sold by Apple, that runs only on older PowerPC machines. Previously called ClarisWorks.

Aqua: Semitranslucent Apple styling for the OS X graphical interface.

ASCII: American Standard Code for Information Interchange, a way of encoding characters in 8-bit bytes that's widely used in modern computers, though increasingly being replaced by Unicode and UTF-8.

ATA: Advanced Technology Attachment. A widely used standard for connecting hard drives and optical drives to computers. A newer version, SATA, or serial ATA, is used in Macs. (Advanced Technology refers to the PC-AT, which is hardly considered advanced any more.)

Automator: A facility in OS X that simplifies the creation of scripts to perform repetitive tasks.

bash: Bourne-again shell. A Unix shell (see also ***shell***) developed by the GNU project, used in OS X. See Chapter 19.

baud: A measure of modem speed that means one symbol per second; bits per second is more commonly used these days. You earn a high geek point if you understand the distinction.

BinHex: An older Mac format for sending binary data encoded as an ASCII text file.

BIOS: Basic Input/Output System. Firmware in a PC that determines what happens when you turn on power. Intel Macs and some newer PCs use EFI instead.

bit: The basic unit of information, with only two possibilities, represented by 0 and 1, or on and off.

BitLocker: A disk encryption scheme in the Pro versions of Windows Vista. See *FileVault* and Chapter 10.

BitTorrent: A popular system for sharing files on the Internet, capable of handling very large files.

blacklist: A list of e-mail or chat addresses you don't want to hear from. See also *whitelist*.

Blue Box: An early code name for what became the Classic environment in OS X for PowerPC. See also *Red Box*, *Yellow Box*.

Bluetooth: A wireless networking standard for short range uses such as connecting computers, keyboards, mice, and cellphones.

Blu-ray: An optical disc the same size as a DVD, but capable of storing ten times as much data. Used for high-definition movies.

BMP: A graphics file format used in Windows.

BNC: A coaxial connector type used in high-end video equipment.

Bonjour: An Apple-sponsored technology (originally named *Rendezvous*) to allow devices such as printers to announce their presence over local computer networks.

boot from CD: To start your computer from a compact disc or DVD. Hold down the C key on a Mac while restarting.

bootstrap: Short for pulling yourself up by your bootstraps. Refers to the complex process by which computers start up when power is first applied. Usually shortened to just *boot*.

broadband: A high-speed transmission technology used with cable modems that allows multiple streams of information on a single coaxial cable.

browser: A program that finds and displays information on the World Wide Web. Macs come with the Safari browser.

BSD: Berkley System Distribution, a variant of the Unix operating system developed at the University of California, Berkley. It's the basis for Mac OS X.

byte: A block of information, usually 8 bits.

cable modem: A small box that connects your computer or router to the cable TV system.

Carbon: A set of application program interfaces provided by Apple to make it easier to convert older Mac programs to OS X.

CardBus: See *PCMCIA* or *PC card*.

CD-R, CD-R/W: A compact disc that can be written on by a computer — for example, a Mac. CD-Rs can be written only once; CD-R/Ws can be erased and rewritten multiple times. CDs store about 800MB of data; DVDs store more.

CD-ROM: Compact Disc Read-Only Memory; a compact disc that contains data that cannot be modified.

CERT: Computer Emergency Readiness Team, a U.S. group that responds to viruses and other computer and Internet attacks.

Claris: A no-longer-existent software division of Apple.

ClarisWorks: See *AppleWorks*.

Classic: A feature of OS X that allowed older Mac OS 9 programs to run. Classic isn't supported on newer Intel Macs or by Mac OS X releases after Tiger (10.4).

client: A computer that uses the services of another computer. Also, someone who helps pay the bills.

Cocoa: A set of application program interfaces provided by Apple for building native OS X applications. See also *Carbon*.

codec: Compressor-decompressor; a piece of software necessary to compress a media file or to process a compressed media file.

Command key: The keyboard key with the ⌘ symbol on it. Located on either side of the spacebar on Apple keyboards.

composite video: An analog video signal standard where all picture information is carried on a single wire (usually yellow).

console: A text stream on which Unix-based operating systems send out messages about their operations. One is running in OS X, but you must launch the Console *utility* to see it.

cookie: A small blob of data that Web sites try to store on your hard drive so that they can be reminded of certain information the next time you visit. You can turn cookies off on the Safari Preferences Security tab.

Core 2 duo: Intel *x*86 microprocessors featuring two processors on a chip, used in many Macs.

creator code: Metadata in the Apple file system that indicates which application should open the file. See also **file type**.

CRM: Customer relationship management software; helps sales and marketing organizations track leads and customers.

cron file: A file in a Unix-based operating system that lists actions to be taken at specific times in the future.

cryptovariable: Another name for a cryptographic key.

Darwin: The Unix operating system underlying Mac OS X.

Dashboard: A feature of Mac OS X that pops up small, useful programs named widgets whenever you press F12. Widgets can be downloaded from Apple.com.

data remanence: The often recoverable traces of information left behind when you think you have deleted your files. Secure Empty Trash reduces the problem, as does the Disk Utility command Erase Free Space.

desk accessory: An older version of Dashboard widgets used in Mac OS 9 and earlier.

dialup: A form of Internet connection where you dial a phone number that connects you to an ISP. Its speed is limited to about 56 kilobits per second.

Diceware: A technique for generating strong passwords and passphrases using ordinary dice. Visit www.Diceware.com.

Direct3D: One of two popular ways for programs, particularly 3D games, to communicate with graphics cards. Microsoft uses this one. Apple uses the other, OpenGL.

directory: Another name for a folder, a named collection of files and other directories.

disk encryption: A method of securing data that scrambles an entire disk rather than individual files or folders.

disclosure triangle: A small triangle icon that increases (or decreases) the information you see when you click it.

distro: Short for distribution; several groups (for example, Red Hat, Debian Ubuntu) assemble and release open source operating systems based on the Linux kernel. Each group's version is a distro.

DMCA: Digital Millennium Copyright Act, a U.S. law that restricts the circumvention of digital copy protections, such as DRM.

doc: The extension used by files saved by versions of Microsoft Word before Word 2007. Word 2007 and Word 2008 use `.docx`, an XML-based format.

Dock: In OS X, a place where icons of frequently used applications and folders can be kept. Running applications are always shown. By default, the Dock is at the bottom of the screen. Roughly the equivalent of the Windows taskbar and tray.

dongle: A small device that plugs into a computer and contains special codes that allow a purchased program to run. Dongles restrict users of expensive software to using only the number of copies they purchased.

DRAM: Dynamic random-access memory. A type of high-speed main memory used in computers. It must have its contents refreshed regularly, but it uses the minimum number of transistors per bit of any solid-state memory.

DRM: Digital rights management. Technologies designed to limit the copies you can make of media you own. Apple uses a form of DRM, named FairPlay, in most of the media purchased at the iTunes Store.

DSL: Digital subscriber line, a form of high-speed Internet access brought to you by your phone company.

DVD: Digital versatile disc or digital video disc. This plastic disc, with the same dimensions as CDs (120 mm diameter), can store an entire movie in pre-HD resolution. Writable DVD-Rs and DVD-R/W discs are available.

DVI: Digital visual interface, a digital video interface standard used in several Mac models and many PCs.

Earthlink: An Internet service provider.

ECC: Error-correcting code; used on hard drives and sometimes on RAM to catch and fix errors.

EFI: Extensible Firmware Interface, a technology used by Intel Macs to start up the computer. Replaces the BIOS in PCs.

EmPower: A connector for supplying low-voltage direct current power to airplane seats for use in powering laptops and other devices; defined by the ARINC 628 specification. An earlier version, now named EmPower Classic, used an automobile cigarette lighter connector.

emulation: One computer pretending to be another with a different instruction set by running a program that knows what to do with each instruction of the foreign computer.

encrypt: To scramble data in a way that's difficult or impossible to undo without knowledge of a secret key.

encrypting file system: See *disk encryption*.

Entourage: The Microsoft mail client and personal information manager for the Mac. Entourage is part of Microsoft Office.

entropy: A measure of randomness; the logarithm of the number of possible states a system can be in.

Ethernet: A method for computer-to-computer communication that requires one computer to be in charge (to support peer-to-peer communication).

Eudora: An alternative e-mail program for OS X and Windows from Qualcomm.com.

Exchange: A Microsoft software product, Exchange Server, that provides e-mail messaging, calendaring, and contact directories in many enterprises. Snow Leopard plays well with Exchange.

ExpressCard: A new standard for small plug-in expansion cards. The MacBook Pro has an ExpressCard/34 slot. Replaces the PCMCIA PC Card standard.

F connector: A video coaxial connector with a threaded sleeve widely used in consumer electronics.

FairPlay: The Apple digital rights management system for music.

fan key: A keyboard key with the ⌘ symbol on it. Also called the Command key.

FAT: File allocation table. A file system used on older PCs. Macs can read and write devices, such as flash drives, formatted in the FAT format.

file extension: A string of letters added to a filename after a dot that indicate the program that can open that file. OS X also stores a file type that serves a similar purpose.

file path: The sequence of folders or directories leading from the root directory or home directory to the file; for example: `~/Documents/Projects/Wiley/S2M4D/Glossary.doc`.

file permission: Codes associated with each file that indicate who can read, modify, or execute the file.

file type: Metadata in the Apple file system that indicates what type of data the file contains. See also *creator codefile extension*.

FileMaker: A database management program for Mac OS X and Windows that's sold by the Apple subsidiary FileMaker, Inc.

FileVault: An OS X service that encrypts a user's home directory.

Final Cut: The high-end, moviemaking Apple software.

Fink: A group dedicated to porting Unix and Linux applications to the Mac. Visit www.finkproject.org.

Firefox: An alternative browser that's popular on Macs and PCs.

FireWire: A high-speed data bus for connecting computers, hard drives, video cameras, and other devices. Also called i.Link and IEEE 1394.

firmware: Computer programs associated with a computer or another device stored in read-only or flash memory that aren't normally changed. "Ware" that's between hard and soft.

Flash: A proprietary format for multimedia data on the World Wide Web. Originally developed by Macromedia, and now owned by Adobe.

flash drive: A thumb-size device that plugs into a USB port and looks like a hard drive to the operating system. Uses flash memory — hence the name. See also *sneakernet*.

flash memory: A solid-state memory technology that retains data even when it isn't connected to electrical power but can be rewritten. Used in flash drives, iPods, iPhones, and digital cameras.

folder: See *directory*.

FOSS: Free open source software.

FreeBSD: An open source distribution of the BSD UNIX operating system. OS X is built on FreeBSD. Other BSD distros exist — for example, OpenBSD and NetBSD.

Front row: Apple technology for remotely controlling Macs and other devices. Run your Mac from your couch.

FTP: File Transfer Protocol, an early Internet technology for moving data files. Anonymous FTP sites let you get data with `anonymous` as the username and your e-mail address as the password. I like the Fetch FTP client for OS X; visit `www.fetchsoftworks.com`.

GIF: Graphics interchange format. An image file format developed by CompuServe that's popular on the Web. It has limited color capability but can complete simple animations.

Gigabit Ethernet: Ethernet operating at a billion bits per second. Also called 1000BaseT.

gigabyte: One billion bytes. Sometimes, 2^{30} bytes or 1,073,741,824 bytes. Some call the latter number a gibibyte to avoid confusion.

GIMP: An open source image-editing program that's available for Macs; runs in X11.

Gnu: Gnu is Not Unix, a project started by Richard Stallman to develop an open source version of Unix. Gnu developed much of the utility software shipped with Linux, and many Gnu utilities are in OS X.

GPG: Gnu Privacy Guard, a free open source encryption program compatible with PGP. It's available for the Mac.

GPL: Gnu Public License, a commonly used legal agreement attached to open source software that requires an improved version to carry the same license. See *gnu.org/licenses/gpl.html*.

GUI: Graphical user interface, a way for humans to interact with a computer by manipulating objects and icons on a display screen using a pointing device, such as a mouse.

H.264: A video data compression standard used in iChat and other Mac software.

hard drive: The main, permanent data store in most computers; uses rotating magnetic disks and a read/write head on a movable arm. See also *SSD*.

hash: A cryptographic tool that mushes data into a small block in a nonreversible way. The hash serves as a signature for the file. It's quite difficult to make two files with the same hash. Some common hash algorithms are MD5, SHA-1, SHA-256, and SHA-512.

HD DVD: A defunct higher-capacity replacement for DVDs. Blu-ray won.

HDMI: High-Definition Multimedia Interface, a standard for high-definition TV cable connectors that includes digital video, similar to DVI and digital audio. Includes provisions for digital rights management.

HDTV: High-definition television. What every couch potato craves.

HFS+: The file system used in Mac OS X. See also *ZFS*.

hibernate: An operating system feature that suspends operation in a way that can survive a power outage. See also *sleep*.

Home directory: The folder that contains all data associated with your user account; abbreviated ~ at the command line.

HyperCard: A programming environment on early Macs that anticipated many hypermedia features of the Web; a predecessor of AppleScript.

hypertext: A system of writing and displaying text that enables text to be linked in multiple ways, be available at several levels of detail, and contain links to related documents.

ICANN: Internet Corporation for Numbers and Names, a controversial nonprofit corporation that administers Internet addresses.

iChat: The Apple instant messaging, voice communication, and videoconferencing software included in OS X.

ICQ: An instant messaging service, now owned by AOL. Users are identified by a number.

IEC standards (power cord, button icons): International Electrotechnical Commission, a standards organization dealing with electrical and electronic technologies.

IEEE: Institute of Electrical and Electronics Engineers, a professional organization that also sets standards.

IEEE 1394: The FireWire standard; also named i.Link by Sony.

IEEE 802.11: The family of wireless networking standards known as Wi-Fi or by the Apple brand name AirPort. See Chapter 9.

IETF: Internet Engineering Task Force, a group that sets standards for the Internet.

IGo adapter: A line of third-party power sources for small electronics such as cellphones that have interchangeable adapters for different devices.

iLife: A family of media-editing and production software included with each Mac: iTunes, iPhoto, iMovie, iDVD, GarageBand, and iWeb. See Chapter 11.

IM: Instant messaging, an electronic text communication system in which both parties of a conversation are at their computers at the same time and send messages back and forth.

IMAP: Internet Message Access Protocol, one of the two popular ways e-mail is handled on the Internet. When you use IMAP, e-mail can be kept on a server and accessed over the Net. The other method is POP.

infrared: A form of invisible light in the electromagnetic spectrum with wavelengths just longer than red and shorter than 1 millimeter.

Intel: The company that invented microprocessors; has long made the microprocessors for most Windows PCs, and now makes them for Macs.

internationalization: The process of adapting computer software to work in different languages and cultures.

Internet: All the computers in the world talking to each other.

iPod: The Apple line of portable music players.

IRC: Internet Relay Chat, an early form of instant messaging that's still used on the Internet.

ISA bus: A type of plug-in card used in early PCs; replaced by PCI.

iSight: The Apple line of video cameras, now built into many Macs.

iWork: The Apple office productivity suite that includes Pages word processing, Numbers spreadsheet, and Keynote presentation software.

journaling file system: A file system that separately keeps track of recent changes. In the event of a system crash, the journaled changes can be used to reconstruct a damaged file system, significantly improving overall data reliability. Used in OS X.

JPEG: Joint Photographic Experts Group. A body that developed a widely used standard format for photographs (.jpg).

kernel: The innermost part of an operating system, the stuff that talks to all the hardware. OS X uses the Mach kernel.

kernel panic: An unrecoverable failure in an operating system's inner workings. In OS X, it's often a sign of underlying hardware problems. Reboot and back up your computer.

key: As used in cryptography, a block of information needed to encode or decode a message.

keyboard shortcut: Pressing two or more keys to initiate a command without selecting an item from a menu.

Keynote: The Apple presentation software that one-ups the ubiquitous Microsoft PowerPoint.

kilo: The standard prefix meaning 1,000. In computing, it sometime means 1,024, which is 2^{10}. Another prefix for the latter number is *kibi*.

KVM switch: A box that lets you use a single keyboard, video display, and mouse to operate more than one computer.

LDAP: Lightweight Directory Access Protocol, a system for finding people and resources on computer networks.

Leopard: The Apple code name for Mac OS X 10.5. See also ***Snow Leopard***.

line in: An analog audio signal amplified to a certain nominal level for connection to other audio equipment.

Linux: An open source computer operating system inspired by Unix. See also ***Gnu***.

Lisa: A short-lived Apple computer that was a predecessor to the Macintosh.

LocalTalk: An early Apple wiring standard for AppleTalk networking that used telephone wires. It has since been replaced by Ethernet.

location: In Apple networking, a way to group settings so that they can be easily changed when moving to a different locale, such as from home to work.

Lock icon: A small image of a padlock that's shown in Web browsers to indicate whether the current connection is securely encrypted, in which case the lock is closed, or is not securely encrypted, in which case the lock is open. It's worth checking before entering personal information on a Web form.

lossless: A data compression mode that allows all original data to be recovered. Higher compression levels for music and video discard some data and are lossy.

Mac OS X: An operating system developed by Apple, using technology from NeXT, BSD UNIX, Mach, and earlier versions of Mac OS. Now available only for Apple Macintosh computers. A server edition also comes with Xserve.

MacBinary: An older Mac format for sending binary data over the Internet.

Mach: An operating system kernel developed at Carnegie Mellon University and used in OS X.

macintouch.com: A popular Macintosh support Web site.

MacPaint: A classic drawing program included with the earliest Macs.

MacWrite: The earliest Apple word processor for the Mac.

MagSafe: The power connector used on Mac Intel laptops. The connection is magnetic and is designed to safely pop off if someone trips on the cord.

malware: A computer program that's up to no good, such as viruses, worms, or spyware.

McIntosh: A type of edible apple that's popular in New England. Also a brand of audio equipment. Not to be confused with Macintosh, an Apple, Inc., brand name.

mega: The standard prefix meaning one million. In computing, it sometimes means 1,048,576, which is 2^{20}. Another prefix for the later number is mebi.

metadata: Information about data, such as what it means and where it comes from.

MIDI: Musical Instrument Digital Interface, a way to communicate music as named notes rather than as digitized sounds. It's used to connect digital instruments to computers.

MightyMouse: The Apple concession to mouse multibuttonness. For decades earlier, the single-button mouse was Mac dogma.

MIME: Multipurpose Internet Mail Extension, a standard that allows Internet e-mail to carry information in a variety of formats other than plain ASCII text.

Mini DisplayPort: A video out connector used on many Mac models. A smaller version of the VESA DisplayPort that supports the encryption of video signals to protect HD movies from piracy.

mini-DVI: A smaller version of the DVI connector; used in some Mac models.

MobileMe: The Apple online service for file sharing, e-mail, personal Web pages and more. Not free, but handy.

modem: Modulator/demodulator. A device used to send digital signals over analog circuits, such as a phone line or television cable.

Mono: An open source effort to develop Web service tools, compatible with Microsoft .Net, that can run on non–Windows platforms, such as OS X. Visit `mono-project.com`.

MP3: A popular compressed audio format; stands for MPEG-1, Audio Layer 3.

MPEG: Motion Picture Experts Group, a body that sets standards for video compression.

mpkg: A file format used to distribute OS X software.

MSN: Microsoft Network, the Microsoft collection of Internet services.

MySQL: A widely used open source database system. SQL stands for Structured Query Language. MySQL runs in OS X. A commercially supported version is also available. Visit `www.mysql.com`.

Newton: A short-lived Apple product that created the personal digital assistant market.

NextStep: An operating system, developed by NeXT, that Apple evolved into OS X.

NTFS: NT File System, the file system used in Windows NT, Windows XP, and Windows Vista. Macs can read NTFS disks.

NTSC: A standard for standard-definition television signals used in North America, Japan, and parts of South America. *See also* **PAL video**.

NuBus: A standard for plug-in cards used on older Macs.

object file: The output of a compiler. A version of a program in machine language that the computer can execute.

Objective C: A variant of the C programming language that's widely used in OS X and its application programs. It takes a different approach to object orientation than does C++.

Octet: A fancy name for an 8-bit data field. See *byte*.

Office Open XML: A controversial standard for electronic documents proposed by Microsoft and based on its Office suite's internal format. Also called OOXML. Competes with OpenDocument.

Ogg: A nonproprietary multimedia file format. See *www.xiph.org/ogg*.

open source: An approach to software development where the original, human-generated instructions and comments are publicly available. Visit Opensource.org for the official definition.

open source license: One of several copyright licenses under which open source software and documentation are distributed. They typically allow wide use but require the same copyright notice to be included on redistributed versions. See *www.opensource.org/licenses*.

OpenDocument: A nonproprietary file format for electronic documents. Also called ODF and the OASIS Open Document Format for Office Applications. Competes with Office Open XML.

OpenGL: A nonproprietary way for programs, especially 3D games, to talk to graphics cards. OS X supports OpenGL. Competes with Microsoft DirectX.

OpenOffice.org: An open source suite of productivity applications — word processing and spreadsheet, for example, that runs in OS X.

optical digital audio: A replacement for analog sound wiring in home electronics that uses fiber optics rather than shielded copper wire. No more annoying hum loop.

OS 9: Short for Mac OS 9, an earlier Mac operating system. Earlier systems include 4, 5, 6, 7 and 8.

Outlook: The Microsoft e-mail client for Windows. See also *Entourage*.

package: The Apple way of distributing applications for OS X that combines numerous files and folders associated with a program into what looks like a single file. Sometimes called a bundle.

PAL video: Standard-definition broadcast video signal standard used in Europe and much of the world. See also *NTSC*.

pane: A simple window in a graphical computer interface.

Panther: Code name for Mac OS X 10.3.

parallel port: A printer interface once common on PCs but never used on Macs. Also known as a Centronics port or IEEE 1284 port.

Parallels: A virtualization package that lets Windows and other operating systems, such as Linux, run at the same time as OS X. See Chapter 16.

partition: To divide a hard drive into two or more smaller disk volumes, sometimes done with a hacksaw or an ax, but Disk Utility is the preferred method.

passphrase: A longer form of a password, often made up of several words. See also *Diceware*.

password: A string of characters you type into your computer to let it know for sure that the person typing is you. See Chapter 10.

PCIe: Peripheral Component Interconnect Express, a third-generation interface standard for computer expansion cards, used in the Mac Pro. Replaces PCI and PCI-X.

PCMCIA or PC card: A standard for small, credit-card-size cards that plug into laptops to add capabilities. MacBook Pro uses a newer standard, ExpressCard/34.

PDF: Portable Document Format, an Adobe standard for digital documents that can be read on most computers using a free Adobe reader program. Mac OS X uses PDF as its document format, and the included Preview application can read .pdf files.

perpendicular recording: A method of increasing the amount of information that can be stored on a hard drive.

PGP: Pretty Good Privacy, a popular public key encryption package that's available for the Mac, Windows, and Linux. See also *GPG*.

phone plug: A type of audio connector that consists of a long, cylindrical sleeve with one or two insulated contacts at the tip. it comes in ¼-inch, 3.5mm, and 2½mm diameters. Not to be confused with the cube-shaped RJ series telephone plugs.

phono plug: See *RCA plug*.

PhotoBooth: A small but fun application that comes with OS X and takes pictures using the iSight camera. Operates much like the old four-for-a-dollar photo booths found in amusement parks and arcades.

Photoshop: The powerful Adobe image-editing software. Photoshop Elements, a much lower-cost, less-capable version, is also available.

PHP: A scripting programming language often used with database programs such as MySQL to create Web applications.

PICT: A graphics file format used on older Macs.

PKI: Public key infrastructure, a way to distribute keys in public key cryptography.

PlaysForSure: A DRM-protected music format promoted by Microsoft but not supported on its Zune player.

plug-in: A piece of software that can be easily incorporated into an application to increase functionality.

PNG: Portable Network Graphics, a nonproprietary format for exchanging images.

POP: Post Office Protocol, the most common way e-mail is handled on the Internet. See also *IMAP*.

pop-up: An additional window that appears when accessing a Web site. It's sometimes used to add functionality to a Web page, but more often for advertising. Also pop-under, a window that's added behind the window in use so that it appears only when that window is closed or moved, sometimes known as a leave-behind.

pop-up menu: A menu that appears when you click a button or icon that displays a double arrowhead; similar to a Windows drop-down menu.

POSIX: Portable Operating System Interface for UNIX. A standard application program interface (API) promoted by the U.S. government to enable programs to be easily ported to different operating systems. OS X supports POSIX.

PostScript: A printing file format developed by Adobe.

PowerBook: An earlier brand of Apple laptop.

PowerPC: A microprocessor architecture developed by a consortium of Motorola, IBM, and Apple and used in Macs until the switch to Intel microprocessors.

PPP: Point-to-Point Protocol; connects two computers and is most often used in dialup Internet access. Also PPPoE — PPP over Ethernet.

PRAM: Parameter RAM, a small block of storage used to save information needed during startup. Resetting PRAM is a common Mac nostrum. See Chapter 20.

Pre: A new, smartphone from Palm; competes with iPhone.

preferences: Application settings in Mac OS.

propeller key: Another name for the *Command key* (cmd).

protocol: An agreed-on way that computers use to talk to each other.

PS2: A second-generation IBM PC. The electrical connections it used for hooking up a mouse and keyboard are still used on some PC models. Macs use USB instead.

public-key cryptography: A method of sending secret messages and electronically signing documents that uses two keys, one that can freely be made public and a second that's kept secret by the person who receives the coded message or signs the document.

quad core: Having four separate CPUs in one chip.

Quartz: The Apple name for the display-rendering technology in OS X.

QuickTime: The Apple format for multimedia content. It competes with Windows Media and Real.

RAID: Redundant Array of Inexpensive Disks, a way to build large, reliable storage systems from PC-grade disk drives.

RAM: Random-access memory; the main fast memory in a computer.

RAW file: Image data from a digital camera in its original form, with no compression or other processing that can lose information. iPhoto has some support for RAW images; Aperture has much more.

RCA plug: A push-on coaxial connector invented in the 1930s by the Radio Corporation of America to allow phonographs to be played through table radios. Also called phono plug and jack.

reality distortion field: A humorous reference to Steve Jobs' ability to sell ideas convincingly.

reboot: A shutdown and restart. See also *bootstrap*.

Red Box: A code name for a long-rumored project that was supposed to allow Windows applications to run in OS X, somewhat like Wine. See also *Blue Box, Yellow Box.*

regular expression: A Unix term (also regexp) for a cryptic but powerful way to specify search criteria as a string of characters. It was popularized by the Unix program grep.

RGB video: A way of transmitting video signals as three separate analog channels for red, green, and blue.

RJ-45: A cube-shaped electrical connector used on twisted-pair Ethernet cables. Not to be confused with the similar, but smaller, RJ-11 connector used with telephones.

root: The top-level directory in a file structure; the highest level of access privilege in a Unix system.

Rosetta: The Apple method for running older PowerPC programs on Intel processors.

router: A box that helps direct information packets among connected computers to create a network.

RS-232: A standard for serial ports used on PCs. It's increasingly replaced by USB.

RSA: Rivest, Shamir, and Adleman, an algorithm for public-key cryptography based on the difficulty of factoring numbers.

RSS: A set of standards for delivering Web content that's updated regularly. Users subscribe to different feeds that are aggregated and displayed by software in their computers.

RTF: Rich Text Format, an older Microsoft word processing format used by TextEdit and other OS X programs.

RTFM: A suggestion that people read the manual before asking for assistance.

rumors community: A group of Internet sites that speculate about Apple Computer, Inc., and its products and sometimes publish what they claim to be inside information.

SATA: Serial ATA, a high-performance connection standard for mass storage devices, such as hard drives, used in many new computers, including Macs.

SCSI: Small Computer System Interface, a connection standard for mass storage devices used in older Macs.

SDRAM: Synchronous dynamic random-access memory, a variant of DRAM that offers higher performance by tying its operation to the CPU's clock pulses. Think of the galley scene in *Ben-Hur,* where the slaves pull their oars to the beat of a drum.

serial port: A computer connection that sends data sequentially, bit by bit, over a communication line. **See also *RS-232, parallel port.***

shareware: Software programs that are freely distributed over the Internet, with the expectation that people who decide to use them will voluntarily pay a fee to the authors.

shell: An operating system program that listens to commands typed by the user. The Windows command line interpreter is a shell. OS X uses the bash shell by default, though others, such as the Korn shell, are available. Before GUIs, the shell was the outermost, visible part of an operating system. The innermost part was and is the kernel.

shut down: To turn off the computer.

sleep: The temporary suspension of the operation of a computer, usually to save energy — particularly, battery power on a laptop.

SMTP: Simple Mail Transfer Program, the basis for electronic mail on the Internet.

snd file: An early Mac audio format.

sneaker-net: The system of transferring information between computers by having someone carry the data on removable media — originally, floppy disks, but now flash drives and CD/DVD optical discs.

Snow Leopard: The code name for Mac OS X 10.6.

socket: A software port that one program uses to connect to another program running on a different computer.

Software Update: The Apple facility for distributing revisions to OS X and its application programs. It automatically notifies users when new stuff is available — by default, once a week.

Spaces: A feature in OS X Leopard and Snow Leopard that supports multiple workspaces for a single user. See Chapter 16.

spam: Unsolicited commercial e-mail; the e-mail equivalent of junk mail.

Spotlight: The OS X search technology.

spring-loaded: An icon that pops open or takes some other action when the cursor hovers over it.

spyware: Software that covertly gathers personal information about a user, such as Web-surfing habits, without the user's consent, and conveys it to a third party.

SSD: Solid-state drive, an alternative to hard drives that uses memory chips rather than rotating magnetic disks.

SSH: A program and a set of standards for establishing a secure connection between two computers. It relies on public-key cryptography. OS X has SSH support.

SSL/TLS: Secure Socket Layer/Transport Layer Security. Two names used to describe the most commonly used method for securing Internet connections.

startup disk: The disk drive that contains the operating system that will be used to start the computer the next time it's turned on or rebooted. Set by a pane in System Preferences.

StuffIt Expander: A free program that unpacks a number of compressed file formats, including .sit files.

sudo: A Unix command that prefixes other commands, causing them to execute with superuser privileges. It requires an admin password in OS X.

S-Video: An analog video signal standard that has separate wires for color and brightness. See also *composite video*.

SYLK: Symbolic Link, an older Microsoft spreadsheet file format that's still used at times to exchange data with other programs.

tar file: A compressed archive format used in Unix systems.

taskbar: A Windows feature, located along the bottom of the screen, that's somewhat similar to the OS X Dock.

TCP/IP: Transmission Control Protocol/Internet Protocol, the way computers communicate with each other on the Internet.

telnet: A program that lets you log on to other computers on the network.

tera: The standard prefix for one trillion.

Terminal: A program in OS X that gives you access to the underlying Unix operating system by using a command-line interface.

terminal emulator: A program that communicates with legacy systems by pretending to be a dumb computer terminal, such as a VT-100 or IBM 3270.

text file: A computer file that contains only characters, usually encoded in ASCII. Uses the `.txt` extension.

thumb drive: A finger-size device that contains flash memory that plugs into a USB port and looks like a hard drive to the computer. Also called flash drive or keychain drive.

Tiger: Code name for Mac OS X 10.4.

Time Machine: The Apple automated backup system for OS X Leopard.

trusted platform chip: A tamper-resistant microprocessor chip on Macs and newer PCs, designed to hold cryptographic keys and certificates. (The rub is, trusted by whom?)

Unicode: A computer character code that attempts to include all written languages in use in the world.

universal binary: A way of distributing computer programs so that they can install and work on both PowerPC and Intel Macs.

Unix: A computer operating system developed in the 1960s at AT&T Bell Labs. Mac OS X is based on Unix.

USB: Universal Serial Bus, a means for connecting peripheral devices to computers, used in Macs and PCs. USB 2.0 is considerably faster than, but backward compatible with, USB 1.

V.92: An ITU standard for dialup modems operating at speeds up to 56 Kbps. Used in the Apple Modem.

VGA connector: A widely used analog video cable connector with a D-shell and 15 pins in three rows. Most Macs come with a VGA adapter cable.

virtual memory: A technique that allows an operating system to assign more random-access memory than the computer physically has by writing to disk storage any sections of memory that haven't been used recently.

Virtualization: A way of splitting the resources of a computer among more than one operating system so that each one thinks it has a separate computer all to itself.

virus: A program that attaches itself to another program or document and then transmits copies of itself to infect other computers.

Vista: A version of the Microsoft Windows operating system that followed Windows XP and is being replaced by Windows 7.

VNC: Virtual Network Computing, a standard for the remote control of a computer desktop from another computer. Used in Apple Remote Desktop.

watermark: A collection of bits hidden in a media file that allow digital rights management software to detect copyrighted works.

WAV: A Windows audio file format.

WEP: Wired equivalent privacy, a broken encryption scheme for Wi-Fi. See *WPA* for better security.

whitelist: To specify addresses from whom you welcome messages. The opposite of black list.

widget: A small program run on the Dashboard layer of OS X.

Wi-Fi: The brand name applied to devices that meet interoperability criteria for wireless networking based on the IEEE 802.11 standards. Apple uses the brand name AirPort.

Window Shade: A feature in OS 9 that lets users collapse a window to just its title bar.

Windows CE: A Microsoft operating system for small devices, such as PDAs and smart cellphones.

Windows Genuine Advantage: The Microsoft program to discourage people from using unlicensed copies of Windows; considered too heavy-handed by some people.

Windows Media Player: A Microsoft program and file format for handling multimedia content, usually with the .wmp extension.

Windows XP: The version of the Microsoft Windows operating system that shipped with most PCs from October 2001 until Windows Vista was introduced and, because of public outcry, with many PCs for about a year afterward.

wireless access point: A base station in a wireless network.

WMP: See *Windows Media Player*.

worm: A self-replicating computer program, usually malicious. Differs from a virus, which attaches itself to another program.

WPA, WPA2: Wireless protected access; encryption for Wi-Fi that's quite strong if you use a long enough passphrase. See Chapter 10.

WWAN: Wireless wide-area network, a way for mobile computers to connect to the Internet by using the cellular telephone network.

X11: A windowing standard developed at MIT that's used in Linux and Unix systems and can optionally be installed as part of OS X so that it can run programs created for those systems.

XLR connector: An industrial-strength audio connector, typically with three pins.

yarrow: A high-grade, random-number generator used in OS X. High-grade random numbers are essential for computer security programs.

Yellow Box: An early code name for what became the Cocoa environment in OS X.

zero configuration: See *Bonjour*.

zero-day exploit: A computer security attack that appears at the same time as a vulnerability is announced.

ZFS: The new high-performance, ultra-reliable Sun file system. It has limited support in OS X — for now.

Zip archive: A file that's a collection of other files compressed with the Zip algorithm. Look on the Finder File menu.

Zip drive: A computer mass storage system that used removable cartridges and could store 100MB or more on each cartridge. Used on some older Macs; USB versions are still supported by OS X.

Zune: The Microsoft personal music player, competes with the Apple iPod.

Zune Marketplace: The Microsoft equivalent of the Apple iTunes Store.

Index